PRAISE FOR

This Is Major

"A hilarious, heartbreaking, and endlessly entertaining homage to black women's resilience and excellence."

— *Kirkus Reviews* (starred review)

"An insightful collection. . . .With sharp insight, Lawson elevates the discussion of race in America."

— *Publishers Weekly*

"In *This Is Major*, Shayla Lawson skillfully illuminates the unparalleled influence black women and girls have had on mainstream culture. I learned so much from reading this book while also relishing the humor and fearlessness of Lawson's inspiring voice. It's a must-read for anyone interested in pop culture, history, or politics."

— Camille Perri, author of *The Assistants* and *When Katie Met Cassidy*

"Shayla Lawson's *This Is Major* is part cultural criticism, part pop music history, part memoir, part ethnography, and all conscious humor. What I love most about this book is that for all its mastery of various subjects and genres, it is always searingly honest: 'I have always been a woman on the verge of a gun. My anger is quiet. Reserved . . . I grip a pen instead. . . . I do not consider this strategy for assassination a passive action.' This is a brilliant book by a black woman aware that there is a long history of her special brand of genius, from Phillis Wheatley to Nina Simone."

—Jericho Brown

"Written as a prose love poem in essays to black girlhood, black womanhood, and black femmehood, Shayla Lawson's fourth book is required reading for all, but especially for black women and girls trying to hold space for their whole selves, the whole of their blackness. Lawson lunges into full-bodied critique and historicization of the hurt of white patriarchal supremacy and the white gaze with cunning wit and a fresh scalpel."

—Nafissa Thompson-Spires, author of
Heads of the Colored People

THIS IS MAJOR

THIS IS
MAJOR

NOTES ON DIANA ROSS, DARK GIRLS, AND BEING DOPE

SHAYLA LAWSON

HARPER ● PERENNIAL

NEW YORK ● LONDON ● TORONTO ● SYDNEY ● NEW DELHI ● AUCKLAND

HARPER PERENNIAL

THIS IS MAJOR. Copyright © 2020 by Shayla Lawson. All rights reserved. Printed in the United States of America. No part of this book may be used or reproduced in any manner whatsoever without written permission except in the case of brief quotations embodied in critical articles and reviews. For information, address HarperCollins Publishers, 195 Broadway, New York, NY 10007.

HarperCollins books may be purchased for educational, business, or sales promotional use. For information, please email the Special Markets Department at SPsales@harpercollins.com.

FIRST EDITION

Designed by Jamie Lynn Kerner

Library of Congress Cataloging-in-Publication Data has been applied for.

ISBN 978-0-06-289059-7 (pbk.)

20 21 22 23 24   LSC   10 9 8 7 6 5 4 3 2

Racists always try to make you think they are the majority, but they never are.

—TONI MORRISON

CONTENTS

Introduction

AMERICAN GIRLS

The summer of 1992, more than anything, my sister and I wanted American Girls. I was ten, my sister was six, and the dolls were the only thing en vogue for us, other than En Vogue. In the same way the R&B group represented what it meant for us to be proud, confident black women in mainstream America, the American Girl dolls solidified for us what it meant to be, well, girls. The dolls looked like they were made from porcelain, but were actually plastic—young, feminine, diplomatic envoys to early Americana. The dolls came neatly accessorized by the Pleasant Company franchise and its inexhaustible list of historically relevant clothes, furniture, and children's novellas—each sold separately.

My sister and I devoted multiple summers to reading the American Girl tween period dramas, dedicated to the saga of the dolls, sans dolls. Each girl was a symbol of our American legacy, playtime elevated to patriotism. We sat riveted reading

Molly Learns a Lesson, where World War II Molly schemes ways to support the home front, and gasped reading *Felicity Learns a Lesson* when the eighteenth-century colonial heroine takes a stance against serving tea, tea parties pivotal to her grooming as an English lady. We devoured all we could of the series, buying the books at Joseph-Beth, our local bookstore, or checking out from the library what the bookstore didn't have. When we weren't reading the books, my sister and I were combing through the American Girl catalog, which I had ordered myself, detaching the mail-order postcard from the back of *Samantha's Surprise*, filling in our address and slipping it into the mailbox—no postage necessary.

Unlike many other toys, which my parents provided in abundance—a Nintendo Power Pad, a Yamaha keyboard and matching synth drum set—my mother bided her time before calling the number in the catalog and opening up the family checkbook to order two porcelain-faced plastic dolls. The dolls were expensive and we considered all their additional, exorbitant accoutrements essential to our make-believe: you couldn't, for instance, dress Victorian Samantha Parkington in Kirsten Larson's prairie shoes—that was treason.

My mother had little use for dolls. Although she was proud of my Cabbage Patch Kid—a bit of a coup for her, scored during a Minnesota winter when I was three years old: the doll the lone chocolate-brown face in a Toys "R" Us aisle filled with apple-white cheeks—she was less than enthusiastic when, a few years later, my then three-year-old sister plucked a blue-eyed, towheaded Baby Alive from the shelves during a sweltering

Kentucky summer. She sighed and put the baby's cellophane-screened box into the shopping basket, resigned to it as an enemy of progress. Baby Alive was a brand-new toy, and it would be at least another season before Hasbro created the doll's dark-skinned version. I imagine my mom tried not to think about her baby girl, a portrait of a young mammie, learning to wipe fake poo from the baby doll's bare pink bottom. *Okay*, she said, sucking in through her teeth.

When the American Girl catalog came, I would circle everything I assumed I'd need for my new life as the owner of an elite playmate, and my sister followed along. Unlike me, she barely asked for anything, living instead inside other people's happinesses—the joy my father got from bringing home the Yamaha synthesizer or the glee I took from the elaborate musical numbers I'd stage to songs programmed in the keyboard's demo buttons, remixing the lyrics to the Disney song "The Girls on Minnie Street" to the tune of Shocking Blue's "Venus." My sister would have rather gone fishing or collected rocks. I was better suited for consumerism. I had a want in me that could only be filled by the possibility of toys. It was difficult to tell if my sister was as excited about the dolls as I was, or if it was an extension of how she loved the things other people in the family loved, but the dolls soon co-opted the time we'd previously spent rehearsing scenes from *The Phantom of the Opera* or *The Little Mermaid*, the soundtracks blaring in the background. We silenced the CD player to consider which American Girl we wanted to be.

We decided my sister was Molly: the plucky tomboy with a

stubborn streak. I fancied myself a Samantha, austere, pinafored, and stockinged—in fact, there are quite a few photos from my early childhood in which I'd dressed in Edwardian frocks, petticoats, and white gloves. I begged my mother to sew my sister and me matching Victorian sleeping lappet caps and nightgowns, which she did. I dreamed of having a kerosene lamp so I could read by the flicker of candlelight—like the one in Samantha's "nighttime necessities" kit from the catalog—to which my mom said *no*. I forsook the dream of an end to electric lighting, but I didn't give up my pursuit of an American Girl.

I attempted subterfuge—inserting copies of the books into the pile my mother read to my sister at bedtime, as if there was no story more important to a first grader than, say, a Swedish immigrant surviving her dangerous cross-Atlantic voyage. My sister would wholeheartedly agree that she wanted my mother to reread the story, I am sure now, just to please me, although she would have preferred reading any other book, any book that prominently featured a bunny.

Gradually, my mother's resolve against the American Girls weakened. I would catch her browsing the catalog late at night, putting aside her knitting to pore through pages of photos of dolls sitting in the serene glow of a fake fireplace inside a cardboard log cabin. She confessed to us that, when it came to the dolls, she was confused. My mother didn't see her two small girls represented in any of the images that composed the catalog. I, however, didn't understand what was taking her so long to hop on the John Philip Sousa bandwagon of American history.

At the time, I was becoming a white supremacist. To be

clear, I wasn't out defending statues of Robert E. Lee with tiki torches, but when we associate "white supremacy" only with extremism we miss the point. My defense was neither intentional nor malicious. White supremacy, the belief in white migration and white ideologies—and the very existence of "whiteness"—as the benchmark for greatness is the majority narrative, and it was all I knew. Even if I didn't understand this as a child, I bought stock in the idea that what made America "America®" was all things white. It is in our history books. It is in our media. It was the primary message of the American Girl® franchise.

Driving a carpool of me and several friends home from school one day, my mother overheard me say to the other girls that America should abolish the welfare system. I was nine years old. With the exception of my mother and me, the entire carpool was white.

I grew up on welfare, she told me, once all the white kids had hopped out of her Volvo station wagon and headed into their suburban homes. I rolled down the windows in the back seat so the wind patted softly against my face. *Your grandmother raised all of us—your aunt, your uncle, and me—on welfare until she got a job at an elementary school and was able to buy her own house.* I let my fingers ride the air.

I was only kidding, I said, but I could tell what I said hurt her; I did not understand its insidious prejudice. Like I said before, I am a consumer. I want too much of everything and, as a young girl, I wanted to be on the side of the mainstream right. If the rules of America®, both stated and tacit, applied differently to black people, that did not mean us black people who lived in such close proximity to whiteness that I had no other black kids in my neighborhood to carpool with.

For my West Coast–raised mother, rural 1980s Minnesota couldn't have been the easiest place to raise two black dolls. Much like the state was for American Girl Kirsten in pioneer times, it was a new frontier. Back while my mother was still pregnant with me, she and her Ghanaian friend Nana took one of their first outings together to a Hallmark greeting card store.

Fantastic! said the store's owner, standing behind the counter. *I'm so glad you two showed up. Would you mind watching the store? I need to run across the street to pick up a cake.*

Oh, sure! Nana tells me my mom said, with patented Minnie Mouse cheeriness, rubbing her pregnant belly, the grateful owner leaving the Hallmark shelves of puppy calendars, Thinking of You cards, and Precious Moments figurines in the careful hands of two Black women.

Nana was flabbergasted (Flabbergasted.). *Doesn't she know we could rob her?*

They assume we're all either doctors or computer scientists here, my mom told her. At the time, Rochester, Minnesota, boasted a corn-shaped water tower and two big industries: IBM and Mayo Clinic. Nana and my mother were both doctors' wives—two among dozens of out-of-state imports, often black or brown. I imagine my mother continued nonchalantly through the aisles of Get Wells and Thank Yous, seeking out the right card for whatever situation she sought to commemorate, until the owner returned.

In Minnesota, it wasn't as important for my mother to teach

her own American girls what blackness was as it was to remind us we were black. I had a very limited understanding of what race was. I was aware of a different array of skin tones at my family's backyard barbecues versus the neighbors', but I didn't fully understand this bothered anyone, since we ate at the same tables in our townhouse complex's communal yard.

On the rare occasions when my mother would allow me to eat lunch with the policeman's straw-blond daughter next door—either on their back porch or in their kitchen, where she could still see me at the table through the bay windows. The girl's parents would ask me questions about the difference between *our house* and *yours*.

Do your parents have a coffee table? they asked. I looked around at their bland, but neat, furniture in the nearly identical layout of their townhouse, and at the blue ceramic plate of microwaved nachos. My mother never asked their daughter questions any more politically loaded than how long she'd preferred to eat macaroni and cheese with ketchup. I thought their questions were stupid. But I understood they wanted answers from me about how to feel, blue-collar whites now living next door to a black doctor's family.

By the following summer, my mother, the policeman's wife, and my mother's friend Nana were all pregnant—all expecting girls. While riding in the front of a shopping cart my pregnant mother was guiding out of the local Target, I spotted another black girl, the first black girl I had ever seen in my town, my age, and screamed.

Mommy, look! It's a black girl! A black girl! I shrieked and pointed. Perhaps I was giddily anticipating the two infants who would soon be entering my world. I had no idea hollering *Look! Look!* at another black girl was wrong. My mother tried to stuff me into the back seat of our wood-paneled Chrysler sedan, buckling me while I continued to squall. I couldn't stop. I couldn't hide my elation. I couldn't end its loudness.

I knew kids who were biracial, like the children of the hyper-academic hippie couple we'd sometimes visit in the country. I understood they were, like me, African American by definition. But their father was white. The girl and boy looked like Precious Moments figurines lightly bronzed by gold crayon. Even their mother, who would bound through the farmhouse in long, quilted skirts that occasionally flashed her bushy legs, had a bright gold complexion and a loose curly Afro, which were a stretch for me to see myself in.

Soon after my Target sighting, my mother organized what either she or I christened a "Black People Party," importing girls from as far away as St. Paul and Minneapolis. I think she felt she had something to prove. My parents grew up in a working-class, black and brown town just outside Oakland, California. She needed to know that in the midst of her own adjustment to the staunchly white Midwest, she had not neglected her duties as the parent of black kids.

We moved to Lexington, Kentucky, right before I turned six. The first morning in which we awoke in our new home, my sister and I ran down to my parents' bedroom to wake them up with a song we'd learned in Rochester from television and had been rehearsing for months: "We're going to Kentucky, we're going to the fair, to see a senorita with flowers in her hair. . . ." Choreography and everything. We'd expected the serenade would make our parents happy. But what looked to my sister and me like something new and promising must have looked to my parents like dangerous recidivism. Up until my father accepted the job, my West Coast parents had believed any good American could, with the right mix of upward mobility and selectiveness, avoid communities with a right-wing political majority, schools with high illiteracy rates, proudly displayed Confederate license plates, and a downtown city center where a charmingly renovated main street preserves the name of what it once was—one of the largest slave markets in the south before the Civil War.

It wasn't that Rochester, Minnesota, wasn't racist. In the months leading up to our move, I was called by my first racial slur. *Monkey, look at that little brown monkey*, two boys sang, circling around me. But I looked at the boys. They both had brown faces. What they said hurt because I knew it was meant to, but I didn't get why being black made my dark skin different from anyone else's. I told my mother about what happened. She stormed up to the school demanding both boys apologize. I delighted in how much she seemed to terrify the teachers, parents, and students at my school. It was the kind of thing that made me feel that "black" was setting ablaze a school campus or a department store or a stranger's ego to defend justice. In Minnesota, the town still feared the clout my mother carried as one of the racial émigrés its economy depended on. It mattered to them, if only slightly, that she was happy with how they handled her daughter. In Kentucky, this would not be the case.

As soon as I started second grade, white kids began making fun of my overly enunciated Minnesota English—*Yew talk funnie*, they'd say, in an accusatory drawl that meant I sounded suspiciously white. I was chastised by both teachers and students for behaving as if I were smarter than them. My mother had to make frequent trips to my local public school to address what the administrators saw in me as "defiant" behavior, but she was nothing like the firebrand I had seen swooping to my aid through eight feet of snow. The school officials, who seemed prepared for the presence of "uppity Negroes," met my mother's anger with impenetrable composure.

Now, Mrs. Lawson, if your daughter only . . .

Now, Mrs. Lawson, we know you're from out of town, but . . .

Mrs. Lawson, we believe your daughter is . . . your girl is . . .

It was becoming clear that, if we were meant to survive, I was going to need to change to fit this place, which held none of the joyous music I anticipated. At some point, someone suggested to my mother that I might need to be held back a grade, an idea she staunchly opposed. When we were in Minnesota, my parents had had my IQ tested by a Mayo Clinic psychologist to see if I was ready to start kindergarten at the age of four. After receiving my test results, the psychologist suggested I was ready to begin the third or fourth grade. So, she knew the Kentucky school's protests about my aptitude had less to do with the student I was than *who* I was, but I didn't. In Minnesota, there hadn't been other black kids in my elementary school, and kids of color banding together on playgrounds as a united front—a

United Colors of Benetton—was still nearly a generation away. The boys who called me "monkey" in first grade had faces nearly as dark as mine but they would never have thought to befriend me because of our similarity. I can only assume that by taunting me they hoped to distance themselves from the complexions that distinguished us among our classmates.

The second week of second grade in Kentucky, I sat next to Ollie, dark-skinned, pristine and thoughtful—each of his Polo shirts lovingly ironed with creases at the sleeves. I had a six-year-old's crush on him, but I was also afraid, afraid of what it meant for the two of us to be connected by the presumed inadequacy that seemed the only option for black schoolchildren at the time. Our teacher was openly hostile to Ollie, an acrimony he didn't deserve: he was polite. In fact, he barely ever spoke. I decided to distance myself from whatever caused Ollie to be despised. I shot up my hand and made sure it was clear I had all the answers, even when I didn't have all the answers. I didn't realize this too was offensive. I didn't realize Ollie's quietness came from heedful parenting. Almost no town in America looks at black children and assumes we are destined to be doctors and computer scientists. By the time I started third grade, Ollie was gone.

It wasn't until fourth grade that I remember having black girls to play with, but by then I was frightened of leaving the tiny space I had carved out for myself among a group of white girls who loved Lisa Frank stickers, the colors purple and pink, and horses. I spent a lot of time drawing and pretending to fantasize about horses—a regional animal I never really cared for—an early form of the code switching that would character-ize my future, my multiple moves across the country and the Atlantic, reflecting back whatever version I think people want to see in me. During recess, I'd run back and forth between my two new friends and the Lisa Frank girls, whose favor was dan-gerous for me to lose. Most of the kids played kickball during recess, making it the perfect neutral ground between groups. Chloé, queen bee of the two other black girls in fourth grade, was most interested in the kickball concrete because it had the best view of Mrs. Blackwell's classroom, which harbored three of the school's cutest fifth-grade boys. We would flirt with them from outside the window—or at least Chloé, who had an older sister, and thus some idea of what flirting was, did. I would stand doll-faced next to her, hoping no one would actu-ally try to speak to me.

He thinks you're cute, Chloé would say of the boy with the killer white teeth and soft cheeks who smiled at me in a way I can only describe as fifth-grade suave. I thought he was cute but knew my mother would call Chloé's flirting back one of the things "only fast girls do," and I was only ten. I had gan-gly limbs and big eyes, I was still fantasizing about obtaining my very own American Girl. Mrs. Blackwell, who had taught Chloé's older sister, shooed Chloé and me away from the boys and closed the window. Then Mrs. Blackwell went back to ig-noring the boys while the rest of the class learned math. As sum-mer vacation neared, I moved farther and farther away from that window, immersing myself instead in a game the Lisa Frank girls had invented, galloping around on one leg, pretending to be ponies—a game I knew even then was completely asinine. I was scared of getting closer to any world in which boys kissed me. When I could no longer keep up the façade, I diverted my sexual energy to chasing the fastest boys. I pinned the shoulders of a boy who looked vaguely like a *My Girl*–era Macaulay Culkin to the concrete. I couldn't tell if I was deeply attracted to him. I never moved past my expectation that he would reject me because of my color. Unlike boys in Minnesota, Kentucky boys were generally raised to never hit girls, no matter what, a chivalry I tested by inflicting pain on them that spread a glee through me that was muscular, lustful, much less tragic than a kiss.

You need to be with your own kind, Chloé said to me with pity in her voice one day as I stood in the playground panting, a tired pretend-horse.

They are my "own kind," I said, trying to sound plucky and contrary, like a Melissa Joan Hart character. In truth, Chloé was less worried about me chasing down whiteness in one form or another on the playground than flirting with the older boys by herself. It wasn't that I believed what I tried to convince Chloé, that I was no different than the white kids. I just wasn't ready to accept my blackness as a limitation. If this meant that I alienated myself from black people, so what?

This, again, is where I feel we associate white supremacy with something too rigid. As early as second grade, I understood I had to be an exemplar of whiteness in order to be a good student. I had to communicate that I valued the superiority of this education over all other forms. I had a responsibility to hold

whiteness above even myself. This made me a white supremacist; it took me an entire childhood of racist discrimination to
learn anything different. I had to believe that white history,
white English, white geography, white science, white math—
and by extension white books, television shows, religious icons,
and movies—were the only ones that mattered. The more credible rendition of our story, in which human advancement is the
shared gift of all people, not solely the moral and intellectual
property of one made-up race, was taught in school as an unsup-
ported interpretation adhered to by the minority.

It is a lot to make our children conquer, on their own, the
white supremacist system we inherit through their schools and
popular culture, through their toy companions and trusted teachers. As kids, we learn we are lesser people only to spend the rest
of our lives unlearning it. Our children may find that counter-
education in our communities and families, but our institutions
do not invest in teaching them that without our contributions,
what we call America would have never existed. And the absence of us in the future will mean this country's absolute death.

I was eleven when Addy Walker first appeared in the American Girl catalog. I was young for sixth grade, hadn't yet started
puberty, and was still secretly obsessed with the Girls. *There's
a new American Girl doll*, my mother announced one day, as
if my sister and I hadn't heard. Addy Walker's arrival marked
the first time my mother drew our attention to the catalog instead of the other way around. She would hold the centerfold
picture of Addy up to us as she knitted in the living room while

we watched television. My sister and I kept busy, pretending not to notice our mother's shift in topic. *There's a new American Girl doll*, she mentioned again a week later while my sister and I finished our homework in the kitchen, *and she's black*. To ignore that a black American Girl had entered the negotiation we'd been trying to have with our mother for ages would have been a bigger offense than back talk. Addy was our sister. The only one of us gazing back from the depths of the glossy pages of American Girl history. But Addy Walker was a slave. A freed slave, to be clear, at least by the end of the *Meet Addy* book, but to get to that part of the story, Addy first watched her father and brother be sold off their cruel North Carolina plantation and *then* escaped with her mother to Philadelphia through perilous nights of wading in mud and running from dogs. My sister and I never said as much to each other but we both knew that Addy was the American Girl we were destined for, and neither one of us wanted her.

I heard the rest of the Addy Walker books are going to be written by Alice Walker, my six-year-old sister said to me diplomatically as we packed our school lunches in the kitchen one morning. That wasn't the case, but our knowledge of black writers consisted mostly of the authors whose names we scanned on the bookshelves of our parents' home, on the spines of books with fantastical titles that my mother said were still too grown-up for us to read: *The Color Purple*; *Black Feeling, Black Talk/Black Judgement*; *The Women of Brewster Place*. My sister was trying to tell me the doll had been approved by the kinds of black women I longed to know. But I still didn't want to play a slave. I had spent all of elementary school trying to distance myself from slave narratives, from singing "My Old Kentucky Home" in music class, from Kentucky's plantation history. Although no longer concerned with mimicking white superiority, I needed to keep myself apart from the fate of girls like me in history. Girls like me, meaning, black.

At home, I avoided telling my mother why I did not want an Addy Walker doll, still looking for ways to please her. At the library, I checked out *Sophia Scrooby Preserved*—a book about a young African girl, typecast as the heroic daughter of an African chieftain, who is captured and sold into slavery.

Is this what you want to read? my mom said, turning the cover of the book over in her hands.

Uh huh, I said—big, glass doll eyes. I didn't realize that *Sophia Scrooby Preserved* was written by a white woman, any more than I was aware my most beloved set of black children's books were written and illustrated by a Jewish man, Ezra Jack Keats. It was only later, in middle school and early high school, that I was exposed to the work of Alex Haley and Frederick Douglass, and Nikki Giovanni and Gloria Naylor and the women authors on my parents' bookshelves. I found Phillis Wheatley, drawn to the iconic etching of her face in profile on the pages of my fifth-grade literary reader. She looked smart. I started writing poetry. The more I wrote and read about her and the other black women whose biographies my mother began to buy to fill the shelves of our advancing girlhoods, the less I wanted to uphold the white supremacist education that "celebrated" the "achievements" of a few black individuals. I looked at the reports our teachers proudly assigned to me, my sister, and black classmates on

Mary Bethune, George Washington Carver, Muhammad Ali, and Benjamin Banneker with more cynical eyes. Black culture is not a shortlist of people whose exemplary conduct, despite their race, earns them a place in American history; I started to see I was a history I had not been taught and I knew very little about. By sixth grade, I assigned myself a report on Ghana during our geography class world history unit. I shot up my hand during a class lecture on Egypt, saying, *if Cleopatra was queen of the Egyptians, she had to have been black*. It wasn't the right answer but I wasn't concerned with having the right answer. I demanded to see a history that had me in it.

In the 2017 episode of the television show *Black-ish* "Toys-Rn'tUs," Tracee Ellis Ross' character, Rainbow, takes up the anti-slave-doll mantle when the show parodies the American Girl franchise with a brand they call Girlstory. Rainbow protests the store with a one-woman picket line and burns a stack of white dolls in effigy. Before being carried off by security guards, she spouts lines from Maya Angelou poems and Sojourner Truth. The show, whose title means "kind of black," is based on the presupposition that the family's wealth and social privilege are at odds with their blackness in an America where these things cannot coexist. The show's premise is not much different than what I parsed out of America as a child in Minnesota— that my brand of blackness was special. It reminds me of how often we educated, higher-class black people change the tone in our voices, like we're getting ready to sing an old Negro spiritual anytime we quote from "Ain't I a Woman."

Sojourner Truth never said "Ain't I a Woman." She said, "I

am a woman's rights." The phrase that elucidates how Truth saw herself—an enslaved black woman—as central to any conversation America can have about the law. She did not need to be rich or privileged to do this. She did not ask anyone if she was human enough to be of consideration. Truth's speech, which was published in the *Anti-Slavery Bugle* weeks after her extemporaneous delivery, was "translated" by a white female abolitionist twelve years later to sound like minstrel black English. The transcription from the *Bugle* looks nothing like "Ain't I a Woman." Truth's speech was originally delivered, and printed, in scholarly American English. Yet, here we are, Truth inscribed in even our memories as some white person's version of her. I think of "Ain't I a Woman" as a metaphor for the America® we are. Well or poorly educated, black or not, malicious or well-meaning, we all perpetuate the stories circumscribed in our histories. That it is our color that decides if we are main characters or caricatures in this country's beginnings. But America has never wanted us to have a full record of its people, especially its people of color, a chronicle of full human beings. Sojourner Truth worked diligently to inscribe her words in the *Bugle* so that we would be armed with our anti-slavery history. Imagine if Rainbow had been carried off by Girlstory security guards asserting, "I am a woman's rights," when quoting Truth instead of "ain't I?" The latter requests we make the stories of black women central to this country. The former demands it.

What I saw in American Girl Addy Walker was the America I associate with the support of white superiority as a brand. In the same way America preserves the history of its reservations as territory it bequeathed to indigenous nations (characterized in different accounts concurrently as both bloodthirsty and noble savages), America presents emancipation as a gift it gave black people. This history shows no accountability for how white America® got here, through the abuse, humiliation, and massacre of our bodies. The American Girl franchise didn't "give" us a slave doll. The slave doll is not their humble nod to black history. It is the preservation of a neat and tidy American slavery that can be seated beside the warm fire glow of a bedtime story.

Despite what America thinks, we, the people, shall not, will not, and never have been owned.

Of course, this was all Rainbow was fighting for in the doll store, a world in which us seeing ourselves in American history did not begin and end with white people telling our children they own us. It wasn't until 2016, a year before the episode aired, that American Girl introduced a new black doll into their historical series. (In 2011, the company roster briefly featured a black Creole doll named Cécile, but she was discontinued in 2014.) The doll's name was Melody Ellison. She was a Civil Rights–era singer living in Motown Detroit. (We don't have time here to break down the hodgepodge of black Americana that makes up Melody's backstory.) It took nearly twenty years for America® to find a second story about black culture to make the story of an American Girl.

I wrote *This Is Major* because we are major. Black girls have contributed to every step of America's development from conception to consumerism. We set the benchmark for beauty standards, language, and music, and have been pioneers in politics, invention, and industry. *You* are here. You are every girl and doll, in the make-believe that reclaims our unwritten origin story. Who dares to tell us black girls aren't real? This book is for the little girl who deserves a story in which a girl like her isn't concerned with being whipped or singing hymns or taking the moral high ground, because she is actually free. She can sleep. She can linger over a couplet as long as she wants. Her hands are soft. And she may scab when she rides her bike, but most of her scars are on the inside. And she has a lifetime to stitch them back. She has all the time in the world to sit in the sun and sip the sweet tea someone else made for her. And her mother is there and she never has to lose her. And her sister is there wearing the prettiest dress. And she braids and she braids and she braids the hair of the girl and the girl and the doll who looks like her and they all hold on, like they have no other American® purpose.

As for my eleven-year-old self, it is nearly winter when my sister and I decide to reveal our American Girl truth to our mother— that neither of us is ready to be a playtime abolitionist. My mom seems to understand.

Couldn't you just buy an Addy Walker doll and pick out the clothes from another character's closet to give her a new story? No, we say. In our minds, American Girls come with prescribed stories. My sister and I ask our mother to look through the catalog and choose the two dolls that remind her most of her two daughters. We are on winter break when our boxes arrive, containing Molly and Samantha. I don't know how my little sister felt, but the minute I opened the package and saw Samantha's stringy brown hair and velvet derby hat, the only thing I wanted was Addy. I wanted two Addy Walkers so my sister and I could hold each other in doll shape, trying on each other's dresses and plaiting our kinks. These were the ways we had always looked after each other—as family—the things that made us complete.

We played with our Samantha and Molly dolls for a week before we put the girls back in their boxes, and put the boxes under the bed, and our mother never scolded us when over a year of petitioning amounted to one winter afternoon of playtime heartbreak. I think she got it. I think she understood that, with each discovery, with each minor triumph, we were moving ourselves closer to the lead role of a major narrative. We have always been here. We were already American Girls®.

THIS IS MAJOR

YOU ARE HERE

The color of this book is Grace Jones
strapped into an electrical socket. The patron
saint, a black & white photograph of *Diana Ross
enjoying a rib*. This book's therapist-of-record Paris, Josephine
Baker. The official art
piece of this book is Lorna Simpson's *Wigs*.
The official hairpiece of this book is 100%
Kanekalon, Tank and the Bangas, the official
sew-in. The cheat code to this book is drop-it-down.
This book's favorite nickname is SZA.
This book once got lost in the forest of Noname's
blowout, only to come out a Simone Biles medalist.
This book's sister wrote a Mary Bethune report
by hand in the third grade. (This book is for her.)
This book's first crush was fast cars, then Tracy Chapman. This

book's favorite role play is
reverse femme dominant. Favorite country, Dominique
Jackson. This book lost its virginity to the remix
of "I Get Lonely" sung by Janet Jackson's crochet braids
(feat. Blackstreet). This book knows the meaning of
nay-hu. It does not speak in tongues, but it does understand
"How Did You Get Here?"—Deborah Cox.
This book can't decide if the weather today
is Michelle Obama side arms or Michelle Obama side-eye,
but it will show up laid, pressed, and dressed—you best
believe. One time this book almost got pregnant.
This book's Plan B would be knitting mittens
out of covers from platinum Motown albums—
The Supremes. Lupita Nyong'o is its best season.
And if this book goes to jail, it will be for
reciting the entire *nothing but death* monologue from
The Color Purple. This book will bring the
best peach cobbler
to your funeral and the best fried whiting
to your Caucasian House Joanne the Scammer
Christian picnic. Instead of *Get Better*, this book says:
Ida B. Wells. This book's favorite hair
salon is Kayla Newman *(On fleek!)*. And if this book had one
wish, it would be that every day is
the day dark-skinned Aunt Viv wore a lip-pink leotard and
danced the Dougie.
This book discovered the equation for dark matter
between Slick Woods' teeth: Zadie Smith's

On Beauty ÷ Betty Shabazz. This book's Rite Aid shopping list
reads: DREAMS-WINE-
CARMEX-KOTEX. A Lynn Whitfield soliloquy is its favorite
convenience store. This book's Shondaland
TGIT turn-up is *Another Round* cooking up their version
of Sandra Lee's Kwanzaa Hate Cake. This book's favorite hair
care regimen is The Lady of Rage.
Tyra Banks—its favorite financial institution.
This book's favorite gang sign is FKA twigs.
This book wants a selfie with Deana Lawson's
living room. This book still smokes Blacks
and writes Venus Williams love letters in chocolate
Sharpie, and if you're broke-down, the service manual for this
book is Erykah Badu's interview
for *Pitchfork* (Underrated!). This book's fertility
notification is a picture of Minnie Riperton fisting
melted ice cream. And when it gets busy it Audre Lordes, Nina
Simones. This book's favorite
pastime, Jenifer Lewis. This book's favorite temple is
Eartha Kitt. The official book club of this book is Edna
Lewis—biscuits—and the unofficial
ordained reverend of this book
is a Maxine Waters' filibuster. This is your June
Jordan. Your Rosa Parks. Your Billy Porter Met
Gala Realness Elementary School. Your senior high
yearbook superlative crossed out and scrawled
down as Fenty. This book's favorite scripture is Song
of Solomon 5, but it blots out "comely" for "fly"

—look, this book Toni Morrisons. This book just got married
to a picture of Tracee Ellis Ross &
wrote Lisa Bonet as its +1 on the "Save the Date" e-vite.
This book asks every story, *What Would Pat Evans'
Shaved Headed Do?* And the moral of this story is
you're welcome.

FOR COLORED GIRLS

Safiya, Kadijah, and I kept a notebook called THE CHRON-IC(LE) all through high school, pre–text message era, a spiral-bound group chat. We'd pass it between classes, the teachers mostly slick enough—or afraid enough—to keep us out of the same honors courses at the same time. We ruled the school, and THE CHRONIC made sure the fifty-minute interludes sepa-rating our three-part harmonies were still filled with musings, mayhem, and conspiratorial nonsense.

Like that time we stayed in the lunchroom during the first half of eleventh-grade English—our one class together—when a substitute was present, and ended up in the vice principal's of-fice. Even without a moment to collude, our lie was perfect. I blessed to THE CHRONIC, the place where we'd grown so accustomed to hearing each other's inner dialogue that it didn't take a lot for each of us to guess what the other one would say: that Safiya had an asthma attack, that the rest of us stepped in to help, that it was all a matter of confused circumstances—none of us had any intention of skipping Mrs. Underwood's eleventh-grade English class to begin with.

Of course, they didn't believe us. But our well-spoken, advanced-placement, code-switching, social-butterfly ubiquity was tolerated out of tokenism, which we accepted because we all had aspirations far outside our midsized Kentucky town. Maligning the three of us did the school little good, and we took what advantage we could of the situation. By the time we hit senior year, we each held designated offices that carried with them the responsibility to speak at graduation. The convocation, the benediction—like, I'd convinced the vice principal—on my own—to make the post of poet laureate so I could keep up at the speed with which my girls were running things, we were that big.

Senior year, we also all had parts in the school play, Ntozake Shange's *For Colored Girls Who Have Considered Suicide/When the Rainbow Is Enuf.* Safiya, Kadijah, and I were ladies in yellow, red, and blue, respectively. The cast also included the cheer captain (Angie in green), girls we knew from grammar school (Sequoia in purple, Jacqueline in brown, Chloé—my girl from fourth-grade recess—in orange), and an ensemble composed mostly of juniors, who all wore black. Twelve girls in total.

Of course, the show didn't go up in our middle-American high school without a hitch. There was plenty of complaining from the Drama Club that the school putting on a play that required an all black-girl cast was discriminatory, even though there was still the school musical to audition for in the spring, even though pretty much every musical we did was some rendition of *Guys and Dolls*. But the cast list was posted and we moved into rehearsals regardless. *For Colored Girls* was our drama department's competition play, which meant it was only scheduled to run for a month or two during the high school theater's early fall season, but our cast performed so well that we moved from local city competitions to all-state competitions and then toured the southeastern regional circuit for more. The run lasted all the way through spring, and the "colored girls" grabbed more accolades than any previous production in Paul Laurence Dunbar High School history.

Paul Laurence Dunbar: that was always the irony. Whenever we took to the road, the other schools assumed we were a bunch of black girls from a black school doing the blackest Broadway play to come out of the Blackcentric seventies. Instead, we were the only black girls at an all-white school in one of the richest suburbs in horse country, and most of us were bused in just to boost race and income demographics—their affirmative, action. The school was called Paul Laurence Dunbar because decades ago there *had* been a Paul Laurence Dunbar High School on the colored side of town (let's not play, Kentucky is the south, it *was* the "colored side of town") but that school had been condemned, then closed, despite active protests from community members at local government council meetings. Since the name carried some state significance (Dunbar was the son of Kentucky slaves), the school board promised it'd build another school in Dunbar's honor. It eventually did, on horse farmland a good forty-minute bus ride from any members of the community it was meant to serve.

But sometimes, we *were* Dunbar's jubilation. We were not just reciting poetry. We were poems. One time that fall, the whole cast was on a competition trip to Tennessee and held a Kentucky Fried Chicken hostage when it ran out of drumsticks at an all-you-can-eat buffet, singing a chicken song we improvised, Chloé and Jacqueline clucking around the buffet display case. We caught hell for that one, the drama teacher sitting us all down when we got back to the school with some saccharine speech about how *sometimes when we're having fun we assume everyone is having fun with us*, essentially asking us not to act so, well, colored. Of course, she hadn't been there, in the KFC, because the all-white all-school musical was in full swing by then, and because the number of requests we got to keep performing *For Colored Girls* was so unprecedented that the school arts program wasn't set up to support the school's only full-time drama teacher staying with us on the road. Much of the wrangling was instead left to our moms—who would rotate the responsibility of chaperoning us on out-of-town trips—and the play's director, Peggy Stamps. Peggy, a soft-spoken woman who'd been raised Bahá'í, was primarily a full-time artist, and she hadn't really signed up to corral rambunctious teenage girls. She was black and patient, but also gave us this look like she'd never played the dozens in her entire life. We knew we wore her out with our shouting and our digs and laughter, but we were so giddy, so high on our own momentum, we couldn't stop. This one bright instance we had in our brief lives to be essential. We colored girls took up as much room as we could in the temporary spotlight.

For all of us, learning to survive as black women felt larger than everything we were trying to become. We weren't treated right. We didn't always feel good. We didn't always love ourselves. We felt tangled in our skin tones and costume sizes as if caught in the coil of our hair. We spent our whole lives trying not to get noticed: not to get put on blast for having a kinky natural or big lips or no booty or all-ass—for possessing, in lack or abundance, what it meant to be a colored girl. On stage, we felt ordinary—or some variation of it—as if we didn't have to be anything better than we already were. It was as if being in costume gave us liberty to be real, and the version of us everyone knew—at school, at home—was somebody else.

I think a lot of these girls aren't virgins, my mom says, catching me outside the restaurant bathroom, alone, while we're out on the road with the cast, girded with freshly applied lipstick and a one-sentence precautionary "sex talk." She'd just seen Angie seduce a group of sailors at a Joe's Crab Shack with what I recognized as some of the choreography from her lady-in-green dance solo. I shrugged, thinking of Ntozake Shange's poetry—filing through my images of the unyielding patriarchal notions linking a woman's virtue to her chastity rather than her character. The colored girls weren't. A lot of these girls had seen a lot of shit girls our age shouldn't have. A lot of these girls had been hurt. By the time the show wrapped, at least one of the leads had clocked her sixth abortion and another found out she was pregnant. And these were the things I had been told directly, not the other tragedies I'd only heard whispers of. And my mom didn't know as she whispered to me outside the restaurant bathroom how much the dangers she wanted to protect me from had already hurt me. We never talked about the time she'd caught me masturbating at the age of nine. Shocked, we took out the Bible and we prayed and she told me this was not the kind of thing that good little girls do. I tried to tell her this had been done to me, taught to me, when I was much younger, only two. She couldn't hear it; she said it hadn't—so we prayed, a pact, and I locked up the words until, by the time I was a teenager, I'd repressed it so deep I didn't know anymore why I carried this pain in me, wrapped tight inside that I clung to instead of good company. I couldn't remember my broken girlhood. What I knew was, we were the first black family to live in the gleaming new suburban neighborhood right beside Paul Laurence Dunbar. Set between the rolling hills and white trim, my family was supposed to be picture-perfect. I tried to hold up my end of the heavy brass picture frame that surrounded our house and everything inside it; my mother, father, and sister; the horse farms that peered through each window; the immaculate china cabinet; the two-car garage that neatly stored a Jeep, a backup refrigerator, a regularly tuned Volvo sedan, and all our old toys. My place in the first black family to integrate our rich, white neighborhood was to not cry. In *Colored Girls*, I did.

Each night, I smudged thick, blue, midnight eyeshadow on my lids before each performance, the sensation of it so close to how I was in my life back then—always smearing on something beautiful to protect myself from my memory. Our cut of *For Colored Girls* included one long lady-in-blue monologue, "around midnight," about an abortion the character suffers through after a rape. Every time I performed the piece, I cried one fat, real tear on the stage. I maintained my makeup. I let go a little of the hurt I felt I'd kept inside me forever. *[A]nd nobody came/ cuz nobody knew*, I said, *once I was . . . ashamed of myself.* Although it was a feeling I knew well, the gift of *Colored Girls* was that it wasn't the end. Peggy had choreographed the piece so that, just before my blue lady broke down completely, Kadijah, in red, and Safiya, in yellow, came to the stage and wrapped me up in their arms. They'd help me offstage, the three of us linked arm-in-arm, as Sweet Honey in the Rock's "Balm in Gilead" played in the background.

It would be more than a decade after the play before I remembered what happened to me in my childhood, but I think the play began to untie me from a heavy grief. As a girl, I was singled out and vulnerable. As a colored girl, I felt like part of a formidable front line. Although keeping up with school and our private lives exhausted us, none of us quit the play. We suited up all through our fall semester, and into half of the spring.

In the spring, we were invited to Norfolk, Virginia, to compete in the southern regional high school theater colloquia's final round. In honor of our success, the drama teacher worked it so the whole school would see the play; we performed *For Colored Girls* in the Paul Laurence Dunbar High School theater for an entire day during every class hour, our fellow students ushering in and out during their English periods.

Near the end of that day, a group of junior boys gathered in the front rows to heckle Sequoia—lady in purple—about something they said she did with a boy. They booed ferociously as she stumbled through "sechita," the lines she'd rehearsed hundreds of times. She finished, only to cry something vicious backstage once her scene was over. I was angry they did that. I was angry they had taken *the time* to do that to her. Like we needed to understand what we really were: alone, worthless, and brown. But even to this, Ntozake Shange had an answer. As soon as Sequoia exited the stage and the stage lights lifted on my next monologue, "sorry," *if there's one thing I don't need it's any more apologies,* its opening line.

If there's one thing I don't need, I said, then paused as Sequoia's hecklers jostled to compose themselves, *is any more booing.*

What?

I heard scattered gasps expelled across the tar-dark theater. A couple of the other colored girls on stage broke character for a moment and cocked their heads. A certain tension invaded the audience as I continued, replacing "sorry" in the monologue with cues for how an audience should conduct themselves.

I got "boos" greetin me at the front door. You can keep yours, I said, now fully ensconced in my revision. The audience roared. The boys got read. The colored girls committed to the improvisation quickly, as we leveraged more gusto from the lines we knew by heart.

At some point during our rehearsals, it had become a tradition for lady-in-red Kadijah to regale us with stories about Ntozake Shange at our age. Kadijah's parents were academics and local black activists. The entryway to their house contained whole bookcases of first editions by black scholars. You couldn't take your shoe off without hitting an impressive carving filmed in light dust, or one of several large wooden ankhs. Kadijah's family treasury of books and ancestry qualified her, among our *Colored* cast, as our resident black girl historian. According to her, a teenage Shange, née Paulette Williams, had spent a few years living in our very town while her parents worked for the same federal hospital as my dad and Safiya's mom did. Paulette wrote poetry and breathed our same very air. She was one of us, we whispered. She was.

Ntozake Shange's name didn't appear anywhere in the set of Encyclopedia Britannicas lining the basement shelves of my parents' home. It was the era of dial-up internet and AOL, and none of us had the patience to fact-check the biography Kadijah had given us against the World Wide Web, or the reference texts at a public library. We didn't want to. The story sounded as true to us as being part of her play. I wanted to believe Ntozake knew me, that I could grow up in my Kentucky town but attend college at Barnard (like Zora Neale) and then move to Harlem (like Zora Neale). This was all I wanted. That—and to tie my hair up, like Shange in a yellow scarf, and wear long billowy skirts. With Shange, I felt I was both looking into my future and hollering back to the past.

⁓

Kadijah came to me backstage on the final night of our performance at the Southeastern Regional Theater Fest in Norfolk, her skin aglow, light sweat beading between her eyes, after delivering the show's final monologue, "a nite with beau willie brown," a piece Shange wrote after listening to her neighbor's screams and her neighbor's husband's laughter as he beat her.

I really felt it this time, she said. *I really felt what she was saying.*

I must admit I did feel the air still as Kadijah embodied the beating beau willie gave to the apartment's invisible door, which Kadijah then cowered behind, playing his girlfriend and kids. In the monologue, brown, a Vietnam War vet who returns drunk and damaged, terrorizes his young family. In the final lines of the lady-in-red monologue, he dangles his two children out the fifth-story window of their mother's apartment because she says she won't marry him. My stomach bottomed out when I realized—for the first time, maybe, in all those performances—that he *actually did* "drop them." But I was too worn out to mention it past a sweaty hug. We were all tired, the trip had done a number on us, and we were coming apart.

We lost the Norfolk competition the night before we headed home. It was our first and only loss during our run, and we felt crushed. It wasn't that we believed we couldn't lose—losing was pretty much what we'd been geared up for our entire lives—it was that our losing felt so particularly tied to our *Colored* coloredness. At the end of our performance, the judges asked us questions we couldn't answer about *the maturity of the play's subject matter for a cast of high school girls*, the choice to use *so many blackouts for transitions*. We shrank back into the carved spaces of our girlhoods, cumbersome and familiar. The warm approval of the spotlight no longer reached us, in the glare of this new critique.

You girls should feel so good you made it this far, a judge said to us, enunciating each syllable like she was pinching our cheeks. We were high school students. Untrained actors. We probably weren't anywhere near as good as we thought we were. But up until that moment, we'd felt as large as the accolades we had so far won, like our full-page spread in the *Lexington Herald-Leader*'s section on culture and arts. It had meant something to us, to our community, to hear a dozen young women say, *i found god in myself and i loved her fiercely*. Even before the criticism, as those house lights flooded our final performance, we knew we would have difficulty landing, leaving behind the chronic high, returning to the knowledge that we touched the ground.

We left the theater conference with two awards, one for Kadijah's performance (she deserved it), and the other a company award for costuming, a consolation prize—a yearbook superlative—"Best Clothes."

⁓

I want to dance with the midget, Sequoia whispered in my ear at the awards banquet after-party. It was 2000 and we were Kentuckians, she knew no other way to describe our fellow high school actor as we swarmed a circle around the two leads from the victorious schools—a little person and a guy who played a speechless hobo. We started play-grinding all around them and heard the hobo utter the first words we'd hear from him the whole long weekend: *I feel like God*. Of course, we danced and laughed and cheered on the winners until the last song, doing our imitation of the most gracious group of carefree Black girls the southeast had ever sent to represent. That was who we were. The carefree way we kept everyone in our lives together, our one true art.

Post-after-party, Sequoia, Safiya, Kadijah, and I all returned to our hotel room, and it was well after midnight when we tried to settle into a restless sleep before the next day's long ride home. Over the past six months, we'd seen a cruelty growing in Kadijah, but assumed it was her adjusting to her status as the Best Actor of our successful tour. But on the ride to Norfolk she'd yelled at the chorus girls, some of the youngest castmates, in a disagreement about politics. *You're f—ing ignorant*, she'd screamed, lowering her voice in the center of her F-bomb since the mothers were so close. The anger cramped up the bus, us each sitting either panic-stricken or seething.

In the hotel room, Sequoia and I had been sharing one bed, Safiya and Kadijah the other. Although there'd been tension surrounding Kadijah's outbursts before this trip, Safiya and I were confident we could handle the close quarters, and Sequoia, who had almost gotten into it with Kadijah weeks prior, agreed she could watch her mouth as long as Kadijah didn't say anything mean to her directly. Had Kadijah said anything to me that night, I probably would have shrugged it off or cried. But once we all got into bed, she started in on Safiya.

The two lay back to back as Kadijah shot insults at her sobbing friend. *Why don't you just hit me?! Hit me!!* Kadijah hissed. By the time the words were out of her mouth, I'd leapt from the bed and I'm pretty sure I already had. Kadijah covered her face with her palms. I continued to strike my fists toward her empty hands. Our mothers beat on the door, our screams pulling them from the droll of late-night television.

I can't remember where, or if, I slept that night. The next morning, I listened to Prince's "Purple Rain" on repeat the whole bus ride home. Safiya sat next to me, resting her head on my shoulder, but I told her she'd be better off comforting Kadijah, whom Safiya hadn't spoken to since the fight. I attempted a stoic acceptance of my own actions, pretending I didn't need anybody. I wanted to cry. I hated myself. I couldn't believe I'd laid a hand on a girl I loved.

A few days later, my mom took me over to Kadijah's house to apologize in front of her parents. The first thing Kadijah did when we arrived was run to the door and hug me, tightly, her body guileless and soft. She was used to situations like this, Kadijah confided in me, she was suffering from a version of Tourette's syndrome and was burdened with an inability to keep herself from blurting certain things out at the wrong time, a condition that was heightened by stress and lack of sleep. I'd had no idea. But then again, I'd never told either of my closest friends that I was self-medicating with blister packs of Klonopin and Zoloft I found in bags my dad got from pharmaceutical reps, attempting to feel less or nothing at all. THE CHRONIC, the notebook that defined our high school dreams, only covered certain chapters.

Despite Kadijah's attempts, I wasn't ready to reconcile. Even then, I wished my indignation had allowed me to act differently. Safiya, Kadijah, and I meandered the halls of our high school alone. There was no more CHRONIC, though I think Safiya— torn between her two best friends—held on to the notebook and kept writing in it long after I'd stopped talking to Kadijah, or even talking to myself. I was troubled by how our separation pleased the teachers at school, how relieved they were to see our sisterhood dissolve into solitude.

I know what you did, the new part-time drama teacher whispered to me, giving me a thumbs-up. The school had recently hired him during the theater department's upswing. He and his colleagues were happy I'd hit Kadijah, as the incident had torn away some of how they no longer wanted to see her, as a proud girl. If you're wondering what kind of adults would feel that way about a kid, remember that we were never children to them, Kadijah, the most outspoken and often the most courageous of us, especially. That year, Kadijah had been the president of the student council, and convinced the school to let her read one fact about notable Black figures on each day of Black History Month, over the loudspeaker, during homeroom. Throughout February, every time she took the mic, both students and teachers cringed.

Black people endured four hundred years of oppression, she finally said halfway through the month, tired of the insults she received after each morning's broadcast, in the lunchroom and in the halls. *You can at least get through four minutes of educa-tion during Black History Month.* I was sitting with Safiya in AP English. Ms. Repass quickly fired back at Kadijah's voice above our heads.

Slavery did not last for four hundred years, Ms. Repass said, *and if she wants to make such a scene she should at least get her facts right.* That was that. The rest of the class nestled back into white comfort, Safiya and I looked to each other and said noth-ing; we all opened our copies of *Beowulf.*

It was not yet the end of March when Safiya stopped coming to school altogether. She'd been in and out a lot that year for *For Colored Girls* and with illnesses, but in the final months of the year, the state board served her parents with a truancy notice. She hadn't exactly been skipping school. She'd just stopped coming. Unsettled by their daughter's shift in mood, from bright polyester to ripped paper bag, her parents let her stay home.

Even though I wasn't supposed to drive that far without permission, I took my silver Volkswagen Golf to her house one day, right after school. She was sitting on her bed looking at magazines, a circular fan in the corner turning the pages back to where she started. I offered to straw set her hair; she was in between a relaxer and growing her hair out and her thick dark naps carried a radiant sheen as I parted it. I didn't know what I was doing as I took the pin tail comb, stretching each section of her curls before wrapping them around the drinking straws we'd cut into sharp sticks of plastic. We tied up the roller set in a yellow head scarf and put her under the hooded dryer we'd pulled from the basement.

I'm depressed, she confessed to me under the batting sound of the dryer.

I am too, I said. It came out like I was trying to best her sadness, but I didn't mean to.

No, I mean I'm really clinically depressed. I am on medication. I knew what she needed me to hear, but I was too young to understand what to say, and I too was depressed in a way I had not named until I heard her say it.

Safiya came back to school the next day. The set never took, so she'd taken out the straws herself, and slunk in late to our history class, looking like the watercolor portrait of young Ntozake on the cover of our copies of *For Colored Girls Who Have Considered Suicide/When the Rainbow Is Enuf*, her hair tied in the yellow scarf.

❧

Have I ever considered suicide? Absolutely. When I was young, I had no plan to live past seventeen. I was afraid to watch myself fail and I was afraid my life wouldn't amount to much. A life in which I was loved and got to be a colored girl felt unfathomable to me. As early as the mid-1970s, studies have shown that, although average suicide rates for black people are still lower than for their counterparts, suicide is still more common among black girls ages fifteen to nineteen versus white girls the same ages. In 2018, the *Chicago Tribune* reported a 71 percent increase in suicide rates among African American children from 2006 to 2016. Yet many black people are still raised with the assumption suicide is something black people just don't do. Black people don't kill themselves. They never get depressed or go to therapy. It is not that we are taught we are happy, or taught to *be* happy. We are taught to not feel pain. Because of this, even in my twenties when I was diagnosed with depression, taking medicine, and going to therapy, I didn't understand why I felt pain more than my ancestors who had lost limbs and got doused with fire hoses and survived without expensive medication and a therapist's couch on which they could contemplate their existence. I felt a deep sense of unworthiness; I felt this way throughout most of my teens and twenties. I never committed suicide because I couldn't get myself to come up with a suicide plan—another weakness for which I hated myself. So instead, I stopped eating. I became anorexic. I developed body dysmorphia. Both acts at the time were completely devoid of vanity.

As a black girl, the only thing I wanted was curves, our signature womanhood. I knew that starving myself would make me less attractive, but I didn't feel I was worth wanting. I didn't feel good that I was still alive. I wanted to disappear. It was easier to wake up in the morning with less of me to hate than it was to take up more space. I fantasized about dying. I decided that if I didn't have the courage to kill myself, I could make it a brief, disconsolate existence. My hunger for suicide was a disease; how did I not see this, then, as oppression? I was a sad person. I was a sad little girl for a very long time.

Ntozake Shange came up with the full title of *For Colored*

Girls after attempting suicide several times in her early twenties. This all changed when one night, while she was driving through Oakland, California, she saw a huge rainbow and knew right then that black women have "as much right as the air and the mountains do" to survive. It wasn't until I was in my early thirties that I decided I wanted to live. I was recently divorced. I was recovering from ACL surgery. I was in my house alone, my leg layered in gauze and connected to a large machine that pushed ice into the sack surrounding it to keep the incision from swelling. Under the weight of the bag and the new scars, my leg felt like it was splintering. I needed assistance to lift it and get myself out of the bed, but there was no one there to help me. Desperate to use the bathroom, I rolled from my king-sized bed onto a stack of pillows I'd placed on the floor, then scooted all the way across the carpeted hallway and to the tile floor. It took me fifteen minutes to travel a distance that was at most twenty feet. I screamed the whole time. I didn't think I could make it. Although this would have been a stupidly simple thing for me to accomplish on a day when I was healthy, on that day the task felt insurmountable. That's exactly how staying alive in depression feels, blisteringly painful, sometimes, to stay here; back then, I constantly thought about giving up. But, I finally grabbed on to the toilet seat. I lifted myself up and scooted my underwear as far down as I could over the bandages and tubes that extended up my right leg. I expelled. I couldn't say that I felt joyful but I felt relieved. I couldn't understand how, as much as I didn't want to, my body continued to will itself to live and waste, to hurt and push. I didn't know I had years on the horizon ahead where I would feel I had as much right to be here as the air and mountains do, but something about the way I battled to piss that day turned on a switch inside me that said—*Love yourself. Please.*—that the reason black women have survived is so I can do exactly this.

⤖

I pop back in on Facebook every now and then to see how my colored girls are doing, and it was through Facebook I first learned of Karyn Washington, who founded the dark girl appreciation blog *For Brown Girls* when she was just eighteen. Amid my Facebook feed of colored girls, pictures of the roles they now play in real life—as early-education teachers, mothers, pastors' wives, sociologists, college professors, health care professionals, engineers, and police officers—I saw an article posted by one of my friends, reporting Karyn's death, alongside a collage of photos.

In the pictures, Karyn wears a black tank top, like she's one of the junior girls in my high school production, thick twists crowning in a loose bun at the top of her head. Although she wears the same shirt in each image, she strikes a different pose. She looks like she could have played the roles of each of the girls, all by herself, but I imagine her most in yellow. I can see her understudying Safiya's role, the way Sequoia once had to when Safiya was too sick to rehearse, practicing her pimp walk entrance, exaggerating Safiya's snuff and head tilt, all of us dissolving into fits of laughter we could only resolve with heavy breaths and tears. Perhaps being a colored girl would have saved her; the communion it gave me.

Although I don't know for sure if Karyn chose *For Brown Girls* as the title of her blog because she was drawn to Ntozake Shange, she called her site an "inspiration destination." She wanted to bring us together in a place on the internet where we could be held—just like I was.

"She really wanted to get people past judging themselves . . . to the point where you saw your body as more of a vessel for the work that you were going to do to help other people," said Karyn's close friend Yumnah Najah in an interview for *Madame Noire*. I know how that feels. There is something about being able to stand up on stage, or behind a screen, and begin. To speak of the force you know you are—not small and sad and colored, but a conduit connecting the gravity between the earth and heavens. I believe that's the way Karyn felt every time she sat down to rally us: like the day she took down A$AP Rocky for an interview he did saying dark-skinned women should leave wearing red lipstick to "the fairer skinned." Karyn was incensed by the comment's insinuation that rouging full lips makes us look apeish. She got her brown girls to Twitter and Instagram, to flood the internet with pictures. Red lipstick on their faces dolled as emblems of empowerment. Karyn the architect, her hashtag: #DarkSkinRedLip.

Despite the fact that Karyn's work as an activist for dark-skinned girls had been covered by *The Root*, BET, the *Washington Post*, and *Cosmopolitan*, by the time I knew her name, Karyn had already left us. At the age of twenty-two, Karyn Washington took her own life. Crusader that she was, she was battling a deep depression. According to reporter Anita Badejo, while Karyn was running the blog, she was also the sole caregiver to her single mother, who was suffering from cancer. When her mother died after a five-year battle with the disease, Karyn's depression was coupled with the weight of an incalculable grief. Although she sought help, Badejo writes in a *BuzzFeed* article, it was hard for people to see beyond the façade of the "carefree black girl" whose bright lipstick charmed them in pictures because "Karyn projected what seemed to many an unwavering air of happiness and security." That's what spoke to me in Karyn's photographs. The face I knew from my youth that read, *I am here. I am unsinkable. I can be whoever you need me to be.* But we can't.

The myth of the carefree black girl has taken many of us. We may live inside the moment where we laugh but we are always performing. Not in the way we colored girls did, where we were stretching and pushing beyond what we were told we could be, but in the way we were asked by our parents and our teachers and our towns to project the kind of strong, resilient womanhood that for a little girl is impossible. It is us saying to the world *you do not need to protect us* when in fact it does. Karyn reached out to her friends and her adult mentors. She learned that another black woman blogger, Ty Alexander, had also lost her mother, and had recently published a book titled *Things I Wish I Knew Before My Mom Died*. Karyn struck up an email correspondence with her. "Because I was so deep in my own grieving process," Alexander writes on her blog, "I replied with two posts that I had written. It was all the comfort I could give her at that time." When she learned of Karyn's death through a Facebook post in April, she says, "I went to Karyn's profile page and instantly broke out into an uncontrollable . . . cry. . . . I cried because I couldn't save her. I was way too busy saving myself."

I'm not calling anyone out. We are all capable of missing signs. Just as my mother thought telling me some of the girls in the show "weren't virgins" would protect me from the possibility of rape or violation, unaware that she was staring right into the face of a trauma she could not see. And just as I couldn't see until now how the coy dance Angie did at Joe's Crab Shack was probably her way of signaling that she felt safe with us—that she could climb to the ledge of whatever reason she needed, as a teenage girl, to dance for adult strangers, and we would all be right there: munching on fried fish and biscuits and ready to shout out loud, or hold her back, or do whatever we needed to save her, just as we had done for one another on stage. Or how I couldn't see how much Kadijah and Safiya, in their own private sadness, needed me. That THE CHRONIC, that tattered book we carried, might have been the first chance we'd had to say, *Hey, I'm here.* I can't say if Karyn would have lived any longer if she had had the colored girls, but I can say I did. I am here, in part, because so many people have loved me fiercely.

I saw Ntozake Shange read a few months before she died, at a theater in Brooklyn, my first time seeing her in person. She was seventy, and a young woman held her hand as she walked to the stage. Until she sat, I felt unable to breathe. I was convinced that if I breathed too hard I would break what, in the audience, had become a quiet reverence. *Thank you. Thank you*, we all seemed to say in the awed patience in which we listened to her footfall. She took her chair, center stage. She opened a notebook. She said she wanted to read us something new she was working on, the pages pale as a yellow scarf. Blue stage light. Red lipstick.

I TRIED TO BE TWITTER FAMOUS

I did. Not hard. More like the way I learned all the steps to the dance break in Sisqó's "Thong Song," watching the BET Countdown every day after school for as long as the song charted. I was ready—in case the song ever played in the high school cafeteria—to shuffle toward an imaginary dance floor as soon as I heard *That girl so scandalous*, like my white JNCOs were full of sand. I pretended I'd end the sequence trying to land a backflip, knowing that I never could. I never practiced my moves in the mirror but I thought I looked good. If you ever watched me dance in the noughties, though, you'd know that, no matter how much I aimed for video vixen, I looked like Jack Skellington, a thin, dark fantasy battling the top of a helical hill. All limbs and rhythm and no direction. This is me on Twitter.

    I first heard about Twitter around 2008. I was at an MTV taping of a *Making the Band* reunion special at a studio in

Times Square. I'd been writing freelance articles for a culture blog and the girl who usually covered the hip-hop beat was sick, so I'd been armed with her questions, her press pass, and a digital camera. (I didn't own an iPhone, the smartphone was still in generation one.)

The press box was a who's who of hip black bloggers, none of whom I'd ever met, in impeccably curated outfits and twist-outs. I'd just moved to Brooklyn from Kentucky with a pair of well-worn cowboy boots and skinny starter-locks. Though I'd barely learned what a MySpace page was, MySpace was already irrelevant, and I had never really watched reality television. As the A-list bloggers tapped away madly at their phones, I scanned the box for a conversational ally, and saw a girl with a spiral note-book smile at me.

Busy night, I said, gesturing toward the in-crowd. She rolled her eyes. We talked a bit more before I felt comfortable enough to expose my ignorance. *What are they doing?* I asked.

Oh, she said, surprised. *They're all on Twitter.*

Diddy came out on stage to the sound of dancehall air horns and his own eponymous song. He hopped from one side of the stage to the other, convulsing in a Harlem Shake. He catapulted wads of black T-shirts that read NO BITCHASSNESS from a cannon. The crowd loved it. The Young, Black, and Bloggerful posted live tweet after live tweet on their iPhones. I watched them while everyone else watched *Making the Band*. I tried to pretend like I fit in, pulling out my Blackberry and furiously live-texting my sister. From that point on, Twitter has always been a place for a swag I do not carry. When I say swag, I mean I can't pull off a Sisqó backflip. When I say "Twitter," I mean Black.

Black Twitter is the place where Twitter goes to have a social life: the coolness of black culture reconstructed in memes, social insights, and pop culture commentary. Black Twitter has, essentially, become Twitter. I say this as someone whose job it used to be to write social media content for agencies whose client lists included Nike, Adidas, and Google. My first day on one new job, I sat down to read the company's onboarding materials—a roster of strategic data collected about every viable social media platform, including Twitter. What was listed for its demographic? "95 percent Smart Black People." I wondered about the polling data and percentages that delineated how many "smart black people" were on Twitter when none of the other social media platforms included a metric for race. I wondered about the implications of a company's on-boarding materials calling for the exploitation of smart Negroes. But I needed a paycheck. I sat through multiple PowerPoint presentations whose title slides incorporated gifs of Oprah and scenes from *Black-ish*. I sat through creative brainstorms where white folks suggested we turn some big company's new product into the "Bye, Felisha" of products. (I still don't know what that means.) When I say "Twitter" is Black Twitter, I've collected the receipts.

Even before it was my job to know Twitter, I studied it like a groupie. I did this the same way I approached black barbecues and house parties I was way too awkward to be at—standing in the back, pantomiming the slick dance moves I saw other people do, waiting to practice them later in the privacy of my own room. I didn't know all the words to the hit songs but tried to come in real strong at the harmonies. I used to consider Twitter an online version of a black Greek banquet, an HBCU home-coming where everyone except me knows the right things to say. Where everyone is gorgeously aloof and perfectly pressed. Because I'd spent years feeling like this kind of outsider in my extended family, and really at every black social gathering, I wasn't in a hurry to log on to a community in which my jokes were too slow, my pedicure too jacked, a place where it would be easy for people to call me out for the ways I wasn't living up to black cool.

As is often the case with my insecurities, I know now I was wrong about those expectations of cool being all that Twitter had for me. If I go back to the MTV press box, I'm certain many of those kids still had the tags hidden inside their expensive jackets. Some of them were probably recent arrivals from the South or Midwest. Some were probably texting their sisters to look like they were going viral on Twitter, or live-tweeting to an audience of almost no one.

Had I understood years ago that Black Twitter was a house party invite I missed out on rather than a party nobody wanted me at, it might have been good for me. It's a social common ground for everyone hip enough to get a house party invite, as well as their uncool cousins, as well as their aunties who live in rural Iowa with no other black people on their block. We mourned together. We watched *Scandal* together. We let people in on our inside jokes, our nerd cosplay, the quirky expressions that came out of our children's mouths. We made our private lives public so that we could become more intimate with each other despite our physical distance.

I could have used Twitter when I was living in a small village in the Netherlands, listening to NPR on a small world band radio, when I heard that Trayvon Martin had been shot. I didn't know any other African Americans there, and I deeply grieved both the loss of Trayvon and the loss of an America many of us had hoped Obama's presidency would foster. I thought of Harlem, where I was living the night he was elected, and waking up the next morning to the streets still filled with ticker tape. Even when I found an empathetic ear in the Netherlands, it was lent to me in a different context, a different native language. It wasn't the same. I needed more; an international network of black voices would have helped me.

Maybe I am a little wistful about missing out on Black Twitter's earliest stages as an agent for communion and change. When I finally joined Twitter it was 2013, and my first poetry book was coming out. I was in an MFA program and the students in my cohort were using the platform to connect with small presses, journalists, editors, agents, and other writers, and I realized I should be doing the same.

Of course, it takes a lot of hubris to start a Twitter account in 2013 and think you'll be welcomed with open arms. Twitter will humble you. The music is loud and the dancing is already in full swing and everyone has already clustered off to two-step or sway in their own little groups or watch two famous people break-dance battle in the middle of the living room. No matter how many people I thought I knew on Twitter, no matter how many poems and articles I had published, no matter how good of a writer I thought I was, the people of Twitter were in no hurry to become my audience. Although I'd secretly hoped my arrival on Twitter would generate a tiny ripple of excitement, I wasn't offended when my following stayed low.

From the outside, Twitter can seem like a place where strangers will immediately validate you with two thousand "likes" just for listing what you had for breakfast, but that only happens when you have invested time in it—true for Twitter celebrities and bona fide celebrities alike. There are a lot of ways to become Twitter-famous, but it can be difficult for a late adopter to build up a following without developing a persona or brand, and without knowing the social behaviors. Many of the people who have gone viral have done so because they understand Twitter's norms and have cultivated their followings accordingly. They're the people you always expect to see on the Twitter dance floor.

That said, Twitter was a place where I could see what writers I admired were thinking without having to fan out in front of them obtrusively. I liked this path because it let me be quiet. I was there, on Twitter, but I didn't feel the compulsion to become someone. My feed mostly consisted of me tweeting lines from books I read, "@-ing" the authors as a citation. As my visibility grew a little as a poet, I started to feel the same pressure to be presentational on Twitter that I had back in 2008 texting my sister on my Blackberry while watching *Making the Band*.

It can be hard to tell if you meet me, but I suffer from pretty strong social anxiety. I survive my misgivings about always saying the wrong thing and trying to decode everyone's micro-expressions by performing. I can exude confidence and charm and humor even when I don't feel like it, especially with the buffer of a couple of cocktails. During a networking evening at a conference in Washington, DC, I ran into a group of well-known authors, some of them Twitter-famous. They found me engaging, in my moment of wit and jazz hands, and asked me for my Twitter handle. A few months later, I ran into one of those writers, an older white man, at an event in Portland. He told me he had stopped following me on Twitter. *When I met you, I thought you were going to be interesting on Twitter*, he said, *but you aren't.* As a fan of his work, it hurt me. I thought I had made it. I thought exchanging Twitter handles meant we were now in each other's orbits—like adding someone on LinkedIn or Facebook, a process that I was also late to adopt but found easier to comprehend.

Although I still look at Black Twitter with some awe for its early days, I am frustrated by how it has created yet another space in which black people are critiqued. As the platform has grown, I've watched mainstream media distill the candor and colloquialisms that gave the platform its black authenticity into a quaint minstrel show for whites. This version of Black Twitter manifests itself frequently. Black people are often exceptional cultural performers. Without noticing it, we code-switch into what we are told to be. For me, having a famous writer tell me I wasn't interesting enough on Twitter read the same as him telling me *I* wasn't enough. I didn't understand then that he'd followed me so I would entertain him by performing my blackness, that I was supposed to use Twitter as a way to work toward his approval. This is the exact reason I avoided Twitter to begin with. I am always worried this is the way people feel when they read my feed.

I decided I needed to start flexing my Black Twitter swag, although I was still saying "swag" and had none. I created my best imitation of what an interesting black tweet should say. I sat at home trying to figure out how to turn my Twitter feed into a living journal of black inner thoughts. I was home alone listening to Sun Ra and Mozart, but I couldn't tweet that I was home alone listening to Sun Ra and Mozart. So, I carefully prepared a tweet about how it's hard for me to get down with a full Cardi B album because all her brags sound like how I felt the first time I got a job with dental. I posted the tweet and waited for the like count to go up—twenty people. Not only did I feel bad at Twitter, I felt like a fraud. What I had wanted to do that day was write an essay about how "Bodak Yellow" cuts through the narrative of mean-girl bullying with a vulnerability that makes my neck ache from bobbing "yes" so hard. I wanted to sit down and write that while listening to Sun Ra and Mozart. But I didn't. Instead, I kept refreshing the "like" count, so fixated on the idea of having a cool idea I no longer felt the drive to explore it.

There is the type of writer who is brilliant at Twitter and then there is the type of writer who is, tweet-unfortunately, me. I am a highly social introvert—a personality type that is usually very good at Twitter as a medium—but I am also an internal processor. I'm not good at thinking through what I want to say by saying it. I might have witty thoughts, but I edit and overthink them before I can ever transcribe them and by that time the moment to tweet has fluttered away. I will never be the first one to have a clever thing to say on the hour—or multiple times on the hour if I'm live-tweeting a Diddy concert or the scandals of Olivia Pope.

Black Twitter is by no means a monolith. What I'm describing is one of the many ways people use the social platform to communicate. I'd be remiss, for instance, if I did not mention the number of offline political movements that began as hashtags: #BlackLivesMatter, #MeToo, #MuteRKelly, #DarkSkinRedLip. Black Twitter contains so many conversations of short-form liberation. But the part of Black Twitter that often lives on in infamy is its minstrelsy. That "95 percent Smart Black People" marketing demographic enmeshed in the white gaze. As a free public platform, Twitter provides mainstream culture unfettered access to black conversations when they have traditionally had to pay us to "be interesting" through concerts and movie tickets and cocktails. White culture sees the cool black party, and unlike me, they open the door and step right in. The problem isn't that they want to join us. The problem is there is a difference between their allyship and their adoption of our viral gifs, hashtags, videos, and catchphrases to recognize them. They refuse to acknowledge the political damage this does to what we are saying. There is a massive difference between a white person hearting a gif of Beyoncé's Coachella performance to show support for the visibility of women and a white person using a gif of Beyoncé smashing cars to highlight a white contribution to the feminist movement. One version of this conversation is Twitter alliance, the other is Twitter erasure. One version of this conversation supports Black Twitter, the other version of this conversation makes Black Twitter a meme.

Just as I will never understand the type of white person who tells me I don't give good black person, I will never understand the type of white person who fetishizes Black Twitter. I do not understand how one relishes the opportunity to crash a house party, either not realizing or not caring about the imposition they create in an intimate space. At its most innocent, the insertion of the white gaze upon Black Twitter conversations results in a loss of engagement after @RainbowBriteWhite hops into the thread with a post she thinks is clever but completely misreads the conversation's nuance. (Threads in which, it is important for @RainbowBriteWhite to understand, her "freedom of speech" has no relevance because it shuts down opportunities for other free-thinking people to communicate out of necessity, rather than a desperate attempt to stay socially relevant.) At its least innocent, the white gaze in Black Twitter spaces has created what's known in online communities as "blackfishing," white people who create personas to disguise themselves as black people—darkening their skin for photographs and mimicking black slang in their tweets to gain a larger following—a social media of Ariana Grandes. In some of Twitter's worst moments, black people blackfish *themselves*—taking cues from the authentic style of popular black tweets to transform into cool black caricatures, hoping this derivative version of who we are may earn them a shot at viral fame—the new, digital blackface.

The appropriation of Black social creativity without proper attribution (and in cases as extreme as the adoption of Kayla Newman's phrase "eyebrows on fleek," without proper credit or compensation) is rampant, and carries a foreboding irony. Black people took to Twitter and Vine and YouTube and Instagram and blogs because the white mainstream media continued to relegate our stories to the sidelines. In response, we created an internet dialogue in which our stories were regularly featured, a platform where those of us with the talent to be journalists, influencers, and culture critics could make our own content. And as we laid a flag upon this lush digital country, with its hashtags and new nomenclature, white people—willing to recognize the power in our thoughts but not our thinkers—started moving in to colonize. Working in advertising, this reality was never lost on me: I, a non-tweeting black girl who went to graduate school to study poetry, was hired by a white company who stole from Black Twitter conversations to sell products rich white people would only buy if we talked about them like the actual Black Twitterers they refused to hire.

Despite how much I failed at Twitter, I was still convinced I needed to be Twitter-famous if I ever wanted to make my mark on the literary world, a world in which the popularity of your online persona often becomes a major factor in what your writing career looks like. I started working at a social media marketing agency because I saw the shift in the publishing market and thought it was the best way to learn how to build a better online presence for my second book. It wasn't that I needed the book to succeed to support my ego. I was also pitching an essay collection (*this* essay collection) to big publishers, and my agent informed me some of the editors who had been interested passed because I didn't have a large enough social media following. Perhaps this is too meta, but I'm sharing it because I was surprised this was something no one else had ever told me. I knew that models and reality TV celebrities needed to maintain large social media followings in order to get gigs these days, but I didn't know that the same was true for poets and essayists. Even if it wasn't the only factor in the success of my work, it was another way in which I saw myself as Twitter inadequate, and so I wondered if there was anything I could do to bolster my Twitter account.

You know, you could just buy followers, a white former colleague said over cocktails after I told her about my social media concerns as an author, looking very pleased with herself for having provided a solution to my problem. *I saw a story about it on* Dateline *once*. She took my phone from my hand and started scanning Twitter pages of authors with high follower counts. *See*, she said, *you can tell a lot of these "people" who "follow" them are bots*. I didn't care whether other authors' followers were real or not. I wanted to appear Twitter-successful. I was putting myself in the mindset of being a marketing strategist for myself.

What my former colleague didn't know was that I had already tried to buy followers. I felt sleazy about it, the same way I felt in middle school when I tried to stuff my bra. Even though I didn't believe I was fooling anybody, I hated being the girl with the flat-chested Twitter account. Under the guise of studying up on brands that used fake follows for flash promotions and influencer accounts, I researched companies that sold follows as a side project at the social media agency. After weighing the options in terms of price and legitimacy, I finally selected the company that looked the least like a credit card scam. In addition to the Better Business Bureau logo at the bottom of its main page, it boasted the guarantee that all (which I generously interpreted as "some") of the followers they offered though their site were real Twitter accounts—people who were paid a nominal fee to pretend like they were interested in their clients' social media accounts. I hovered my mouse over the options for what my new Twitter following should look like. 10k. 5k. I finally settled on a modest one thousand. I wanted it to look like my following had grown, but I didn't want the growth to seem phishy. The website asked if I wanted to opt-in to a feature in which my new followers would also scroll through my old tweets and bolster them with likes. *Why, how thoughtful*, I said to myself, daydreaming how to introduce me to my newly acquired throng of real and imaginary followers.

How long would it take to become Twitter-famous? The company's FAQ page said about a week. I spent the next ten days filling my Twitter account with my thoughts on eating meat, J. Cole's latest album, waking up in the morning, and hoping I didn't get frostbite after stepping in a puddle in my Doc Martens. I @'ed every product I mentioned and celebrity I wrote about, hoping the added name recognition might help my musings go viral. When nothing happened on the eleventh day, I reached out to the customer service department, convinced I'd been duped.

We tried to fulfill your request, miss, said the patient customer service agent, *but we couldn't find enough followers who would willingly seed your account. We will try again in two to three days. If we don't succeed, we'll give you a refund.*

They gave me a refund.

I couldn't even pay people to follow me.

I have not yet become Twitter-famous. Twitter is a battle I have tried to fight and have lost in so many ways. But I think that's alright. Although social media is filled with commercialism and fake representation, my experiences with Twitter convince me there still exists within in it an authentic space. It may never be mine, but if I don't earn the right to be listened to, to dance and talk with people, that's okay. Perhaps I still haven't figured out yet, out there, what I want to say. But if you're out there, too, maybe we can talk about it.

Twitter at me, America.
Shamelessly,
@blueifiwasnt

TAMMY FROM HR

You are here because you are cool. You have arrived. You've finally landed a career in some transparent millennial advertising agency with the pinball machine and the snacks and the sliding glass office spaces. After three to six interviews and a probation period that amounted to an extended six-month half-paid internship—so you could shadow the girl whose new position comes with a pay bump meaning she will earn four times more than you—you have made it: a job with health care and vision and dental and sick pay and the opportunity to quit at least two of your four to six side jobs.

You understand you are a commodity. You are meant to keep your hair big, your nails hood, and someone more obscure than NAO on the company turntable. You are here to give your company street cred. You are here to be . . . not enough so that anyone can get you snapping your neck or popping your gum like a black girl sitcom stereotype but . . . enough so that your officemates can visit the bar where you DJ on weekends and ask you who to call to cater in collard greens.

Lucky you.

And you've probably watched a lot of movies. The ones where Kate Hudson or Katherine Heigl is at the helm of some transparent millennial advertising agency where she "has it all" and "works hard" and points her finger at things she likes to make important decisions; where the ad campaign she's developing hints at the romantic mess in her personal life, and by the end she'll have to choose between a job in Paris—one that she neither applied for nor is qualified to do—and some vapid neighborhood heartthrob. And when that man arrives at her office unannounced, carrying a bouquet of wilted carnations, she throws down the red wax pencil she edits with—the kind no one uses anymore—to jump into his arms. You stay through the credits, contemplating why Hollywood movies don't want women to have jobs. You lift your feet from the sticky floor, impulse-folding your empty containers of popcorn and Raisinets, realizing that the office where Hudson/Heigl worked had no black people.

It did. We were all visiting HR.

Your first trip to HR begins the moment you're paired with Becky with the Massive Inferiority Complex. Becky follows women on Instagram who make their own nut milk, and she adopted her dog from a disaster relief area because the lead production assistant in your office—a girl Becky Single-

White-Femaled into best friendship—did too. You and Becky are assigned to complete a series of projects that only a natural-haired black girl and a desperately overestimated, entitled thirty-something convinced that becoming a "creative" is going to launch her career as a freelance wedding planner can accomplish.

Becky spends a lot of time doing who-knows-what on her smartphone. She is exceedingly nice and chatty with the other people who share your sustainable reclaimed bamboo workstation. Everybody except you. You accept this, suggesting to Becky that the two of you should "lock in" a half hour on your Google Calendars for some "face-time" and although she's sitting right next to you, although she's not busy—and you know this because you just peeked at her Google Calendar—she shrugs.

Much like in middle school, you do the project yourself, assuming that once you're finished, you'll walk Becky through it, having left gaping holes in obvious tasks so she can feel like she's contributing, and make sure you both receive full credit. You know this doesn't exactly make you a "team player," but you recognize it's been a little bit harder for Becky to pass the ball since she's not used to point-guarding somebody black. For your half-hour meeting with Becky, you bring a list of ideas, hoping to assist her down the court to the play you've got as your end game. You put on your "smile face" (maintaining the psychotic steadiness of a Batman villain) and share ideas.

Becky has not had time to come up with any ideas. She has been too busy. You say you understand this, this project being

a less-important part of her workflow (it's not) than the obviously rigorous schedule she's been maintaining (she hasn't).
She grunts, knowing you have seen her empty Google Calendar. She blurts a half-assed idea off the top of her head. You
think, that's a stupid idea, and agree it's a great idea, directing
her toward the list of reasonably executable advertising campaigns you spent most of the night working up, looking for the
thought most similar to hers. She says if you'd been working in
creative longer, you would know why your idea wouldn't work.
That may be so. You ask her if the two of you can keep cracking
at hers. You tighten up your smile face and pull out a new piece
of blank paper, diving in to her piece of an idea with a preschool
teacher's enthusiasm. You know you sound pedantic, but past
Beckys have made it clear to you that Beckys like to be spoken
to this way. It reminds them of *The Help*. You have spoken to
Beckys other ways in offices and it has always resulted in *You
made Becky cry* or *You made Becky feel like she knows less than
you do with her associate's degree and your graduate school education and her previous customer service job at Macy's and your
more senior position in this company* and so you bob up and down
on the pink carousel horse of Becky's preferred communication
style, holding close to its spiral pole.

She gets frustrated. You do too. You suggest the two of
you take a break and reconvene the next day since you've both
worked hard (well, you did) and you have plenty of time to
finish up the project tomorrow (no, you don't) which she, be-
grudgingly, agrees to, returning to her nicey-nice conversation
with the project manager at the other end of the sustainable

reclaimed bamboo table about whether Madewell or REI carries better knit beanies.

You come to work an hour early the next day with your half-finished PowerPoint and, in your pocket, your best campaign idea. You don't know if it's best to introduce the idea to Becky as if it called to you while you were standing next to the kombucha tap in the kitchenette that morning, or if you should wait and "bust it out" as a last resort when you two sit down with your creative director. The first version sounds achingly tedious. The second version sounds like throwing her under the bus. Your smile face expands at the mention of it, but you decide it is much better to give your colleague the benefit of the doubt. When she comes to the table with her latte in a white paper cup, you are brightly typing away.

She opens her MacBook, and then pulls up a more-than-half-completed version of the PowerPoint you two began on her desktop. Apparently, during the night, Becky has come to the same place you did about the best campaign idea to push forward—either because she saw it on the list of ideas you previously shared and you successfully incepted her subconscious, or because she came to a reasonable conclusion on her own. You are elated. You ask Becky what she wants to "bust out" and then ask her what she'd want you to "bust out" and you both dive in.

The project idea you present to your creative director is solid. The pitch gets pushed through. You and Becky are set to lead a team that will help flesh out your vision. The mood is all backslaps and high fives. You return to your sustainable reclaimed bamboo table workstation expecting this will be your and Becky's moment right out of an ebony and ivory buddy movie, but based on the way she slams her MacBook down onto her desk, it appears this is not the time.

You never let me talk! she screams. *You are always taking credit for all our ideas.* You distinctly remember the moment in the presentation where you gave Becky all the credit for your ideas, and since this is the first time you have ever worked together, you are unsure why Becky is using the plural. *I have ideas,* she screams. Becky is unstable. You try to dial down this confrontation. By this time, all the workmates Becky plays nicey-nice with are off at barre or SoulCycle. There are no witnesses to Becky's tirade in your corner of the office. You apologize to Becky although you do not know what you are apologizing *for* to Becky and you tell her maybe the two of you can talk about it the next day over a matcha.

You meet Becky at the coffee shop, two blocks from the office, that hands out the sustainable white bamboo paper cups and lids. You buy her a latte (she doesn't drink matcha) and keep the receipt. You and your maniacal smile listen to stories about her small-town upbringing—her recollections of which sound vaguely racist—and stories from her undergrad days, which you have no interest in. You ignore the fact this bitch just yelled at you. You show you are willing to be all welcomes and fixed smiley faces. You assume that you and Becky have made up.

But it isn't enough. Having identified that yelling is one way to get what she wants—and recognizing that, as the only black girl in a glass office, you can't yell back—Becky begins to yell regularly, at the top of her lungs, her most accessible superpower. She yells at you if you ask her to work late. She yells at you when her disaster-relief rescue dog eats crumbs from your gluten-free muffin off the floor. And if she isn't yelling, she is cutting her eyes, which means she might yell. She has stopped trying to hide her contempt for you from the rest of the office. But given that you are black and she is "so nice," everyone continues their clicking away at their workstations, content to let you two "hash it out."

Did you try to "hash it out" with her? asks Tammy from HR as she pulls out an empty folder from a pristinely organized filing cabinet. She draws a fresh incident report form and a retractable ballpoint pen from her desk drawer. The actions themselves are comforting, almost Zen. Like the affirmations you imagine she conducts each morning, presented on sticky notes assigned to specific corners on the bathroom mirror, or that thing you've seen people do before TEDx Talks where they raise their arms in the air and shout: *I CAN!* and *Be it, Do it! Believe it, Dream it!* or just *Michelle Obama!* You look around Tammy's minimalist office—the only opaque walls in this millennial workplace—searching for one of those HANG IN THERE! cat posters (a staple of dentist's offices in the eighties), but Tammy's office is tastefully empty of motivational memes.

One wall is painted an unobtrusive light slate or yellow or mint green. Tammy's desk is uncluttered by personal paraphernalia, save for a few family photos that include, but are not limited to, a portrait of a girl relative whom she connects to you. *I know how you're feeling right now*, she might say, *I have a daughter about your age*, but Tammy typically doesn't, so "daughter" is replaced in conversation by the word "niece," or "cousin," or "Rotary Club sister" to establish kinship.

Did you try to take her for matcha? Tammy asks. Yes, you did take her for matcha. This is not your first ride on the Becky carousel. You take out your receipt. *Well, I don't really know what else you can do then.* Tammy sighs. She clicks her pen and puts a check mark through all the incident report squares. She reminds you of how important it is in this office to be "collegial." You consider asking if Tammy might think Becky's distaste for working with you might be "racially motivated," but you know this is a transparent millennial office and you would be, essentially, drafting your own termination letter and you have neither hired a lawyer nor gotten your nails done, and are too tired to search for a new job.

Becky's assigned a new partner. You are assigned to no one. Becky moves her things from your shared bamboo workstation to that of her new workmate's with the smugness of a grade school girl who just acquired a dozen crisp new Lisa Frank folders. You have weekly check-ins with your creative director about the drop in your productivity now that you have no new campaigns to develop and are working as a team of one. You see Becky with her new partner, giddy as a power bombshell in a Kate Hudson flick. In the next fiscal year, Becky will get promoted—the rose that grew from white privilege—and you'll be out of the transparent creative sustainable millennial advertising agency entirely.

The next time you see Tammy, she comes to you. You are still adrift in the transparent millennial office space, cutting your eyes every now and then at Becky, who seems happier than

My Little Pony. You use the time to make yourself as invisible as possible so that everyone forgets you work there. You still have no assignment. Occasionally, you are called into a meeting where you try to convince your British boss the "cool" new tagline he's developed, *Dyn-o-mite!!!*, sounds like a derivative reference to the seventies show *Good Times*. Occasionally, you shut down an office brainstorm by explaining to the new strategist who created the client brief the company cannot pitch the paid content on a rapper's Twitter feed to a music company as "woke Kanye West." But most days, you go unutilized. You sit at your desk without a project for weeks at a time. You show up and shut down. You wear the same turtleneck and jeans to the office for days in a row, drafting spirals in your notebook like a sad, black Steve Jobs. You barely remember who you were when you interviewed: your bomb-ass portfolio of independent contracts, your tech-forward intuition for trends and fine art. You barely remember the days in the office, pre-Becky, when you would beam when talking about your work—the huge winter campaign nearly ready to launch or the new social media widgets you'd been toying around with—drinking kombucha and dressed to the millennial nines.

You become convinced the company keeps you on because letting their one black full-time employee go is a millennial company no-no. It's not true, actually, that you're the only black employee; Tammy's team has at least one half-black female employee who is super-awesome but whom you almost never see unless you take a detour on your trips to the bathroom, and only talk to if she is not with another employee and only if you two whisper. You should have developed a code language, you reflect. But you don't need it the day when the first of two black freelancers start in the office and you lock eyes with Tammy's protégée as you realize the first of them is a "him."

Surprising. Because although you are here because the only thing any millennial company seems to be selling these days is some palatable version of black cool, black men are scary, so—there you go. But you get it. They've decided to take the risk of temporarily hiring a black guy so he can write about soft drinks or basketball—or both in tandem—for the new "cool" office client and maybe, if they're lucky, compliment them on their choice of shoes.

If you and the temp pass in the kitchenette, you nod at each other cautiously. Three days before his contract is finished—and not renewed—you finally speak. He recognizes you because he frequents the coffee shop a block from your apartment and you both start laughing—talking about the scones and your mutual friends. Tammy joins in. She wasn't in the kitchenette but seems to have manifested herself with an expression that reads *May I help you?* that perhaps she means a bit more beseechingly, like *You fine Negroes know you can't have these white people seeing you laughing and talking like this*, which makes sense since Tammy has black friends—the one half-black girl on her HR staff.

What are you two chatting about? says Tammy. This time, she makes her own smile face.

Dogs, you say in unison. *Dogs.* You look guilty about whatever you did—or didn't do—and return to your workstation to pretend to work.

They place the next black freelance employee near your workstation. She has an anti-gentrification bumper sticker on the face of her laptop, and she mutes, but doesn't remove, her Beats headphones when people stop by her desk to chitchat. She is the better version of everything you used to be before you worked here. Before you swallowed down your instincts with big gulps of on-tap rosé and an insurance plan that allows you regular visits to your favorite naturopath. You find this new black girl enviable and are amazed by her as you sink deeper into your gray wrap sweater, gray scarf, fake work, trying to out–*Invisible Man* Ralph Ellison.

It's the day where you are all supposed to convince the new "cool" client how "cool" you are by showing up at another obscenely expensive in-office cocktail party. The party needs a playlist, a task left to the interns and the guy from strategy who gels his hair back and owns a pair of Yeezys. By three p.m., the party is a rager. It is loud and there is liquor and the music theme is basically any B-side from any rap album by any artist whose name starts with A$AP or Lil' and somebody's put out a strobe light and gunned up the volume. You remain seated at the sustainable bamboo table workstation, snuggling into your work scarf. Like 40 percent of the office, you have decided what's going on in the kitchenette is much too "cool" for you and your plan is to hide out, scrolling through music videos, until you slide out the door around 4:25 p.m.—when all the senior office members are good and drunk.

Group emails start flooding your inbox from executives, typing on their smartphones. Re: OFFICE PARTY. A lot of This is not cool, guys and Way to show team spirit, guys, and the importance of being "collegial" in front of the new clients.

Funny, your new black girl colleague replies-all to the entire staff, all of this talk about team spirit and keeping up appearances when every song on the playlist has the word "nigga" in it.

Transparent millennial <<mic drop>>.

Had they asked you to DJ the office party (which you are glad they didn't) this would be exactly the time you cue the sound that goes *pew* *pew* *pew*, followed by *Bullet! Bullet!* and dancehall air horns. You seize the opportunity; you pack up your bag and leave, at 3:25 p.m., crediting the hour and a half you reclaim on your office timesheet to REPARATIONS. You watch notifications for the email thread Re: OFFICE PARTY pop up on your phone the whole walk home. You only stop to read one, an email from another black employee—a person who has mastered invisibility so thoroughly you forget he works there. He enters and exits the fray with a one-word reply-all:

Amen.

The next morning, it is you sipping a coconut-milk latte from an all-white paper cup when Tammy arrives at your chair. You are the first at your desk, already "working." She is nervously hanging on to a cat mug.

Yesterday was something, she says, easing into the conversation she feels obliged to have about "the n-word." You turn your smile face toward her and keep pounding at the keyboard. She leans into the bamboo. You slide into a state of feigned sympathy. Poor Tammy. All of those diversity luncheons she's had her half-black assistant arrange, and now this. What do you think we should do? her eyes ask as she hides her mouth behind the lip of the cat mug.

Maybe we should stop letting people add whatever they want on the office playlist, you say.

I thought of that! Tammy commiserates, the contents of the cat mug sloshing. *But then* [Yeezys] *said that would be* [racist] *because we can't censor black artists.*

Excuse me, what? you say, your smile vanished. You can't do this shit anymore.

Tammy recognizes she has stepped far outside the league of her retreat-acquired HR training. She remedies her part in the "n-word" debacle by explaining that she started in the office as a "creative"—just like you—and remembers when making playlists was her full-time job. The glory days. Not all these new young people, she adds. You say nothing and nod. *Thank you*, she says. She knew you'd understand.

The last time you see Tammy, it's not Tammy, but her half-black assistant from HR. It is the beginning of the new year and you've been approached by an executive. You are somehow convinced the time he spends speaking to you is belated recognition for the work you have done in the outside world, where you cease to be invisible. This is a chance for you to merge your inner black girl cool, with your office black "cool," as product-

placement. He's been following you on Instagram. He starts re-
lating the grassroots work you're doing to his time following the
British punk underground or starting the first blog for surfers
and you think, perhaps, you have finally been seen.

*Hey, we're starting up a new series featuring employee stories
at our Friday group lunch meetings. Would you want to be our
first presenter?* Certainly.

*Maybe you can mock up a presentation and we'll kick around
ideas?* Most definitely.

The executive schedules a follow-up meeting on your Google
Calendar for two weeks later. He never shows. Instead, Tammy's
half-black assistant sits across from you on one of the millennial advertising agency's minimalist Bauhaus couches, clicking
her ballpoint pen and leafing to a new page in her steno book so
you can "brainstorm." She pens down the title to her meeting
notes. You have somehow been chess-pawned into giving the
featured presentation during a BLACK HISTORY MONTH
EVENT.

What "Black History Month Event"? you say. You two have
developed a code language. She shifts her eyes. She looks nervous and resigned. For music, she is thinking Fela Kuti. She has
been asked to ask you where to call to cater in collard greens.

We're thinking the first week in February, she says cheerily.
You ask when the event that follows yours in the "employee stories" series is scheduled. *There's nothing on the books, yet!* she
says. Nothing on the books for the foreseeable future, she says.
Is the first week of February okay for you? she asks. This is awkward. You both lean in and lock eyes across this transparent

black-and-white checkered board, unclear who should make the next move. And that's the game. You remember how much you used to love playing chess before your coolness became a commodity. Before you took on a career in which your blackness was something your employer could sell. You pull out your black queen. You slip into your real smile. You think of all the things you would like to say to them in a sharply worded Power-Point. You open up your Google Calendar.

How about March? you say.

NO, MY FIRST NAME AIN'T WHOOPI

(It's Shayla—Ms. Lawson, if You Ask Me)

Oh my God, it's Oprah! It's OPRAAAAHHHHH!!! screams a man holding several large bags of books. I'm not there. It's 1991 and my family has made an excursion to a book fair at the Frankfort, Kentucky, convention center. I'm nine years old and off with friends waiting in line to get a children's book signed by Ken Kesey. *Oprah!* the man continues to scream, grabbing and holding up my mother's wrist. Gripping my four-year-old sister's arm with her other hand, she calmly talks down her new fan, explaining to him that she is not Oprah, encouraging him to let go of his vise grip. When my mom and sister join us, my mom tells us what happened, making a joke to the other adults about how she, newly emerged from her Jenny Craig weight-loss transformation and wearing a pair of blue jeans, wishes she'd been mistaken for late-eighties Oprah instead.

He should have known Oprah wasn't on the guest roster for the book fair, I interrupted. To my nine-year-old self, it seemed like a *Harriet the Spy* case I'd already solved. My mother clearly wasn't Oprah. I didn't understand the gravity of this stranger's offenses: the amount of attention he'd drawn toward my mother's dark-skinned body, how scary it must have been for her, how much she tried to soften the blow for both her and her youngest daughter by joking about her minor public assault.

I hadn't known this as a nine-year-old but mistaken-identity encounters would become a part of my adulthood. Regularly, somebody white and ordinary will be standing behind me in the checkout line of a chain store and convince themselves I am someone black and famous. When my presence calls to mind a black celebrity for a white person, instead of assuming I *look like* that person, they quickly assume I *am* that person.

Once, in a drugstore waiting room, another customer spotted a picture of Whoopi Goldberg on the coffee table right as I entered. He looked at the magazine then back at me. He smiled and began shaking with excitement, getting up to introduce himself. *Hey . . .* he said, waving a finger at me while he cocked his head. As I drew closer to him, his face soured. He didn't think I *looked* like Whoopi Goldberg. (If he had, he would have continued wagging his finger with a little *Hey, has anyone ever told you you look like . . .* by way of introduction.) He thought I *was* Whoopi Goldberg.

Argh! he said when I wasn't. He couldn't hide his resentment, the energy he wasted, approaching a regular black person with admiration. Every time someone assumes I am a celebrity, I am the one to blame when I am not.

People get touchy when women use "assault" to describe their daily interactions with strangers, but intentionally touching someone who you don't know and who is not in danger—and who has not asked you to—is assault. If you get angry at someone you don't know because they are not who you think they are, if the person you approach feels attacked by your unpleasant reaction, this is, by definition (if not mainstream connotation), assault. It is not okay to scare people just because you want their attention. It is not okay to scare them further when you realize you thought they were someone else. This behavior isn't accidental. It has been common practice for white people to assert ownership over black bodies by gripping and touching us as if they know us, as if we are still property. Strangers touch our hair or faces. They grab our butts and arms. These actions aren't meaningless: America's system of chattel slavery was sustained by white people telling themselves black people were a commodity they owned, as indistinguishable from one another as livestock; America's system of law enforcement still wrongfully incarcerates black people just because they look close enough to somebody white people *think* they recognize, someone who looks guilty, black as charged. Aside from an egregious sense of entitlement, I have no explanation for why anyone white living in a small town like Frankfort, Kentucky, would believe they were running into Oprah on the regular. Had my mother been her, she would have been surrounded by several bodyguards to prevent a man like the one my mother encountered from getting anywhere close. Oprah would have been flanked by security to prevent this man from treating her like property, to prevent his minor public assault.

⁓

Has anyone ever told you you look just like Whoopi Goldberg? says a Dutch Realtor. My then-husband and I are living in the Netherlands and trying to finish up rental paperwork for a house. I don't respond, focusing instead on filling out the forms. Engaging this stranger in a conversation about how I look is low on my list of priorities.

You do, he adds. I shrug. This is always the thing that irks me, the moment after I have chosen to ignore a "you look like" remark. My silence is meant to be gracious. My temper rises when it's not enough for me to let the observation pass. White people don't tell me I look like Whoopi Goldberg because they are trying to tell me I am powerful or radiant. They don't tell me I look like her because they are big fans of some specific part of her career. I'm a huge fan of her role as Guinan on *Star Trek: The Next Generation*, in which she runs a bar and wears badass jumpsuits, and the sexual tension between her and Captain Picard is so thick you could beam through it with a phaser. But people who tell me I look like Whoopi Goldberg don't want to start a dialogue about her EGOT greatness. They want to tell me I have dreadlocks and wear glasses. I know that. I also know if I had come to the same Realtor with my hair pinned back and a face full of makeup, the same he would have told me I looked like Whitney Houston.

—*like Whoopi Goldberg—except prettier*, the Realtor goes on. He assumes I haven't answered him because I was insulted by the celebrity look-alike mention, and continues to assert his opinion of my body, as if it matters. I lift my head to stare deep into his eyes as he grapples with the discomfort that I will not be weighing in on his opinion of what I look like. Mistaking my response as blatant rudeness, my husband thanks him using a Maastricht dialect, a gesture meant to counter it. He only speaks up once the Realtor left the room.

I could have told him he looked like Gene Wilder, except uglier, I said. *But I didn't think it was necessary to turn a business transaction into a celebrity sighting.* My husband laughed. I've spent enough time living around Europeans and Americans to know that white people, especially white men, tend to think that by pointing out black women in public, they're doing us a favor. Aside from Whoopi, I have been called Florence Griffith Joyner, Jackie Joyner-Kersee, and Macy Gray. I have been called Janelle Monáe, Erykah Badu, Serena Williams, Kelly Rowland, and Gabrielle Union. I have been called "that black woman from *Mr. Robot*." I have been called a number of black women who look nothing like me or each other. And yet, a few weeks after my Realtor "Whoopi Goldberg" encounter, I was at the Red Bull Crashed Ice Valkenburg games and could identify my husband, in a crowd of tall, twenty-something white men, from the back. How do I do it? With a little effort and self-awareness, it is quite easy to recognize anybody. The reason why so many white men misidentify me is because they consider black women generic. One dark blob of a face.

In her 2018 TED Talk, computer scientist Joy Buolamwini uses the term "dark blob" to address the way her dark-skinned features are registered by artificial intelligence. Early in her STEM career, Buolamwini learned her dark face couldn't be seen by the webcam needed for her research (she was building new apps that required generic facial recognition software coding as their foundation). In order to test the new software she was developing, Buolamwini had to wear a white mask. She refers to AI's inability to read the features of darker-skinned people as "the coded gaze," an algorithmic bias toward the recognition of fair-skinned individuals, one that has been built into our AI computer software thanks to skin color bias in real life.

The way computers read dark girls is similar to the way physically and culturally dark girls are seen by white culture. This is no coincidence. Although we like to believe there will be a science-fiction version of our future in which robots offer humans unbiased, logic-driven information, our robots learn from us and carry the biases we uphold. This is what "machine learning" means: machines study human preferences and write those preferences into code. It is no secret that, up to this point, people who look like Joy Buolamwini have been underrepresented in nearly every facet of higher learning, including computer science. The algorithms that determine what our machines learn have been developed almost exclusively through the lenses of white men. A group of people who can't see my face can't teach machines to recognize me.

The "dark blob of a face" Buolamwini mentions reminds me of what sociologist Tressie McMillan Cottom describes in her essay "In the Name of Beauty" as being "dark, physically and culturally." Cottom describes herself as dark "physically" because her "complexion is not close to whiteness" and dark "culturally" because her family roots "reflect the economic realities of dark-complexioned black people." Depending on who you ask and what time of year it is, I am either a brown- or dark-skinned woman. What category I fit into doesn't really concern me, but it is a distinction that matters in America because how "dark" I am often decides my visibility in social situations. Even though I've lived around whiteness and traveled the world, there are a lot of markers of upward mobility that I don't possess. My parents were first-generation college students. I grew up in the south. Like Cottom, I was never groomed by "elite black social institutions" to model certain forms of upper-class sociability. There are many other physical and cultural factors that contribute to the darkness Cottom describes in her essay that do not describe me. But regardless, I read how "dark" white people think I am based on the privileges it affords. One of the biggest privileges denied dark people is being seen as individuals, as who we are.

Regardless of where I have been in the world, I have noticed how physically and culturally white males are held up as the social standard for the majority. Although it's an idea that is mostly promoted by the global North, its power is pervasive. All of us who interact with this belief in a dominant white culture have been trained to assign value to faces based on the things white men notice. What we often call "prettiness" or "beauty" in a face, as Cottom writes, is really just us saying how well that face's features and color reflect a popular, white standard. In this culture dark women are unilaterally considered "ugly" because of the ways they do not reflect white beauty standards. What Cottom renders in her essay on aesthetics as "ugly," I think of, in the context of AI, as "visually irrelevant." But this promotion of the idea that dark women are ugly, irrelevant, and invisible because white men don't notice them is pretty dumb.

Although we are socially indoctrinated with the idea that white males are the majority, they are not. We are trained to treat them as the world's largest population group because of how their subjugation has defined how we think about color and race. For instance, statistics claim that "black" people make up a very small part of the world's population (roughly 14 percent, according to Wikipedia) but that definition of blackness brings in deeply entrenched colonial biases. The phenotypical characteristics of a person's skin are observable physical properties. Darkness is one of those things. Race is not. When we say a person is "black" we are using it as a euphemism to say they are of African descent. Black people come in all shades. But what we aren't doing, if we say the world is 14 percent black, is looking at dark-complected people as a giant swath of this world's population, which is evidenced by the Fitzpatrick scale. The Fitzpatrick scale is a numerical system for measuring skin tones. It categorizes skin shades on a scale of 1–6 ranging from the lowest amount of melanin in one's skin (e.g., "lightness") to the highest. Although it was originally developed (by a white Harvard scientist) to chart the effects of UV light on different skin tones, the Fitzpatrick scale grew in usage and now dictates a lot of things in our lives, from how much sunscreen we are told we need to protect ourselves to which skin-toned emojis we use to send our friends a thumbs-up. The scale assesses human skin tones from dark to light but it also breaks down those skin tones according to ethnicities and regions. According to the Fitzpatrick scale, people of African descent can range in skin tone from Type 4 (referred to as everything from "olive" to "moderate brown" or "deep") all the way to Type 6 ("darkest brown"), but they are not alone. Black people share their ranges of skin tones on the scale with Native Americans, people from Southeastern Alaska, Yemen, New Guinea, Sri Lanka, indigenous groups in Australia, and so on.

If we want to get technical, based on the scale's definition of other phenotypical characteristics associated with race and ethnicity, "black" people extend as far down the range of skin shade possibilities as Types 2 ("fair" or "pale") and 3 ("fair" to "beige") and in some cases 1 ("ivory"); we reside across the entire spectrum of light and dark skin. Because of what whiteness is, white people cannot say the same for themselves. Whiteness is predicated on the idea that having a light skin tone, lighter hair and eyes makes one superior. These definitions are so exclusionary that the totality of this "whiteness"—whiteness that reflects northern European features—exclusively fits into only two categories on the Fitzpatrick scale (Types 1 and 2). If dark people and people of African descent are the majority of the world's range for skin tones, what 14 percent are we calling black?

The UN reports that half the world lives in seven of its most densely populated countries: China, India, the United States,

Indonesia, Pakistan, Brazil, and Nigeria. People with darker complexions make up the majority population in all but two of these countries, and people with olive or moderate-brown skin complexions still make up about half the population of China and the United States. We might not think of Pakistanis or Indonesians as "black" people. Or most Brazilians or Indians as "black" people. But this limited definition ignores phenotype. We share skin tones and facial features (and often, similar degrees of prejudice for the physically and culturally darkest among us) because we are all people of mixed African heritage. The only reason to deny this is to distance the dominant culture from having to see dark-skinned people as the majority. The only reason to do this is to make sure dark people are not seen at all.

As Audre Lorde puts it in her essay "A Burst of Light," "color is the bottom line the world over." Lorde called "black" a "codeword," a "rallying identity for all oppressed people of color." I see the same potential in darkness. "Darkness" is blackness on a spectrum—blackness in degrees. Darkness carries mutability, its presence carries the burden of external racism along with each ethnic group's internalized colonial prejudices. Black people will always carry the largest load when it comes to racial prejudice but that same dark hatred supports the xenophobia, ethnocentrism, chauvinism, and bigotry that render large swaths of the human population unseeable. It is not surprising that the invisibility that comes with being a physically and/or culturally dark person affects artificial intelligence just as much as it has affected our personal lives. We have already witnessed this phenomenon in film and media. Hollywood still casts white celebrities to play the roles of black, Asian, and Latinx characters in varying degrees of offensive darkface—as if there are not enough of us out there to play ourselves.

But this was the same war Lena Horne was waging back in the mid-twentieth century, when Hollywood considered a white woman with dark hair an "ethnic" actress. The glamorous Horne was turned down for playing roles scripted for "mulattos" in both *Show Boat* and *Pinky*, despite the fact she actually *was* a very light-skinned black woman. In both instances, the role was ultimately given to someone white. Studio executives were scared of how audiences would react to seeing Horne, black and unquestionably beautiful, in a leading role that advertised how negligible the difference was between her skin tone and that of her white counterparts. Although the director had already cast Horne in *Show Boat*, film execs replaced her with Ava Gardner at the last minute. In the final film, Gardner lip-syncs over tracks of Horne's voice, and Gardner's face is tinted in Horne's makeup shade, "Light Egyptian." Gardner wears black girl blackface, a watered-down version of Horne's womanhood. Although the times have changed, they have not changed much.

My friend Ava McCoy is an actor. When it comes to her vibe, she likes to pitch herself as a cross between Zoë Kravitz and Drew Barrymore—*the* Never Been Kissed *girl-next-door who could still pull off a badass battle-down sequence in* Mad Max. She bills herself this way to casting directors, so she can get the industry to see her for the spirit she brings to the screen as opposed to the stereotypes they continue to perpetuate. She's ambitious, fresh, and positive, but she's not naive.

We're sitting at an Upper East Side café drinking cups of pink tea when Ava tells me she's heard casting directors and talent scouts say hundreds of times that they *can't cast her in the lead role of an "inclusive story"* (meaning, a film or television show that does not specifically cater to black viewers) because *audiences can't identify* with her espresso skin tone. *Hollywood likes to say, "ambiguity is diversity,"* Ava says, referring to Hollywood's preference for women with complexions closer to whiteness, *as if they're doing enough by bringing me into the room so that film producers and talent scouts can say "Hey, I auditioned a dark-skinned actress." When I do get into the casting room,* she tells me, *I'm usually one of four types of women auditioning for the same role: me, Zoë Kravitz* (yes, Ava often auditions against her black girl idol), *Yara Shahidi, and Amandla Stenberg.* Black, yellow, tan, brown. Ava is rarely—if ever—called in to audition for the kind of "inclusive" role that would pit her skills against those of mainstream white actresses. The black girl casting room still consists of four women of different complexions, a superficial version of the Nina Simone song; our color varies greatly but our circumstances do not.

Ava has, however, been on auditions where her looks play in her favor, like when she shaved her head around the time Lupita Nyong'o was doing press for *12 Years a Slave*, a role that garnered the Kenyan-Mexican actress a lot of attention for her dark complexion. *Casting agents never tell you that "you should play a slave,"* Ava says, of her auditions that followed *12 Years a Slave*'s Best Picture Oscar win, *but they will say, "Have you ever thought about doing a period piece?"* Her reflection reminds me of the summer in my early twenties when I worked as a teaching assistant for a high school arts camp at the Cincinnati Underground Railroad museum. I was supposed to keep the museum halls free of student stragglers but, as I walked through the museum, I would often get lost in a well of tears. I took a step back from the student tour group to give myself some breathing room, and found my left leg a fence-edge away from a black girl sitting on the floor, a bronze body in chains.

Hey, Shayla! Shayla! called out one of the kids, huffing as he shuffled his way back into the tour group. *That slave, that slave I saw over there. It looks just like you!* I know he did not mean this as an insult. I could see it in his face. I'm not saying this to excuse his behavior. I'm saying I could read him. He was doing that thing that so many white men do, when they cannot hide their ignorant pride—ugly, stupid, and disfigured—a pleasure derived from the fact they have seen me at all.

Part of the problem, Ava says, the tearoom we sit in painted pink as a ballerina inside a jewelry box, *people can't fathom a world in which black women get to be soft. They don't see where that is in my range—as an actor or as a person. As a result, in my real life, I have a habit of allowing people I don't know get too close, to be friendly to the detriment of my own safety.* Her own safety. Our own safety: I think of my mother, about the day a man grabbed her arm because he thought she was someone he recognized, someone famous, and she smiled back at him—probably

as pretty and big as if she truly were a television icon, afraid for
her own safety and that of her young girl's.

Our news cycles are filled with accounts of misidentification
of black people leading to assault. Misidentified black people
are arrested and sent to prison for crimes they did not commit.
Misidentified black people are strangled, arrested, and gunned
down by our police. The fact that dark people are not seen for
the uniqueness of our faces, bodies, and vastly varied skin tones
is an ongoing erasure. And the chasm between being seen and
unseen—identifiable and unidentifiable—grows greater as we
bring our cultural biases into the development of artificial intelligence.

Although Joy Buolamwini did not begin her research with
the goal of bringing more visibility to dark girls and rectifying
the "coded gaze," she could not stand by idly. Using her TED
profile picture, she tested her image on major-market facial recognition platforms to see if their algorithms had improved. Two
of the platforms misgendered her as male. Two other platforms
could not even detect her face.

In her study "Gender Shades," Buolamwini created a data
set from a thousand photographs of international members of
parliament on the three main facial analysis platforms: IBM,
Microsoft, and Face++. She used the Fitzpatrick scale to classify
whether her test subjects were "darker" or "lighter" skinned. The
results she gleaned were staggering. Each of the platforms was
able to recognize the face of a lighter/fair-skinned female with
up to 98 percent accuracy, a darker male with up to 99 percent

accuracy, and a lighter male with up to 100 percent accuracy. With darker women, however, the accuracy rate dropped down to an average of 79 percent on the study's best-scoring platform, and 65 percent on the worst. According to Buolamwini, the accuracy these platforms displayed in detecting the gender of a dark woman often "came to a coin toss."

Next, she moved on to testing recognizable photos of many black female celebrities. When Buolamwini input a black-and-white photograph of Sojourner Truth, the AI spat back "a clean-shaven gentleman" as Truth's description. The same type of AI describes Michelle Obama's hair as a toupee. Similar instances of misgendering and misrecognition happened when Buolamwini input pictures of other famous black women on the same platform—Serena Williams, Ida B. Wells, Shirley Chisholm, even Oprah Winfrey—all of whom the AI registered as male.

⬳

I decide to do some low-fidelity algorithm testing on my own. I took several photos of myself—with my hair up, my hair down, my face in profile and head-on, and ran them through the Google Arts & Culture app's face match system, Art Selfie. After the app compared my picture with all the works of fine art in its database, it spewed back a painting titled *Indian Baby*. At 61 percent, this was my highest facial recognition match. In this, I did quite well. Google Photos, which runs on the same algorithmic platform as the Arts & Culture app, had to revise its code because it kept labeling images of black people as "gorillas" in its face match system. To say that how AI sees black people will determine our humanity should not sound like a stretch.

I feel a sinking in my stomach every time I surrender my likeness to the facial recognition in my smartphone. I try and make myself "pretty" for the lens each time I face it, even though I know it's just a camera. I am worried about what will happen if it can't see me. The warning, "Face not recognized" turns my guts. This private moment calls to mind what happens when women like me are not seen, each public assault. By the time you read this, our nation will have shifted even further into a future that involves more widespread use of facial analysis software in the institutions that run our daily lives. The systems that we currently, voluntarily use in our free time are being adapted to advance the reach of law enforcement, school surveillance, professional employment services, TSA and border control— like the worst predictions of science fiction. Algorithmic bias, misidentification imprinted into the DNA of our twenty-first-century intelligence, will be an ongoing public assault.

On her album *MAGDALENE*, FKA twigs says, "I've never seen a hero like me in a sci-fi." When it comes to us black women, maybe it's time. Facial recognition software has been, and will continue to be, a tool of discrimination. It will be used, widely and threateningly, against those of us who aren't in power. As long as this is the fight, dark women need to make sure they are on the front lines of the controversy—heroes—visible and present. The black women in this essay have been champions in expanding how I have seen and been seen—Ava McCoy, Joy Buolamwini, Whoopi Goldberg, Lena Horne, Oprah Winfrey,

Audre Lorde, Michelle Obama, Tressie McMillan Cottom—but how will the rest of us? Science fact or science fiction, the one thing I am certain of is that we must resist what poet and coder Lillian-Yvonne Bertram calls "erasure by algorithm." Dark women cannot leave the fates of our futures up to faulty intelligence—artificial or not. I know you are fighting to keep us from being invisible. I know you are out there, taking this on, as a problem to solve. Wherever you are, I see you. I know we will not survive this fight without you. My advice? Whatever you are doing, make sure they see your face.

BLACK GIRL MAGIC

Uh-uh.

No.

Not a thing.

My friend Lisa, a fine arts professor, sends me a black-and-white photograph she is using in her gallery lecture for the opening of an exhibition, Lorna Simpson's lithograph series *Wigs*. The caption:

PLANTATION SHARECROPPER LONNIE FAIR'S DAUGH-
TER DRESSING FOR SUNDAY CHURCH SERVICES IN
SPARSELY FURNISHED ROOM.

The photograph is from 1936. It was taken by *LIFE Magazine* photographer Alfred Eisenstaedt in Scott, Mississippi.

She is trying to do her little hair, Lisa texts. Kills me.

In the picture, Lonnie Fair's daughter is doing everything

a black girl has ever tried to as she coifs and beautifies herself. She ropes the fingers of both hands around a short, coarse tuft as she looks in the vanity mirror of a crooked dresser that sits beside a shotgun and a pair of workman's boots. The walls of the room are papered in peeling newsprint. She works her magic in a stiff white shift, with a bottle of hair tonic and a shiv of curling papers beside her. Her right arm whirls so furiously it blurs in the photograph. Her feet are so flat her arches inverse, her toes upturn, as if she is dancing on the invisible tips of her father's shined shoes.

Somewhere in this dance, she is happy: for the Sunday, for the sun's rays blistering the wallpaper periodicals sepia, for the spare moment she has to spin her sparse edges. She imagines sitting in the pew of the whitewashed church, her palms anchored under the backs of her legs, her ankles swinging unreservedly, with a tiny scrap of satin ribbon tied around the one curl she fastidiously formed for herself that very morning.

꙰

It is a Sunday and it's raining. Up the street from my apartment, my friend Aaliyah and I sip tea in a bookshop café. Aaliyah raises the timbre of her voice to be heard over the hiss of the espresso makers and the frothy scratch of plastic lids, brought to our mouths, cups brimming with spicy chai.

When people talk about black girls being magic, she says, they're always talking about something exceptional. I always find myself asking, "Where are the regular black girls? Where are the black girls whose stories require them to be nothing short of ordinary?" I've heard black women protect themselves by pretending they are all sorts of magical beings. Mermaids. Unicorns. A solar eclipse. The solar plexus. Even Aaliyah goes on to describe herself as magic. Creature. The kind in preadolescent fantasies, a purple Loch Ness with yellow scales and blunt, protruding teeth. In his documentary *Dreams Are Colder Than Death*, the filmmaker Arthur Jafa looks at the roots of being black in America, at one point interviewing a dancer at Magic City strip club in Atlanta who calls her naked body a "costume."

But that is ridiculous! says a white man, after I work my recollection of the scene into a shiv of dinner party conversation, clearly intoning my agreement with the dancer's logic as we stand around eating canapés. *Sickening even*, he continues. *How could anyone healthy believe that their body is not there.*

    This was not a question. I can recall a number of times a white man has tried to take my body away from me. (Where did I go then? Where was I?) This practice of revision is itself a kind of magic. I go back to Lonnie Fair's daughter. Her hair is short and her heels are planted on the ground and her back is turned toward Alfred Eisenstaedt on a Sunday in Scott, Mississippi, and there is a shotgun propped between her wall and her vanity—because.

❧

I make a brunch date with a woman I met at a music show. She is white. She slinks into the restaurant late, wearing last night's clothes. She is coming from the house of a Cameroonian man she introduced me to at a costume party; she told me at the party that they would be dating soon, which sounded preposterous to me as something someone could predict. I have never possessed that kind of magic, the kind where I can set my desire on someone and they will stay long enough for me to take off one mask, then the other, thoroughly disrobing my costume.

See, I am just such a small person! I have such a small body, she says, comparing her wrist to mine as I pick at our shared plate of chicken karaage. An anger pulses through my body, cools and moods. *I think the universe has always kept me in a relationship because it knows I'm just not built to be out in the world on my own. But you . . . you're such a strong person! I envy you, really. All the things you manage to get out there and accomplish.*

I look at the argument she builds around my body, the heavy magic of my upturned wrist. In reality, it is about the same size as hers. It's not that I ascribe any particular value to being delicate, but saying that only a small feminine body needs protection in this world is intensely cruel. A kind of cruelty that has, for a long time, led to the abuse and neglect of women, of color. Why does she need to ascribe bigness to my body? Because she is predisposed to think of me as a hardened and powerful beast, less a person than a guard wall, or a dragon, a wideness with which to protect her fairy-tale madness. There will always be someone who needs to believe in an impervious black girl. There will always be someone I need to be magic to.

Black Girl Magic relies upon a white conception of supernatural blackness in order to make girls special. Picture the opening sequence to the nineties television show *Touched by an Angel*, in which Della Reese cradles the head of an auburn-haired inge-nue in her bosom—a mammie "Madonna with Child"—while bellowing *Take my hand and I will walk with you*, or think of Michael Clark Duncan's character in the film *The Green Mile*, whom one synopsis describes as a physically "massive" convict who is also "simple" and "naive." Versions of this "magical ne-gro" archetype abound in film, books, and television. On the in-ternet, the hashtag #BlackGirlMagic often extends this magical stereotype but sets ambitious young black women as its stars. Although it positions them at the center of the story, this focus is deceptive. #BlackGirlMagic is an extension of the black girl as the exotic, the nurturer, the seductress, and the conjurer, the archetype made Instagrammable—it requires black girls be one or more of these things in order to be seen.

But the Black Girl Magic movement was originally created to tell black girls they were already great. In 2013, a mother of two named CaShawn Thompson derived the hashtag #Black-GirlMagic from the phrase "Black Girls *Are* Magic" to honor black women she saw doing incredible things and going unno-ticed. The fact that Thompson's initial movement focused on Black Girl Magic as a state of being is significant. To say "Black Girls Are Magic" is to say black girls occupy, represent, exist; it is a magic only they can summon. But #BlackGirlMagic makes black girlhood a commodity, a list of attributes you don't have to be us to reproduce. When you scroll through the #BlackGirl-Magic Instagram feed, instead of a stream of black girls being celebrated for accomplishing incredible things, you find a litany of black girl body parts and accompanying hashtags: #Black-

GirlBabyHair. #BlackGirlGlossyLips. #BlackGirlBoxBraids. Depending on the time of year, the feed is accented with pictures of black girls graduating, opening businesses, and taking on the titles of Miss America, Miss Universe, and Miss World simultaneously, but the majority of the images are still the black girl, white-gazed.

The #BlackGirlMagic photographs often offer non-black women a chance to read us like a spell book for a beauty they can conjure on their own, to absorb our power. Pop stars across the world study hip-hop dance, model their vocal stylings after black girl soul tracks, and darken their skin. Even Madonna, credited with ushering in a new age of pop, studied at Alvin Ailey's dance school and pulled her signature vogue moves from the ballroom scene begun by black queer femmes. Meanwhile, an Instagram search for #WhiteGirlMagic brings up un-ironic images of white women twerking or wearing heavy braided extensions. Worse still, the popular tag using the term "white girls," #WhiteGirlsEvolving, features young white girls posing to expose the roundness of their hindsides—#BlackGirlBooty—their appropriated derrieres. These trends mirror what seems to be the larger tendency regarding black girl aesthetics and triumphs: the world wants everything we have to offer, except us. It is not that Black Girl Magic isn't real, it is that it doesn't set us free.

~

When I consider this kind of Black Girl Magic, our disembodiment rendered as spectacle, I think of Saartjie Baartman, the best known of two or more South African women who were exhibited throughout nineteenth-century Europe under the stage name the Hottentot Venus. Born Sawtche (the name used here for her), she was an ancestor of the Khoisan people of South Africa and was captured from her home and sold into slavery. A Dutch doctor who fetishized her prominent features, the size of her buttocks in particular, purchased her at the age of sixteen from the owner of a plantation, and she spent years as his sex slave in Cape Town, believing he loved her, before he took her to London, then coerced her into traveling across Europe to expose her naked body for profit. The doctor told Sawtche that Europeans were obsessed with her body because its shape differed so drastically from the flat-bottomed women of the West. He told her they wanted to touch and examine her body to absorb its power, its magical blackness. Still a sex slave, she did with her body whatever she was told to; sometimes she was paraded around on all four limbs and, at times, she wore a collar, in a posture so similar to the Khoisan proverb in Bessie Head's novel *Maru* it kills me: "If you catch a zebra, you can forcefully open its mouth and examine its teeth. The Zebra is not supposed to mind because it is an animal." Because she was an animal she could not be hurt.

Because white people believed Sawtche's body was "magic," they treated her, at best, like a domesticated creature and, at worst, a sideshow freak. European men and women of varied social classes and ethnic groups came to gawk at her anatomy, and other fetishists, scientists and doctors among them, paid extra for private examinations of her backside where they would push surgical instruments into her anus and genitals. Detailed drawings of Sawtche's naked body became popular in nature books and European advertisements—caricatures juxtaposing her so-called deformity against the soft desirability of the white female form. The spectacle made of her body was considered so deplorable, a Jamaican anti-slavery activist pressured the British government to place a ban of indecency on the Hottentot Venus tour. The tour ended but the spectacle did not. Sawtche's captor took her to France, where she became a regular sideshow at a Parisian theater, her naked body exposed publicly in between circus acts or music shows. She was never paid the money the doctor promised her. After spending her entire adult life on tour as a sex object, she was eventually forced into prostitution. In 1815, at the age of twenty-six, Sawtche died penniless, suffering from a disease whose symptoms were attributed to alcoholism, smallpox, or syphilis.

Upon her death, a French biologist requested her remains from the police. He made a full wax cast of Baartman's body, then dissected her—preserving her breasts, labia, buttocks, and pelvis in glass jars, bleaching and displaying her remaining skeleton. In the decades that followed, her skeleton and genitals remained on display in the Paris Musée de l'Homme. Sketches and models of her preserved bones eventually became the blueprint for the Victorian bustle. In 1976, two years after Sawtche's body was finally removed from display and put into museum storage, her image was re-created by a French photographer—using black model Carolina Beaumont, her protruded buttocks holding up a champagne flute. In 2014, twelve years after

Sawtche's remains were finally returned to South Africa (after the French government responded to petitions by the Khoisan people), the French photographer re-created the photograph for *Paper* magazine. The model this time? A ubiquitous white influencer. In the Frenchman's original photograph, the black woman is exhibited, naked and tribal. In his white restoration, the woman wears a black sequined evening gown. I look at the images and see only Sawtche—trafficked once again, this time as costume.

～

During the Salem Witch Trials, #BlackGirlMagic was used as a tool for white empowerment. Massachusetts, 1692. It is hard to know what is true and what is not about the trials due to the many conflicting renditions recorded in history but it is widely reported that the slave Tituba was the first person accused. Tituba was most likely an indigenous woman. But over time history has alternately referred to her as "Negro," a "half-breed," and "colored," eventually landing posthumously on the title of the "Black Witch of Salem," weaving blackness and black magic together into Salem's witch trial lore, forever ensconcing Black Girl Magic onto Tituba's myth. Tituba originally pleaded innocent to witchcraft, a crime for which she was severely beaten by her master. To avoid further beatings, she changed her statement, fabricating a story for the courts that aligned with the Puritan prejudices against her dark skin, her presumed knowledge of voodoo and the occult. But unlike the story of witch trial tradition, the court documents expose a vital truth. Nowhere in the courts records is Tituba said to have taught the teenage girls of Salem the "witchcraft" that set the trials ablaze. The girls were practicing divination, not voodoo, a specifically European form of prognostication that involved reading an egg white in a glass of water—a demonic practice by Puritan standards. Tituba's master was the father of two of the teenage fortune tellers. In the face of what looked like trouble for the girls, he offered up Tituba, a woman whose magical influence Salem's lore still exaggerates to hide history's real villains.

Despite its deception bred from desperation, there is magic present in Tituba's confession. It is masterful. She understood that her dark skin and servitude would always carry a stigma in the eyes of white people. She traded on this link between her dark skin and satanic powers, saying the Devil had tempted her to use black magic on the townspeople. She claimed she'd rejected this course in favor of the Puritanical Christian faith. Tituba's confession connected her crime with the narrative of Puritan redemption—the magical negro turned noble savage. Her real "magic" was understanding what being black meant in a hostile, terror-stricken, white society. The Puritans could not kill a repentant sinner. White people expected her to summon magic and so she did. They just didn't expect that magic to be shrewdness, a force powerful enough to keep her alive.

At least nineteen people were hanged or burned at the stake because they pleaded innocent to the charge of witchcraft. The majority of the executed were white women, many of them landowners—wealthy widows with no male heir to inherit their property. Slaughtering these women as "witches" was an easy way to steal from them, since their riches returned to the town upon their deaths. Although there is no single hypothesis for why certain people were hanged and killed during the Salem witch trials, it seems quite likely, given the number of wealthy widows who were hanged, the motivation for killing "witches" was more territorial than spiritual. Under the guise of protecting the new world from satanic influence, the trials were, in fact, a highly devious land grab in which black magic, black *girl* magic, was essential to the grand scheme. Three black slaves were accused of witchcraft. Two confessed. All three women were set free by the courts: redeemed servants of the devil who owned no property. What is Black Girl Magic now? What larger purpose does it serve? How insidious? How are we being used?

∾

In the case of Marie Laveau, known as "The Voodoo Queen," her #BlackGirlMagic is still being used to assert the extraordinary accomplishments of black women can only operate in white culture on the level of myth or religion. Laveau, born in New Orleans in 1801, was the daughter of a freed slave and a wealthy mulatto businessman; she was of the first generation in her family born out of slavery. A well-off woman who augmented her inherited wealth with financial investments and her religious ministry, she considered herself a staunch Catholic, but did not consider the voodoo of her Creole ancestry at odds with her Christian beliefs. She held religious services attended by hundreds of people, both white and black, and privately advised a clientele roster that included "lawyers, legislators, and merchants," all of whom, according to her *New York Times* obituary, attended her funeral. Despite her having been gifted with business savvy and tremendous intellect, most of her legend focuses on her great physical beauty and supposed magical powers. Could she heal the sick? Did she cast spells? Although voodoo is a proud cultural tradition among people of African descent across the Americas, there is little evidence to substantiate the claim that Marie Laveau was a sorcerer or faith healer. What we do know is, in the black community, she was best known for her public service—posting bail money for imprisoned black freewomen, nursing patients with yellow fever, praying with condemned prisoners in their final hours. Did she consider herself "magic"? It is difficult to tell. It was only in the wake of Laveau's reputation as a woman of influence that local news outlets started branding her religious services as "drunken orgies" and uprisings involving the occult. It was Marie Laveau's daughter, Marie Laveau II, who played up the supernatural elements of her mother's mythic image when she took over the family businesses. A black hair salon was among her business holdings. It is rumored that, at this shop, she talked openly with her black clientele about extorting information from the wealthy white patrons of her voodoo business and exaggerated performance as a magical priestess. The "Marie Laveau" referenced in popular culture is a character created by a speculative mix of racist white folklore, her daughter's "costume," and the original woman herself. Even the physical remains of Marie Laveau have found little rest in death: her tombstone was regularly vandalized, and attempts have been made by white fanatics to dig up her body for religious rites. Although the city of New Orleans began restricting access to the cemetery in 2015, she still exists in a state of exhumation through books, TV shows, and music in which she appears and reappears whenever a black magic priestess must be called forth.

What was true of Sawtche and Tituba and Laveau is still true today. Although black women did not create the exploitation of our magic, it has been important for us to sustain it. But "magic" is ephemeral, subjective; its protection is also a myth. Although Black Girl "Magic" has shifted in our conception from summoning the occult to being an exotic unicorn, the expectation is the same: to possess something untouchable so the world believes you have something special to offer.

I call this the Beyoncé Effect, says Marisa, a digital humanities professor at the college where I teach. She comes to campus one day in a fabulous cape; you've got to be mythic to pull off a cape in daylight. As a black woman, you have to come into your job a magical priestess every day. Every day, you take on a world that sees black women as supernatural and simpleminded—capable of witchcraft but not intellect. We have to look superhuman. We break our brilliance down for them; as in the Beyoncé documentary *Homecoming*, we are our own manifestation. Marisa and I talk of how she wields her incisive beauty as both a wand and a scythe. She makes it clear this is *her* vision we witness, *her* shrewdness, her church roots and Creole ancestry, her prestige. Supernatural. We tell ourselves and the world we are limitless.

If my country ass can do it ... Beyoncé says, humbly summing up her multitiered career in a *Homecoming* interview segment. She wears sequins and fishnet stockings. Stretching her arms out to her congregation of adoring fans, channeling Laveau in the voice-over.

In the photo of Lonnie Fair's daughter, I find magic in her solitude, magic in her humming, magic in this moment, the picture's quiet, rumpled buzz. In the time she has taken to pretty herself. To be displayed, like the pale ladies posed on the aging periodicals that surround her from ceiling to baseboard. The infinite pride she carries, a finely calculated enchantment. In the frame of the mirror, the black girl centers herself. The work may seem superficial but it is still work.

(Notice how she never looks at who is taking her picture. Notice how the gun's long body rests in the frame. Notice how Lonnie Fair's daughter could shoot the camera's gaze from the door frame without a curl falling from her forehead. The conjuring kills me. I want to know: what would *that* photo look like—where the black girl turns around—a loaded gun? What do you think? What will her magic be made of? What kind of magic is she then?)

NAMES FOR "BLACK" AND WHAT YEAR IT WAS

Everything "black" has been, for me, since the beginning, a timeline of definitions.

1982 **UNDOCUMENTED**
/ˌənˈdäkyəˌmen(t)əd/
adjective

   1. I am born. The Certificate of Live Birth from the Minnesota Department of Health collects my vital statistics.

   Color or race of the birth mother:
   UNDOCUMENTED.
   Color or race of the birth father:
   UNDOCUMENTED.

1985 BLACK
/blak/
adjective

1. I spy something new from inside my perch in
    the red shopping cart in a Target parking lot in
    Rochester, Minnesota, and point.

"Look, Mommy. A **black** girl! A little **black** girl!"
(My mom says "shush!")

1987 MONKEY
/ˈməNGkē/
noun

1. It is the end of kindergarten and two boys de-
    cide to sing me a song that results in an Eaton
    Hills Elementary parent-parent-parent-teacher
    conference.

Monkey! Monkey! Look at that little brown monkey!

2. BOY 1: the tallest kid in our class. Father, black,
    and mother, white. BOY 2: "Color or race of
    birth mother and father," UNIDENTIFIED—
    skin dark as me.

It is 1980s Midwestern America. Any **monkey** we
can't identify we call "Indian."

1989 ## YOU

/yōō,yə/

pronoun

1. I make new friends in the bus line during my first week of second grade in Lexington, Kentucky. I'm still learning to speak the language; Kentucky is a foreign country.

"Mo-ove!" says a blond white boy as he shoves me. "This ain't your bus line."
"Yes it is," I say, shoving him back. "This is how I get home."
"No it's not!" he shouts. "**You** don't live in my neighborhood. **You** can't."
"Yes, I do," I say, forcing my way into the bus line.
He reaches out again to shove me.
"Yes, she do!" says a bigger boy, deflecting his shove.

1990 ## AFRICAN-AMERICAN

/ˈafrəkən əˈmerəkən/

noun

1. It's third grade and I am hiding out between the beanbag chairs and the bookshelves during a school spirit assembly. I watch a librarian set up a book display that includes a biography of George Washington Carver under a map that

still features the USSR. I approximate grown-up small talk.

"Is this for Black History Month?" I ask the librarian.
She responds enthusiastically, "They are called **'African-Americans'** now!"

1991 **BLACK**
/blak/
noun

1. I don't understand politics but I understand two people are fighting in court on television and all the adults at my parents' dinner party have chosen sides.

"You only believe Clarence Thomas is innocent because he is **Black**."

1992 **NOT BLACK, JUST A . . .**
/blak/
adjective

1. On *The Oprah Winfrey Show*, Oprah is doing a series of episodes on how we perceive race with anti-racism activist Jane Elliott. Elliott asks the audience, "Has anyone ever said to you . . . I

don't see you as 'black'?" The audience members nod. Oprah answers:

"I have some sheep, and sometimes when you have black sheep, the black sheep turn white. I dunno how the hell they do that. (The audience laughs.) Anyway, so my neighbor, who is a farmer, said to me, 'I don't understand. All your black sheep stayed black.' Yeah, I guess cuz they knew they were in a black family. (The audience laughs again.) And he said to me, 'Oh, you're **not black**, you're **just a** neighbor.'" (The audience groans in understanding as Oprah continues.) "I go, 'I most certainly am black.'"

1993 DOWNTOWN
/ˌdoun'toun/
adverb

1. I'm in sixth grade and surrounded by a bunch of older girls at my neighbor Carey's sleepover, all of whom think I'm asleep. The only other black girl is Allison, the adopted biracial daughter of white parents, who really is sleeping.

"Can you talk like a black person?" Carey asks the other girls from the dark under the covers.
"Shhh!!" says another white girl. "Shayla will hear you!!"
"I mean the ones from **downtown**," Carey says.

1994 THEY

/T͟Hā/

pronoun

1. I am at a congregation picnic waiting for a hot
    dog to come off the grill. The Indian daughter
    of white adoptive parents (a girl from India,
    not "Indian" used as a euphemism—see Mon-
    key) comes up to me to discuss the congrega-
    tion's new Ghanaian family, who are sitting
    at a nearby picnic table eating fried chicken
    wings.

"My dad says not to shake their right hand, because
that's the hand **they** use to, you know, *wipe with.*"

1995 NOT GUILTY

/nät ˈgiltē/

adverb-adjective

1. It has been nearly a year since the criminal mur-
    der trial of O. J. Simpson began and we are all
    adjusting to our first exposure to reality TV.
    As one neighbor puts it, referring to his wife's
    absence from the porch where she usually sits
    all spring and summer, resolutely fanning her-
    self, "We've all had a little bit too much of 'The
    Juice.'"

On October 2, 1995, the Superior Court of California of the County of Los Angeles made a landmark decision: blackness may never be innocent but—with enough money and influence—it can be **not guilty**.

On March 3, 1991, when Rodney King was beaten by the LAPD, he was not "**not guilty**." Rodney King was black. (See Black.)

1998 **GHETTO**

/ˈgedō/

noun

1. The summer after tenth grade, I was not in-crowd enough to know why, but the word had taken over Paul Laurence Dunbar High School to describe anything cheap, outlandish, derivative—a knock-off.

I run into Jayran, a Persian girl, at the Express clothing store in the mall, where she's with a blond friend. We acknowledge each other with a smile and nod. As I walk away, she holds a leopard-print halter up to show her friend.

"Ew, my God, this looks so **ghetto**!" she says, putting it back on the rack.

1999 **COLORED**

/'kələrd/

noun

1. My senior year at Dunbar, I listen to Chloé recite her lines as the lady in orange with a full-on
colored sadness:

ever since i realized there was someone callt
a **colored** girl . . .
i been trying not to be that
{Ntozake Shange said. (i was.)}

2001 **AFRICAN AMERICAN**

/'afrəkən ə'merəkən/

adjective

1. As before, but with more gusto.
2. Close to the end of my first year of college, I try
to explain myself to a West Virginian Puerto
Rican friend. I tell him he should stop calling
himself "Thomas" when his name's "Tomas." I
start dating a white boy and Tomas gets testy.
I'm pretty sure he just wanted to kiss me.

It's weird being an **African American** girl.

2002 **BLACK**
/blak/
noun

1. I am African American.

But I feel **black**.

2005 **COLORED**
/'kələrd/
adjective

1. I started watching the American version of
the television show *The Office* because all of the
nerdy black kids I knew kept saying it's "the
most." Episode 2 is "Diversity Day."

"It's collard greens," says Stanley, the office's token
black employee.
"What?" says Michael, the show's token white boss.
"It's collard greens," says Stanley, correcting Michael's
soul food malapropism.
"That does really make any sense," says Michael, "because you don't call them 'collard people'—that's offensive."

2007 **'HOOD**

/hŏod/

noun

1. I am living as an expatriate in Venice, Italy, and
   adore talking about how much I love Buñuel's
   The Discreet Charm of the Bourgeoisie and music by Big Pun. I'm visiting the used bookstore
   with French-Algerian Cynthia, whom I find
   achingly beautiful and, therefore, have coaxed
   into being friends with me. I am her envoy to
   Americana. She is improving her English as my
   Spanish and Italian steadily deteriorate.

"Shayla," she asks, as we peruse the outdoor stack of
a used bookstore, picking up an old Spanish glossary,
"How would you say 'barrio' in English?"
"That's the **'hood**," I tell her.
"Hood," says Cynthia.

2007 **NAPPY**

/ˈnapē/

adjective

1. I'm back in Kentucky after my time in Italy, and
   my sister and I crack each other up with a joke
   that's not a joke. It is the year white shock jock
   Don Imus is feuding with every black advocate

over the inflammatory comments he lodged against the women of the Rutgers University basketball team during the NCAA Championship.

"Dem girls are **nappy**," my sister says, Don Imus' bass in her voice. "Dem some '**nappy**-headed hos.'" I laugh. I laugh to tears.

2008 POST-RACIAL
/post-ˈrāSHəl/

noun

1. I'm working as a junior architect at a firm in midtown Manhattan, and America has just elected Barack Obama as its forty-fourth president. Even though we have no water cooler, the water cooler conversation stays the same:

"Don't you just love Obama?" my white colleagues say to me. "He's so **post-racial**, don't you think?" I call in sick on Inauguration Day.

2009 SOCIALIST
/ˈsōSHələst/

noun

1. My Dutch boyfriend and I decide to drive to Canada, a country that belongs to neither of us, for a romantic weekend. We spend the af-

ternoon walking around the Montreal farmer's market, where I spot an abandoned protest sign on a bench carrying an elaborate drawing of the American president's face. The sign reads:

Obama is a terrorist Muslim **socialist**.

2010 **BLACK**
/blak/
verb

1. After I get married and move to the Netherlands, I am the sole cast member in *The Real Black Housewives of the Dutch Countryside*—my own reality TV show. I binge-watch the Dutch Party for Freedom parliamentary leader promoting xenophobia on television, a return to a pure, red-faced, hate-fueled rage. I have dark skin and speak no Dutch.

Every time I leave the house, I **Black**; I feel like a foreign country.

2011 **BLACK AMERICAN**
/blak ə'merəkən/
adjective

1. I try to explain to the Dutch woman I volunteer with at the refugee asylum center that I'm

African American, not "Black American." She can't hear it. The refugees I'm trying to convince her to stop talking down to are African.

She continues to mention "another **Black American** lady—whose husband is in the military—with whom [she is] friends."

2012 **HOOD**
/hŏod/
noun

1. I keep a world band radio in the kitchen of my Dutch home and listen to NPR while I prepare dinner. My hands are covered in raw poultry. I hear Trayvon Martin's name on the radio. I cry into the roasting pan, not knowing where to put my hands.

Cause of death . . . **hood**.

2014 **ME**
/mē/
pronoun

1. My husband and I have moved to the States and are fogging up the windows of our Hyundai four-door at a McDonald's parking lot in rural

Indiana because our walls are too thin to argue inside the apartment. Our marriage is disintegrating due to his renewed interest in basic blondes.

"I can't believe you are doing this. Do you know what it will be like for **me** to go back into this world? Do you know what it's like to be **me**?"

2015 **BLACKS**
/blak/
noun

1.   I move to Portland, Oregon, after my divorce. I'm visiting a new OB-GYN in hopes of getting treated for a series of infections she attributes to all the sex she assumes I'm having that I'm not having.

"Do you think there are other forms of treatment we could explore?" I ask.
"Not likely," she says. "These kinds of problems are common among **blacks**."
(I get better after I get a second opinion. The new doctor removes my birth control implant, citing, as one of its side effects, chronic yeast.)

2016 IMPLICIT BIAS
/imˈplisit ˈbīəs/
adjective-noun

1. I'm working as a copywriter at a millennial digital marketing agency in Portland where, instead of "cool," everything is "rad." My "rad" boss puts an awkward hand on my shoulder after an uncomfortable diversity training session in which the black instructor informs the whole office that diversity issues will continue until any black person can be as mediocre a boss as your average white man.

"That was quite the lesson," my boss says. "We've really got to work to rid the office of **implicit bias**." (Within the next five months, the company tries to fire me when I speak up against actual bias.)

2017 GANGSTA
/ˈgaNGstə/
noun

1. Another "rad" millennial marketing agency. I take my small dog to work. His outside is a stuffed toy; his inner spirit, a small-dog version of the entire Wu-Tang Clan.

2. My officemate wants to befriend me. She won't hear of it when I explain to her the best way to do this is to not take my dog for a walk.

3. They go for a walk. They are gone for twenty minutes, in which time Sammy Davis Jr. Jr. barks down three pit bulls and scarfs down a peanut butter sandwich from the sidewalk. He takes a shit in a busy crosswalk while the "DO NOT WALK" sign flashes. The dog stares her down as she returns him to my lap.

"Whew!" my coworker says upon their return, "I didn't realize your dog is so . . . **gangsta**."

2018 BLACK
/blak/
verb

1. I've just moved back to the East Coast, to Brooklyn. From the balcony of my East Flatbush apartment, I watch a congregation processing through the street draped in church clothes and Caribbean flags.

I am still, **black**.

2019 **BLACK**
/blak/
adjective

1.   I feel good.

Although I am a **black** girl, I am comely . . . (Song of
Solomon 1:5)

2020

Definition, uncertain.

I believe in an Afrofuture.

BLACK GIRL HIPSTER

I use the word "nigga" to describe things that don't work properly. "Nigga" is my favorite pejorative for smartphones, puddles, elected officials, and bad dogs.[1] For the majority of my life, though, I never used the word—even in my car, alone on a road trip, ripping through the whole *Enter the Wu-Tang (36 Chambers)* album, I'd bleep myself. Since I grew up in the south, people in my community were slow to adopt any kind of affection for the "n-word." We knew our reclamation of "nigger" would do nothing but encourage the ways white people already thought about us. So I didn't use it. And I couldn't think of anyone for whom using even "nigga" felt right.

That was before I moved from the conservative south to the hipster everywhere else. The more I moved around the country, the more my cultivation of a nuanced appreciation for the

---

1 "I don't believe we should use [the 'n-word'] to hurt people; I do believe we should use it to shame our pets."—comedian Ron Funches

"n-word" grew. There's no denying the "n-word" and its vari-
ants carry a hateful inheritance from white America's roots in
slavery. But in contemporary culture, the word also carries an
undeniable gravitas. It is no surprise the word enters the vocab-
ulary of black makers, musicians, artists, and writers as a motif. We restructure the "n-word." We complicate it. We make it
fashionable. We are creating work that is authentic and inter-
rogative and much of that work includes the word "nigga" in it.
But we all know the narrative: the more pervasive the "n-word"
becomes in popular entertainment, the more often white people ask if it's socially acceptable for them to use it. And—if the
answer is "no"—why not?

I believe the answer resides in black performance. At some
point, all black people in conversation with white culture are
asked to perform their blackness so it is easier for white people to categorize them. This cultural presentation decides if we
are cool blacks or acceptable Negroes. It decides if we are dangerous criminals or if we are elite members of the avant-garde.
For artists, performance is employment. Black artists balance
on the tightrope between creativity and diplomacy. But is it the
responsibility of artists to censor themselves in order to protect
a word from the dominant culture? And what does any of this
have to do with the title of this essay, anyway?

Let's figure it out:

The first time I heard "nigger," I was eight years old and watching *Roots* on television with my mom.[2] I don't know what the

---

2 Actually, that is a dramatic oversimplification. By the time I was eight years old, I

white equivalent would be to watching *Roots* with your mom, but I sometimes fantasized about what the white families in my neighborhood were doing during those hours. Eating lamb. Playing Boggle. I imagine a traumatic movie scene in a white child's upbringing would be something like watching the Nazis carry away Liesl in an alternate ending of *The Sound of Music.* Not even close, y'all. Not in the least.

I hated watching *Roots.* I think my mom hated watching *Roots.* But every syndicated Black History February we braced ourselves for a faithful family viewing of at least the first few installments of the eight-part miniseries, which featured all the worst scenes: childbirth, slave ship transport, pandemic infections, whippings, and rape—all culminating in Kunta Kinte losing his foot. Watching *Roots* as a young black kid born in the eighties was basically like getting the shit kicked out of the goodwill I felt toward my childhood icons. At eight, already a budding cineaste, I'd cultivated a measurable appreciation for the method acting of Cicely Tyson, LeVar Burton, Bob Hoskins, and Ben Vereen. Imagine, you're eight years old and:

---

had already been called a nigger, or some variant, by several of my classmates, most, but not all, of them white. The white kids I expected it from, but I didn't expect it from other brown kids. Almost all the white kids in my Kentucky neighborhood had grown up thinking the things they possessed were part of their sole inheritance as white people: country clubs, horseback riding lessons, and all-white public school buses, televisions, parents . . . This embarrassment of riches also included the word "nigger," which they knew was the bad word for black people, which meant it was a word they should never say, which meant—when confronted with new black girl neighbors, apprehensively looking for a seat on the all-white elementary school bus—it was the only word they wanted to say.

ROOTS

THE STORY OF HOW YOU GOT HERE
Episode One

SCENE: A "field" in "Africa."

SCENE: Ma from *Sounder* gives birth holding on to a tree stump in a hut.

SCENE: *Reading Rainbow* hero runs through high grass half-naked and scared—a lot.

SCENE: Oh look! Now the detective from *Who Framed Roger Rabbit* rapes a woman on a slave ship.

Credits
Credits
Credits

NEXT WEEK: Chicken George.

The problem with *Roots* is that you're not supposed to watch it. You're supposed to feel it. You're supposed to register how deeply terrible Black-Americanness is. And if you are black, the only way to properly memorialize the insurmountable torture your people have survived is to sit and watch *Roots* as a child, looking stoic and dignified. *And* you're supposed to get a good night's sleep after you've stayed up late to watch the eight-part miniseries so you can turn around in the morning and achieve, even though you are only eight and you just saw a slave overseer threaten to cut off a little black girl's hand for trying to learn how to read so . . . don't cry, kid, here's a bag of Cheetos.

&

The sky is pouring sheets of rain outside the Irish pub where my date and I have just arrived for karaoke night. The karaoke jockey is a brown-skinned dude with a shaved head and an image from his wife's recent ultrasound in his wallet. He is a man—my date has already warned me—whose hug will involve sliding his hand down my jacket to scoop the high part of my backside. We head to the bar to get drinks and the KJ puts a song on the machine, then walks up to the mic to sing. It's probably important to note here that I usually don't do karaoke dates, considering the activity too intimate—higher up on the list than having sex, holding hands, talking about how messed up your childhood was, and emotional attachment. Karaoke involves making improvised decisions about your dreams and fears in public. That's not the kind of scrutiny I want to subject a stranger to, or ever want from a stranger.

Uh-oh, my date says, taking a sip from his pint glass as he looks at the title "Freaky Friday" on the karaoke screen. I don't know the song. He sets the glass down, coughs, and flashes me a side-eye. *Oh, you will.*

The karaoke jockey's rendition of the song is grinding away at full force. He is shucking and jiving and bucking his eyes. The white audience cheer and slosh pint glasses together like imperialist warlords. Emboldened by their applause, the KJ hits the song's only memorable verse.

If you've never heard "Freaky Friday," you have been blessed. It is a jingoistic tune for the Republic of White Stupidity written by an artist performing as Lil Dicky, a white Jewish alumnus (class of 2010) of the University of Richmond Robins School of Business. If by now you are already YouTubing the video, I take full responsibility for you suffering through it but I've written a synopsis so you don't have to: in the video, Lil Dicky plays himself, a hipster-rapper-you've-never-heard-of, who goes to a Chinese restaurant and fantasizes aloud about racial fetishism. The song takes a plot twist into blatant orientalism as a mystic Asian waiter and a magic fortune cookie turn Lil Dicky[3] into Chris Brown. Brown coons through the second verse pretending to be Lil Dicky, a white man wearing Brown's body as blackface. *Wait . . . can I really say the "n-word"?* Chris Brown/ Lil Dicky asks.

In the pub, the carousing KJ has reached that point in the song on stage. Karaoke night breaks into a gleeful celebration of white supremacy as the mostly white audience watches a black man imitate a white man singing a song that is basically a rip-off of the plot of *Get Out*. The KJ lifts up his hands as if he's Chris Brown in concert, and leads an all-white sing-along. The song goes on. My date and I listen to his white fans "say the 'n-word'" eleven times.

---

3 Yes, his rap moniker, according to the song, is a reference to his dick size.

Kendrick Lamar ran into a similar karaoke disaster while performing at Hangout Music Fest in Alabama in 2018, a month after his Pulitzer Prize win was announced. While performing "m.A.A.d. city," he invited a white girl on stage with him and she nailed the lyrics a little too perfectly, according to *The Independent*, rapping the "n-word" three times before Lamar stopped his music.

"Aren't I cool enough for you?" she asked Lamar. "What's up, bro?" The audience booed. In an act of diplomacy, Lamar offered the fan an opportunity to redeem herself and asked her to start singing the song again. "You got to bleep out one single word, though," Lamar said. The fan feigned ignorance. "Oh, I'm sorry. Did I do it? I'm so sorry . . . I'm used to singing it like you wrote it."

I think of that girl when I hear the lyrics to Lil Dicky's song on karaoke night: "I can't believe I'm in a [black man's] body." It is strange to me how deeply white people need to inhabit blackness as a benchmark of cultural fluency, of social credibility, of cool. The brazenness of a white fan asking a black twelve-time Grammy winner, "Am I not cool enough for you, bro?" She looks at the price on her concert ticket and iTunes download purchases and presumes her patronage puts her on par with Kendrick Lamar in status—Kendrick Lamar, a Grammy and Pulitzer Prize–winning artist—as if her patronage allows Lamar's work to exist.

When in these situations, black people are supposed to perform with Thurgood Marshall–level respectability or as brash coons. Flanked by stereotypes, my date and I adhere to the Black

Respectability Rules of Karaoke Engagement: black person, white song. No matter how much we might have wanted to get into the shits with an Outkast reprise, or a Whitney Houston ballad, we know better. It's better not to be the black person performing black music to the white gaze; once I got caught up in a karaoke moment at a Buffalo Wild Wings singing "Rock with You"—hip pops and finger snaps—and the inebriated Russian woman behind me in the queue switched her song to "Thriller," gurgling into the microphone that I should come on stage behind her to dance and sing backup. That was the last white time that happened to me.

There are two classes of karaoke performers who refuse to adhere to this code of ethics: "uncles"—men like the KJ who so desperately fear becoming outmoded they will revel in minstrelsy to maintain their relevance—and black girl hipsters—who'll take any opportunity to become the karaoke Aretha Franklin or Teairra Marí even when we know we are being applauded for making white people comfortable, even if we can't sing.[4] I used to think I was a hipster. Then I visited an Urban Outfitters, the aisles a blur of twee and kitsch, and realized there is a difference between knowing cool, knowing how to look cool, and having a vague idea of where to shop. As Kendrick Lamar's incident shows, most people's definition of "cool" ends with fandom, engagement that does not extend past what someone can purchase.

Although the word's history is often ignored, "hipster" orig-

---

4 Inversely, black guy hipsters only want to sing songs from Weezer's *Pinkerton* or *Kid A*–era Radiohead.

inally described one particular subset of the American public: the young, black [male], and anti-establishment. A term from the 1950s, these creative and curious young people would have been the classy Negroes of W. E. B. Du Bois' "Talented Tenth"—a philosophical legacy of exceptional blackness—if not for the limits on their opportunities to achieve prominence or success. Recognizing that their blackness rendered their potential inert, early hipsters seethed with laconic rage. They turned to marijuana and cheap booze and jazz and an indomitable knowledge of low-end street culture. (DAMN. Sound familiar?)

In Norman Mailer's 1957 essay "The White Negro"—required reading for anyone who wants to know the white hipster origin story—the author describes the [black] hipster as the American existentialist. "This hipster," he writes, "knows that if our collective condition is to live with instant death by atomic war, relatively quick death by the State . . . or slow death by conformity . . . the only life-giving answer is to accept the terms of death, to live with death as immediate danger, to divorce oneself from society."[5] Mailer heralds the death drive inherent in the lives of smart black people with limited resources, as if their oppression is an enviable state.[6] Mailer writes of

---

5 Interestingly enough, Mailer in 1957 sounds very similar to Tupac Shakur in the late nineties breaking down the difference between "niggers" and "niggas" for a white reporter. "'Nig-*gers*' is the ones with the ropes hanging off the thing," Tupac says, making the gesture of a noose being tied to a tree with his hand. "'Nig-*gas*' is the ones with *gold* ropes hanging out at clubs." According to Tupac, "niggas" recognize the "immediate danger in life" and "divorce themselves from the expectations of society" through outlandishness and materialism. They live this way after watching the "collective condition" of "niggers" and their "quick death by the State."
6 Which would make Tupac an OG hipster.

black hipsters as "rebels," aligning the plight of his generation of young whites with these black "enfants terribles."[7]

I once witnessed for myself the white desire to align itself with the use of the word "nigga" and the plight of black people. At a midnight set for Noodles, a Filipina West Coast DJ, in Greenpoint, Brooklyn, I spotted a hard-looking white woman of about fifty. I was probably about six feet away from her as she stood on the stage with Noodles' crew and rocked through all of the grime and trap music transitions as if each song was her own. When one of the songs hit the word "nigga," we locked eyes for a moment. Being the next-oldest person in the room, I stared her down hard as she mouthed the words, giving her the look. Her fervor was paused for a minute by my indignation, and I could see that she did feel embarrassed. She assessed her position, looking around the stage. She was surrounded by young Asians and Latinxs and bottles of Dom. She was insulated by an audience composed primarily of white people, hipsters and non-hipsters, who did not "bleep" themselves as Kendrick Lamar had asked. *No, I am "cool enough, bro,"* the white woman on stage decided, emboldened by her inventory. She looked me in the eye and went right back to singing "nigga" in the next track. She kept dancing. I took a pause from dancing to cross my arms, stare her down, and lift an eyebrow.

---

7 So, essentially, Mailer is arguing that white hipsters are the "niggas" of white people. I mean, Mailer titled an essay "The White Negro," so, this isn't much of a stretch.

∽

Stuck in impossible circumstances, the contemporary white hipster attempts to achieve equilibrium through curation. They graduated from college with the promise liberal arts degrees would guarantee them social mobility. But as we moved toward the twenty-first century, the economy wasn't ready for the swift shift to a creative workforce and there weren't enough jobs for all those liberal arts grads. Many of those would-be iconoclasts had to move into neighborhoods like Williamsburg, or Central Harlem, or Bedford-Stuyvesant, because they were the cheapest places they could afford and still be close to metropolitan success. As capitalism adjusted to the new creative market, the hipsters began to use the tools of their upbringing to repurpose creative culture. But this progressiveness is mostly façade. As Audre Lorde said in *Sister Outsider,* "the master's tools will never dismantle the master's house." We associate hipsters with things like gentrification and economic appropriation because they have figured a way to use their creativity to reinforce white privilege. They may spend time occupying marginalized neighborhoods, but they don't intend to stay in a deprived state. Hipsters do not intend to remain disenfranchised. They are capitalizing on deprivation as a performance.

"Hipster" is a word for a person who doesn't work or behave properly. I have probably looked like a hipster to some. I wear big glasses. I'm not averse to dive bars or secondhand clothes. But my innate level of coolness, of composure, lives far outside the realm of what I purchase or what I choose to put on my body. Hipsters, however, have branded themselves as the white people who DIY it into the highest tiers of the oppressed classes, and they hate themselves for it because they can always return to being upper-class whites.

᷉

One of the difficulties in calling any contemporary convergence of intellectualism, leftist politics, and grassroots artistry "hipster" in the black community is that black people never divorced themselves from an active creative class. The Brooklyn Boheme, for instance, was a community of young black makers in the 1980s and '90s who inhabited Fort Greene and Clinton Hill, the neighborhoods that white hipsters would start to infiltrate near the end of the twentieth century. But unlike white hipsters, the Brooklyn Boheme didn't move in order to start a movement—they already lived there. In many cases, their families had lived there for generations. Their blocks created black avant-garde theater groups and jazz musicians, poets and political theorists. The Brooklyn Boheme were the children of black New York bohemians. They didn't have to try to attain cultural capital by buying up street cred.

And the Brooklyn Boheme had tribes. The Black Rock Coalition, founded by black music preservationists like Vernon Reid, the lead guitarist from the rock band Living Colour, and film director Spike Lee—people who were indispensably instrumental in shaping the conversations around black identity in the late twentieth and early twenty-first centuries. Situated in this landscape, Rodeo Caldonia was the Brooklyn Boheme's answer to black girlhood. On the surface, the group's members epitomized a version of black girl hipsterdom that wasn't about white commodity—these young radical black women were fourth-wave feminists before Riot Grrrl ever hit the third wave.

After the success of *For Colored Girls Who Have Considered Suicide/When the Rainbow Is Enuf* in the 1970s, Ntozake Shange moved to Texas to ride horses bareback, asserting that the future of black women resided in the freedom provided by the rodeo. Around the same time, B. B. King covered the forties blues track "Caldonia"—a love song to a lanky woman with big feet. It was in the eighties, after unearthing these disparate influences (likely from the record collections in their parents' brownstones or stacks of books displayed by street vendors on Myrtle Avenue), that Rodeo Caldonia was formed. Or, to be more precise, Rodeo Caldonia High-Fidelity Performance Theater. If it is possible to define "black girl hipster," Rodeo Caldonia was it.

Rodeo Caldonia High-Fidelity Performance Theater consisted of a loose confederation of twelve or so black women. The core of the group graced the pages of *Interview* magazine in the late eighties in an iconic photograph: Donna Berwick, in milkmaid braids like a reinvention of *Heidi*; Candace Hamilton, in bowed polka-dot heels and a futuristic Nefertiti cap; Celina Davis, outstretching her arms in a proud *V* and wearing a satirical Miss America–style sash and matching gown; big hoop earrings haloing Amber Villenueva's Afro, her mouth opened wide, like a real-life version of Funkadelic's *Maggot Brain*; Sandye Wilson and Derin Young in black bandeau tops and flat ballet slippers with skirts of tulle, a plastic insect crawling up the length of Derin's leg; Alice Norris lying between all of them, her ankles draped in cowrie shells, her body positioned on the floor like she is ready to be carried off on a settee. Among these women you can also find Alva Rogers and Lisa Jones, the group's founders, and Lorna Simpson, the group's resident photographer.

In the years that followed Rodeo Caldonia, Lorna Simpson became one of the most influential black conceptual artists of her generation, defining where black girl artists would look for black girl representation alongside painter Mickalene Thomas and photographer Carrie Mae Weems. Alva Rogers became a highly sought-after playwright, actor, and muse, with roles in two of the most pivotal films in the black film vault: Julie Dash's *Daughters of the Dust*, the first full-length film by an African-American woman to have a theatrical release in the United States, and Spike Lee's legendary look at black colleges, the 1988 film *School Daze*.

The writer of the collective, Lisa Jones,[8] went on to become a journalist, essayist, and the group's historian. She wrote Rodeo Caldonia's two plays, *Carmella & King Kong* and *Combination Skin*, works that unselfconsciously examined the black existence—from colorism and miscegenation to stereotypes and politics. The girls referred to themselves as a performance troupe, but it is clear that Rodeo Caldonia knew that what happened between them offstage was the real art. "Probably our

---

8 Lisa Jones is the daughter of famous OG poet Amiri Baraka (né LeRoi Jones), who used to run with Mailer and was one of the few cool people I can think of who has been hipster in both ways.

most significant contribution to the world of performing arts was us roaming the streets as a pack, showing up at parties, and talking race, sex, and hair into the night over Celina's barbecue wings and Donna's guacamole," says Lisa Jones in her manifesto "She Came with the Rodeo." The Caldonia girls reveled in their ordinariness—or rather, in the way it is revolutionary for black girls to get together to do the unremarkable. They left behind a slew of unfinished art projects, like the poetry revue *Welcome to the Black Aesthetic*, which never made it to the stage but I imagine was a powerhouse in rehearsal. The Rodeo Caldonia girls brought their high-fidelity energy into the room, each meeting transcendent, each fledgling black girl guiding the others toward the path of their creative adult lives.

When we talk about black hipsters, we're usually talking about black people who have used their status to alienate themselves from their blackness in an attempt to place themselves on a social tier above it. When we talk about black people who weirded- and nerded-out in groups, we talk about them as anomalies or outliers, instead of people who were par for the course in every social and/or political movement. Ntozake Shange, Lorraine Hansberry, Josephine Baker, Diana Ross, Ma Rainey, Bessie Smith, Mary McLeod Bethune: black girl hipsters. Harriet E. Wilson, a novelist from the 1800s—the first African American of any gender to publish a novel in North America—the writer who set the archetype of the free black with the aptly titled *Our Nig*. These were the types of women Rodeo Caldonia admired. These women were not hipsters because of the ways they played up or played against the white establishment. They were hipsters because they created their own standard of cool. "Alternative art-race-rebels," Lisa Jones called them, women who formed the backbone of black girl satire and uniqueness, but none of these women worked inside a cultural vacuum. These black women had radical identities that did not require they be the one hip black girl, the one black girl hipster, in order to make their revolutionary qualities relevant.

As black girls, we've been trained to believe that in order to consider ourselves unusual or individual we have to align ourselves with an existing white aesthetic, but there have always been black women of irony and rebellion. Often, young black girls looking for countercultural edge don't realize that much of what makes America "cool" has been ripped off from black girls, from the slang and swag stolen from our queer femme culture to the lip gloss and nail art pilfered from our chic urban hood. This is a blackness we don't hear enough about; black girls who don't get white hipster cred. We have always been cool. But the conversation recognizing us as hip is bigger than hipsters. Bigger than bohemia. Everything we look to for inspiration, in every way America has learned to entertain and perform, black people—black women—have been the "alternative"[9] at the center of it all.

---

9 I think of the "black girl hipster" as a person in constant peril of tokenism. The identity seems to require that one take up the mantle of "the one black friend" in order to prove their worth. Within this designation, we often mistake an awareness of white pseudo-countercultural conversations as the mark of a black girl aesthete.

I listen to alt-ter-na-tive, my friend Ashiwa would say, sitting cross-kneed on the floor enunciating each syllable through her braces, while the rest of us girls would grind our hips to R&B and salsa music at our college girl basement parties and sleepovers. Senegalese and African American, Ashiwa looked at the limited range of blackness that was her University of Louisville campus and decided blackness was a place where she didn't fit in. In many ways, none of us who'd shown

If you feel being a black hipster is your thing, I'm not here to Doc Marten stomp all over you. But given the history of the word and the broadness of the intellectual black anti-establishment, "black hipster" is an oxymoron. Not all of us come with a Rodeo, but unlike the girls of Rodeo Caldonia, we have access to more anti-typical blackness on television and the internet than ever before. The HBO show *Random Acts of Flyness*. The understated comedy of Eudora Peterson. The international rise of Afropunk (in spite of the critique of its growth as too capitalist) and all the subsidiary black, solidly punk festivals it has spawned throughout the world. I wake up every morning knowing there is black too cool for me to even know about. This makes me happy.

All things considered, to identify as a black person who feels most at home in white culture—specifically in a hipster culture

---

up that night for the sleepover filled with University of Kentucky and U of L girls knew where to place ourselves. We played R&B that night, from the radio, but most of us listened to Skin or Fefe Dobson or Tracy Chapman in our headphones (myself, Meshell Ndegeocello—my burgeoning crush). We saw something in each other but we still made the effort to perform blackness for each other the way we usually did when we hid out during Delta rush week on our college campuses, or hung our heads low while passing the Black Student Union. Somehow, we believed by hiding our black uniqueness we were preserving our black identity.

I was studying architecture. I had a notebook I had plastered with sketches of Josephine Baker done by Mies van der Rohe. I carried a Ben Harper & the Innocent Criminals messenger bag and had regular conversations with a blue and black poster of a young Miles Davis. I was definitely looking for a way to be a black girl I didn't see in 702, but I also loved 702 and knew the best thing to ever happen to music videos was a trash bag brought to life by Missy Elliott. What I'm saying is, we black girls have always been weirdos. We can call "weird" the alternative to standard blackness, but whatever models have been set before us of what a black girl is we've always taken apart and refitted.

that derives its name and angst from the socioeconomic oppression of smart black people—is difficult for me to imagine but not impossible. Keep in mind that the hipsters are the "niggas" of upwardly mobile white people. Why would any black person choose to start at the bottom of a mediocre culture clash? White people don't even want to be there.

In 2010, a bunch of smart, mostly white people got together and declared the hipster dead. *n+1* cofounder Mark Greif published an essay in *New York* magazine titled "What Was the Hipster?" which was followed by a panel discussion at NYU arguing the hipster's metamorphosis—from a derogatory slur for a certain type of young [white] person into, as Greif states in the introduction to *n+1*'s book by the same title, "a set of style accessories repackaged for purchase in shopping malls across America." Since 2010, there has been a wave of endorsements from formerly hipster news outlets confirming the idea that "hipsterdom" was, in fact, a transitory state. In the economic upswing, hipsters have returned to the world of mainstream whiteness as "Yuccies" (Young Urban Creatives) and other subsets that the *VICE* magazine article "What Will Replace the Hipster?" describes as "differently objectionable people," like "The Cutester" and "The Health Goth," as if differentiating these new forms of hipster renders the presence of the white hipster inert.

White culture's rush to scurry away from the "h-word" represents exactly the reason the "n-word" will never be an acceptable term for all people to use. The problem is the people "who call themselves white" (as James Baldwin put it) have made a concerted effort to separate themselves from the dual consciousness that comes with otherness. Code-switching. An embodied understanding that, as a marginalized identity, you perform in this world as at least two people—the person you want to become and the person who is expected of you. The use of "nigga" is not an example of embodied personhood. It is the result of what happens when circumstance limits the fullness with which you can define yourself.

Even though most of the white people who became this generation's hipsters did so because they didn't feel they lived up to America's image of affluent, successful, spectacularized whiteness, people of color—especially black people—will never have that. The "n-word" remains the most common American slur for anyone considered abject or irredeemable. Patti Smith's "Rock N Roll Nigger," a hit song about how Smith, a white woman, considered herself the "black sheep" of the 1970s rock music industry—is a song she still performs. Even as Americans develop new derogatory words for each gender and sexual identity, each religious denomination and ethnic group, for anything this country considers itself at odds with, "the niggers of _____" becomes the go-to metaphor—like when CNN reporter Chris Cuomo referred to "fake news" as the "n-word of journalism."

It is not that the word "nigga" means anything different to black people than to white culture. What "nigga" does is *embody* something entirely different for us than it does for whites. We live with it inside us. I can't say it's in our bones but it is definitely in our skin. White people can't use the word "nigga" because *they have no* "niggas." In her book *White Trash: The 400-Year Untold History of Class in America*, Nancy Isenberg argues that rich white people invented "whiteness" so that poor white people (many of whose ancestors were brought to America on the *Mayflower* as slaves of the Puritans) would think of themselves as superior to "niggers." Instead of seeking restitution for the ways they were exploited, poor people used their status as newly minted "white people" in order to beat, kill, harass, and discriminate against blacks. When the children of the rich and upper-middle-class whites couldn't cut it in America's totalitarian free-market economy, they co-opted poor whiteness, and turned to black culture for a model of how to live in peril—how to be "hung from a noose."[10]

I dare any white person to come to me and say, "I can use the word 'nigga' because I understand its history and I understand what it means *now* to consciously inhabit black thought and black bodies." Try it. Try it and prove to me you are not perpetuating the America handed down to disenfranchised white people to police blacks to begin with. I take issue with the argument that it's a double standard to expect non-black people not to use the "n-word." Of course it is. Damn right it is. Nothing has made America greater than its adherence to a different standard for white people than for everyone else. The problem is that it is now black people demanding that white people hold themselves to a higher standard.

⇌

In my early thirties, my friend Chet'la (pronounced "Shayla," no relation) and I spend a lot of time collaborating as artists, over

---

10 See footnote 5.

my guacamole and her chicken wings. We talk about starting a
web series as an ode to Rodeo Caldonia, "The Bravura Sessions,"
the title taken from Lisa Jones' description of the way, even as
the world changed, the Caldonia stayed constant. Much like
what happened with *Diva De Kooning*, Rodeo Caldonia's never-
released magazine, we never find enough money to fund the web
series. But Chet'la and I do in our together-lives what the series
would have intended: we talk about sex positions and hair care
products and bowel regularity, and we dance and cry—all while
making art.

We write a collection of poems together over the course of
two residencies—Yaddo and MacDowell. It is at MacDowell
that we start to discuss our complex views about the "n-word."
As adults with academic writing careers, it seems improper that
we use the word regularly. We say it when we're talking about
dumb lovers. We say it when we're cursing out a dried-up ink
pen. We invent the term "TЯNT" to describe things that refuse
to behave properly: *This nigga right hurr.* In this derivation of
"thot," seasoned with a smidge of "chickenhead," the two of us
reshape two common anti-feminine slurs. Why is there a "T" at
the end to represent "hurr"? Yes. Why is the whole middle of the
phrase backward? Exactly. The fact the acronym does nothing
to reflect the phrase it represents is the phrase's flagrant enact-
ment of its very TЯNTitude.

In June 2015, an often-bankrupt businessman and reality TV
TЯNT announces his candidacy for the United States' highest office. In 2017, he becomes America's forty-fifth president.

He grips the White House with xenophobia, misogyny, racism, and terror. Trump's reign as a candidate and president bolsters a wave of hatred in this country so great it overturns any farcical notion that white liberals or white hipsters might have had that we lived in a post-racial country, a nation in which the "n-word" posed no credible threat. He fires his one black friend, his reality TV show protégée Omarosa Manigault, from his staff, and she attempts to take him down with recordings proving that he has used, and still uses, the "n-word" in conversation. It does not matter. Trump did not resurrect the "n-word." The "n-word" is America's baby. The "n-word" was birthed here, it has yet to become an old man, the "n-word" is still adolescent at most.

To anyone who believes we must concentrate our energy on the eradication of the "n-word" in order to move forward: we *are* moving forward. And the word is not going anywhere. We do not have to love it, but we have to own it. This essay is the history of its name. A "nigger" is a sketch of a person, the white chalk outline of a body in the street. The outline of a black body in America has always represented fatality—a casualty, a sacrifice. Black people using the "n-word" is less about moving past transgression than it is about how generational cycles of social torment and economic oppression inform how unkindly black culture thinks of itself. For better or worse, every survivor of a tragedy erects a field around their wound, their scar—to shun, to protect, to worship at its altar, to pretend to love. In everything "nigger" has done to not be the "n-word," "nigga" is the best we have done to redeem it. This is not right. This is not healthy or proper. But it is a reality we must face.

For anyone who wants to believe in a post-racial America (in an America at all) the only way to do so is to respect black bodies. This includes using language that respects black bodies, regardless of what language we black people use to address ourselves. No matter how we represent ourselves as we rebuild and repair, our blackness is still in its infancy, its weakest state. If you are a white person who wants to believe in post-racial America, the tools to our reparations demand that *you* transcend race. That you manifest a true appreciation for blackness. White people must allow us the dialectic of our troubled inheritance.

Or ... go on, call me a nigga.

I'll be calling you a hipster first.[11]

---

11 Understand this is a statement made in artistic license. If you are a non-black person who decides to use "nigga," "nigger," or any variant around me, you will get got. For the love of your personal god, I hope you read footnotes.

"BLACK LIVES MATTER" YARD SIGNS MATTER

. . . to Your White Neighbors

While I was living in Portland, Oregon, I was asked to teach *To Kill a Mockingbird* to a group of middle schoolers during a Black History Month freelance gig. The students were bright and eager. When I asked them what they knew about the history of racism in America—slavery, segregation, Jim Crow, and Civil Rights—their arms shot in the air resolutely, in that endearing way we've all lost by our freshman year of high school.

Those are all things that happened in "The South," Ms. Lawson, the kids parroted in the ignorant haze that is how most kids in this country are taught to think about its racist past.

But, little friends, Ms. Lawson is from "The South," I answered. They scrunched up their noses and cocked their heads to one side. They didn't believe me. To their credit, I don't fit the image of what most people think a southerner looks or sounds

like—one concocted mostly from books and movies and inherited prejudices—but here I am. I grew up in Kentucky and went
to college there. I once saw some neighbors hang a bobblehead
toy of a black basketball coach in effigy after the team lost a
championship game. I went to graduate school in Indiana; tech-
nically not the south, but a state that often vied with Kentucky
for the dubious distinction of being the ancestral home of the
Ku Klux Klan.

My name is Michael Lynch, said a neighbor of mine on first
meeting. *As in "lynch."* He explained to me that he was a descendant of the namesake. What Madam C. J. Walker was to the
hair on black people's heads, this guy's distant relative was to . . .
well . . . (?!?). I stared at him. My eyes widened. Michael Lynch
continued to shake my hand. (I guess I could say this has been
a theme for me—white people who believe it's better to stand
directly in front of the racist history that connects us, in order
to prove themselves distinct from it.)

Yes, I told my wide-eyed students, *Ms. Lawson grew up in the
South.* I walked to the back of the classroom to place my hand
on the fried-drumstick shape of Kentucky on the wall map.
*And so often she hears people talk about "The South" as if it is
this place full of evil, racist, bad people. But I want you to know*
To Kill a Mockingbird *isn't a famous book about "The South,"
it is a famous book about America, an America in which, less
than fifty years ago, Ms. Lawson would not have been able to be
your teacher. Right here.* I scanned the room of predominantly
white upper-class students. *How many of you have parents,*

grandparents, friends who are fifty years old? Half the kids raised their hands.

What I knew that my middle school students didn't is that American racism has never been exclusive to region. I considered showing them a photograph from a 1921 edition of Portland's newspaper, the *Oregonian*, in which Ku Klux Klan members in full regalia stand beside the mayor and prominent government officials. CHIEF KLUXERS TELL LAW ENFORCEMENT OFFICERS JUST WHAT MYSTIC ORGANIZATION PROPOSES TO DO IN THE CITY OF PORTLAND, the caption reads. I thought about sharing this image with them, but I did not.

Ms. Lawson, it has come to our attention that some of our students have been . . . disturbed . . . by your teaching of To Kill a Mockingbird, the principal said after inviting me in for a chat.

I'm so glad that you mention it . . . sir . . . I have had my reservations about teaching a book with such mature subject matter to seventh graders.

Mature—Ms. Lawson, that's beside the point. We're concerned that you're focusing too much on the . . . racial . . . elements of the book.

The "racial elements" . . . of . . . To Kill a Mockingbird?

—Ms. Lawson, we've been teaching Lee's classic here for years now and we've never gotten so many . . . complaints . . . Our parents are unsettled by their children's interest in the racial nature of the book, and this is becoming a cause for concern.

Which part? I said.

Which part?

Yes, I do agree the racial nature of the book is a cause for concern.

—*Shayla, we didn't hire you to teach* To Kill a Mockingbird *as a book about "race."*

But it is, I said.

. . . It is?

A book about race.

As an educator myself, I strongly disagree.

If To Kill a Mockingbird *is not a book about race, what is the story?* He opened his mouth to answer, scrolling through his cursory remembrance of the beloved novel: trawling through the high grass of Maycomb, Alabama, with Scout, attempting to catch a glimpse of Boo Radley. He replayed his favorite scene from the iconic movie—Gregory Peck's closing argument—its monolithic depiction of white goodness firmly ensconced in his mind.

It can be hard to talk to people like this, people so squarely convinced they stand on the right side of the racial divide they will do anything to protect it. We've migrated into a time in which it is more important for people to *feel* not-racist than it is for them to *act* not-racist. It almost makes me miss the times in my life when people felt entitled enough to spew their racist hatred from their neighborhood porches. Or maybe not—our country's last ten years have offered up enough new atrocities that I needn't feel wistful for blatant racism, as if it's some distant recollection of the past.

"We're clearly not in a post-racial America," stated publicist

Rachel Noerdlinger on the *Melissa Harris-Perry* show in 2013. "We're in a post–Trayvon Martin America." As much as it pains me to use the death of a young boy—a boy the same age as many of the students I've taught over the years—as the touchstone of an era, I fear she's right.

After a few months in the city, I decided to move to the chic suburban neighborhood of Laurelhurst. I knew little about it other than the apartment I found was stunning—a gut-renovated basement unit with a large kitchen and walk-in rain shower with slate floors. The beauty of the apartment's interior and building's exterior awed everyone who saw it, including the Ethiopian Lyft driver who pulled up to the house to drop me off.

We have finally made it, he said.

I rent, I assured him, *and just the basement.*

Not for long, he responded. I smiled and gave him a tip.

I must admit that for a time the apartment did feel like an achievement. A few months before I finished graduate school, I visited Portland for the first time. I had a couple of job interviews and was trying to figure out if I could live in a city that had the reputation of being absurdly white. Before one of my interviews, I popped into Kure, a juice bar. I spotted an older woman with clean gray twists wearing a beautifully cut white suit, the first black person I'd seen during forty-eight hours in Portland. We smiled and made eye contact. Perhaps this will work, I thought to myself. I accepted the job the following week.

The "perhaps" I was qualifying back then was the time I had previously spent gentrifying black urban neighborhoods.

My old apartment in Harlem had been down the street from brownstones purchased by Kareem Abdul-Jabbar and Maya Angelou (who bought property to invest some of their wealth into a historic black community). I moved there because the street was pretty and the rent was cheap. Forget the fact I was replacing someone who could not afford the now-doubled rent. I was black. I was in my mid-twenties. I hoped I could do some good but mostly I wanted to live in Manhattan and next to all my uptown friends. It was the Recession; the whole city stank of strain and desperation, particularly the blocks around 125th Street, where families who'd maintained those neighborhoods for generations were closing their businesses and losing their homes. My time there was ugly, my guilt like a bad taste. Perhaps, I thought with smug elitism, Portland will be the type of place where I get to choose what it means to be black.

And Portland can be. Black Portlanders call Portland the "town of the one black friend." If you're tired of living in places where other black people ask you to pull out your Black Card, Portland could seem like your kind of place. It has a thriving community of black artists, and bookstore blacks, vegan blacks, So-Cal blacks, cosplay blacks, and black Nike/Adidas/Intel corporate employees—blacks hand-selected to accessorize Portland's pretty, liberal utopian landscape. Portland is small enough that you can curate your own black experience, but Portland counts on people of color to believe that our living in Portland makes them liberal and accepting, and us unique and exceptional. Portland counts on us to cover up the targeted attacks on its indigenous, Black, Asian, and Latinx communities that it continues to make and has made for centuries.

I didn't go looking for a black neighborhood to live in, because I was told Portland *had* no black neighborhoods, something I found momentarily liberating—that I didn't have to choose a neighborhood segregated by skin color. It took me nearly a year to learn enough about the city's history to understand what people meant when they said these neighborhoods *don't exist.*

You know, the joke in Portland is that "Portland's so white even the black people live in Albina," says my one white friend from college as he drives me to my new apartment after collecting me from the airport. But the real joke isn't that all the black people in Portland live in the Albina district. The real joke is Albina's where all the black people *used to* live.

Oregon was established as a white utopia on the North American continent. Laws prohibiting black people to take up residence in the region go back to 1844, fifteen years before the West Coast territory ever became a state. In service to its original utopian mission, Oregon kept the zoning laws relegating people of color to specific neighborhoods on the books well into the mid- and late twentieth century (for instance, it was still officially legal to beat a black person found on the street after sundown until 1996). From 1890 to the eve of World War II, Albina was its own city (not a Portland neighborhood) and home to the majority of the region's segregated African American population. Even after Albina was absorbed into Portland

proper, the district was one of the only places where black people were legally allowed to live. (By "live" I mean rent homes. Although a few black families managed to purchase property, the
houses in Albina were primarily owned by wealthy whites.)
Despite Oregon racism, Albina became home to thriving black
businesses as well as families, but what remains of that history
now is mostly Albina Avenue, a gentrified residential area largely
indistinguishable from the streets that surround it. The Albina
district, however, was not the first casualty in Portland's war
to keep out black neighbors. That dubious distinction is left to
Vanport.

~

About a year into my time in Portland, I finally nailed down a
full-time job at a digital marketing firm working as a content
writer and creative strategist—whatever that means. The job
drew on a combination of the skills I'd acquired as a freelance
writer, designer, and educator. I got pretty good at it. I was put in
charge of a couple of copywriting employees, and it was during
a check-in with one of my staff members that I learned the company was working on a branding campaign for the Vanport Jazz
Festival. A Vanport Jazz Festival headlined primarily by white
acts, most of whom weren't even jazz performers.

Given how white Portland is, a predominantly white jazz
festival might not feel like a particular atrocity. But Vanport,
the location the festival organizers chose, was a disappeared
city of black Oregonians and the site of one of the most horrific

erasures of black Americans in the twentieth century. And the fact you've probably never heard of it shows how deeply the West Coast's racial issues get buried. Of course, the history of America is nothing if not the stories of the bones of dark people buried beneath a gentrified landscape—take for example the New York City African Burial Ground below the building of the NYC Commission on Human Rights, or the Narragansett Burial Ground located underneath a pristine suburb in Rhode Island. But unlike these sites, Vanport was not an unearthing of our dead, but an intentional burial of the living.

During the 1940s, black people moved from the southern U.S. to the north, Midwest, and Pacific Northwest as part of the Great Migration. Vanport, located just north of Portland's Albina district and south of Vancouver, Washington, became a popular destination during World War II because of the shipyards along the Columbia River and because it was one of the few places in the country offering all its employees equal pay, regardless of race. The shipyards employed so many people that the government built wartime public housing for the migrants. Oregon, a state whose racist policies made it impossible for black people to live there, went from having about 1,800 black residents in 1940 to more than 15,000 by the time the war ended, in Vanport and Albina alone. Vanport had become the second-largest city in Oregon and home to Vanport College (which later grew into Portland State University) and to the largest federal housing project in America.

Vanport's black shipyard employees were essential during

the war. But when the war ended and the shipyards closed, Portland wasn't particularly keen on its new dark neighbors. Although by 1947, African Americans composed, depending on reports, as little as 17 percent—or at most 35 percent—of the total population of Vanport, wealthy Portlanders lodged a campaign against the housing project with the goal of closing it. Portland, a city that had, up until that time, maintained its idyllic image as a white utopia, considered the Vanport housing project a physical manifestation of the black public scourge. Vanport was also home to war veterans, Vanport College faculty, white shipyard workers, and all these men's families (as was reported by Portland newspaper the *Oregon Journal* in articles and op-eds during the time, which refuted Vanport's presence as a crime-infested community eyesore) but, unlike these white inhabitants—many of whom moved into Portland as the shipyards laid off employees—Portland's strict regulations around where black people could live made migration into the city almost impossible.

On Memorial Day in 1948, the two rivers that flanked Portland and Vanport—the Columbia and the Willamette—reached flood height. Vanport lay in the basin of the flood zone, and Housing Authority of Portland (HAP) officials knew that its cheaply built tenements wouldn't survive a flood. But they did not say this to its residents. In fact, on that Monday, with the flood imminent, Vanport residents woke up to signs posted all over their neighborhood reading REMEMBER. DIKES ARE SAFE AT PRESENT. YOU WILL BE WARNED IF NECESSARY. YOU WILL HAVE TIME TO LEAVE. DON'T GET EXCITED. Literally,

HAP posted signs that read DON'T GET EXCITED instead of
the flood warnings required by law, or saying nothing at all. Residents only found out about the imminent destruction because
a group of Vanport College students, who had been researching
the dam, came to collect the equipment they'd been using so it
would not be lost in the flood. The people of Vanport managed
an emergency evacuation in the thirty-five minutes that separated them from imminent death. By 4:17 p.m., the dam broke,
and within ten minutes, the entire town was swept away by the
flood. Although it is reported only fifteen people lost their lives
that day, Vanport, Oregon's second-largest city, the home of
90 percent of its black population, disappeared.

I presented the tragedy of Vanport to my direct superior at the
digital marketing firm, having researched the anecdotes I'd
heard. I reread articles from The Vanport Mosaic flood memorial and the *Oregon History Project*. I read recent newspaper articles in the *Oregonian*, *Portland Tribune*, and *Willamette Week*. I
pulled notes from lectures I'd attended led by West Coast historian Walidah Imarisha. My director, a Canadian import, hadn't
heard of any of this.

Wasn't that flood an accident? she asked.

No. No it was not.

Around the same time, Pepsi had come out with a commercial that whitewashed Black Lives Matter protests into something that looked like an urban version of Coachella and the
criticism happening in the commercial's wake made advertising companies momentarily more conscientious about how they

were representing their brands. I mentioned that, in light of this, we should be careful about how we market a white jazz festival co-opting the land where some were killed and thousands of black Oregonians were intentionally made homeless. I went back to my desk and emailed her a *Smithsonian* article citing the involvement of HAP.

After the flood, it did not take long for Portland to relocate the hostility it felt for the vanished Vanport onto the flourishing, predominantly black district of Albina, home to 80 percent of the city's black residents. By 1962, Albina was declared by elected officials to be in an "advanced state of blight." Landlords began to evict tenants, demolish buildings, and sell the land to developers of glossy urban renewal projects, including the Legacy Emanuel Medical Center expansion, which, according to a 2012 article in the *Oregonian*, "razed nearly 300 homes and businesses," destroying "the heart of the African-American community." The new hospital project in Albina was never completed, and the land razed for the hospital expansion remained vacant. Portland's one black neighborhood never recovered. During the anniversary celebration, the hospital invited a group of black community leaders and former Albina residents to a pancake breakfast, in order to apologize for uprooting over half of the city's black residents. A pancake breakfast. Almost fifty years later.

Damn.

When I moved to Portland, I didn't know I was just another instrument of the city's ongoing black erasure, but I should have guessed. I spent a lot of time there walking the streets wearing a hood, often at night. I am dog-mother to a small Havanese. He's black too. Doing this makes me acutely aware of the dangers of being alone and black at night, especially in the places we think of as America's "good," "safe" neighborhoods. After a few months of walking in the dusk in Laurelhurst, where my black dog and I made up the entire black population, the neighborhood started to feel less idyllic and more menacing. I encountered one too many Stepford-looking couples eager to interrogate me as I attempted to pass their homes, the wife on her knees cutting shrubbery, the husband holding a watering hose over the lawn.

What do you do for work? he asks. (Translation: How can you afford to live here?).

How long have you been here? she asks. (Translation: How did you move in without my knowing about it? Have you registered yourself with the Neighborhood Watch?) They fire their questions in rapid succession as I try to keep walking.

The answer to the first neighbor's question is that I was still working at the creative agency, where my office superiors thanked me for my "candor" regarding Vanport and told me they'd get back to me. They decided to continue working on the jazz festival project anyway, adding a hyperlink to the festival website with a letter of condolence written by the Oregon Historical Society to all those affected by the Vanport tragedy. My employer attempted to boost its image as a "diverse" company by shading in its cartoon sketches of all the staff to match our skin tones and publishing articles in advertising journals and interviews in local papers about the "diversity" internship program started by the company's founder. They brought in a local black academic to lead us through "diversity" training. Perhaps this initiative and the jazz festival were incongruous. Perhaps not.

There is absolutely nothing more important to the liberal residents of my gentrified neighborhood, one littered with Black Lives Matter signs, than to protect their sense of feeling "not racist," despite their inhospitable prejudices against our presence. In this, Portland is not alone. Cities across America are carving liberal, predominantly white, enclaves out of what used to be socially and culturally mixed, or predominantly black, neighborhoods in nearly every state. But I question Portland's loyalty to the cause of Black Lives Matter.

When I consider my time living and working in Portland, I remember two situations in which the only responsible thing to do was to speak up at the discrimination against, and erasure of, black people. In both cases, I was met with a clear assertion from the so-called liberal residents of this white utopia that it would be better if I found a new place to go. To work. To live. I lived there for three years. I moved, both jobs and houses, as many times. So often, as I cleared my desk or stuffed my belongings into the back of my car, transporting myself to another part of the city—from education to advertising, from the suburbs to downtown—I wanted to ask them: if the history of black lives in America, in our own neighborhoods, does not matter . . . what does?

Black Lives Matter is an organization founded by three

black women, Patrisse Khan-Cullors, Alicia Garza, and Opal Tometi. In the summer of 2017, the FBI marked Black Lives Matter as a terrorist organization, a "Black Identity Extremist" group. This labeling should scare all Americans, but it should surprise none of us. I never once believed my neighbors kept their impeccable Black Lives Matter yard signs up as a sign of true protest. Black Lives Matter yard signs mattered to my neighbors because, in a world increasingly interested in protecting the rights of a select few, they were looking for ways to feel safe from white guilt. They didn't want to take a hard look at how they too are contributing to this country's undoing, by actively benefiting from the comfort of exclusionary liberal white communities. Communities that don't have to confront their blatant discrimination because they are not forced to ask themselves if the way they treat their non-white neighbors is right. They stay inside their houses, believing they are protecting American democracy like the Constitution-quoting Atticus Finch. Black Lives Matter yard signs do, on their lawns, what signs have always been designed to do: maintain control, to keep whatever is outside out.

Despite my having grown up in the south, Portland is the most racist place I have ever lived. This is because being antiracist isn't about using politically correct buzzwords and giving lip-service to sensitive conversation topics. Being anti-racist is about constructing a landscape that is safe for dark people to inhabit. It is not about white people trying to prove they are "woke" by putting up yard signs. That is not even what "woke" means. "Woke" is a territory of open-eyed, unsuperficial, cultural awareness white people are nowhere close to occupying; they are not even in the neighborhood. But being *anti-racist* in this dangerous era is something they can do, by going out of their way to make non-white people feel safe.

When I finally leave Portland, I am tired of being an outsider. I move back to New York—to Brooklyn—a newly constructed housing co-op in East Flatbush. I am still gentrifying, this is not something I can look past, but I build connections. I patronize its local black-owned businesses, which include wine shops and gluten-free bakeries. And juice bars. I stop and talk to the locals, many of whom still own their townhomes, while I walk my dog. They never ask me what I'm doing here; there is not a single Black Lives Matter sign to be seen. (Why would we need to be reminded it matters that we exist?) I rent. Hopefully, not for long. I have grown enough to understand I can be bigger than the space I occupy. I can be a good neighbor. I take stock in this. I take root.

INTRARACIAL DATING

ACT I

"It feels counterintuitive to suggest that straight black men as a whole possess any sort of privilege—particularly the type of privilege created for and protected by whiteness," says Damon Young in his *Very Smart Brothas* article "Straight Black Men Are the White People of Black People." "But assessing our privilege," Young continues, "considers only our relationship with whiteness and with America. Intraracially . . . our relationship to and with black women is not unlike whiteness's relationship to us."

Perhaps. You take a moment to assess.

SCENE 1
YOU are sitting in a bar in New England that is doing its best impression of one in Manhattan's Financial District. The cast

includes a woman from TURKEY you have recently befriended and her boyfriend, a native of MISSISSIPPI. He derides YOU, saying *you are just like my mother*, when YOU do not respond to a magic trick he wastes on YOU involving sparklers and a flick of the wrist.

MISSISSIPPI: See, that's why I have never been able to date a black girl!

YOU are dumbfounded by the exclamation in his statement that suggests YOU have just agreed with him about black girls.

MISSISSIPPI: See, I was born and raised with all black women: my mom, my sister, my grandma—

MISSISSIPPI continues to elucidate as if this biological predicament only affects black men.

—I could never see black women as anything but—black women are so trained to act like your mom, you know—I couldn't be free with a black girl, you know . . . like, be a kid and just explore.

YOU Exit. But the Scene persists.

SCENE 2
YOU are in Portland having some version of the MISSISSIPPI conversation over and over again with men who barely interest

you. One time, you take a man home, convinced that curing him of his white supremacist intimacy is your patriotic duty. But your allegiance to this flag soon bores you. For a time, YOU find yourself beside a web designer from ANTIGUA—hoping to find a less burdensome self-loathing in dark men from outside the Light Continent.

ANTIGUA: You are the only black woman I've been able to connect with in this city.
YOU: I know.

YOUR tone is chiding, but he'd considered this a compliment, so he looks surprised.

The two of you move to the bedroom. ANTIGUA decides to pleasure YOU unprompted. Proud of his efforts he begins Milly Rocking in front of your mirror; there is no music. A self-impressed beatbox, he repurposes the lyrics of Kanye West's "Fade."

ANTIGUA *(SINGS)*: "You talkin' bout a real-ass nigga . . ."

YOU, half-come, watch the strange display of your bedroom through the sheets, half shielding your eyes as the stage lights go low.

YOU date through your designer phase and your DJ phase, your executive phase, your phase in which everyone reminds you of a skateboarding Malcolm Gladwell and a phase in which everyone looks like Tyler, the Creator—DJs and executives alike.

YOU hook up. YOU make out. YOU dinner-and-movie. YOU Netflix-and-chill. YOU "let's just wait." YOU can count on one finger the number of black men who can rightfully say they have been your boyfriend.

SCENE 3

A BROOKLYN man keeps trying to break up with YOU in analogy.

THE SETTING: A series of iMessages scattered between your phone and your laptop throughout your workday.
BROOKLYN: Your [sic] more like a Manhattan and I'm more like a Hennessy Manhattan.
YOU: But a call-drink is still gonna cost you extra at the club.
BROOKLYN: Haa [sic]. Right.
Beat.

BROOKLYN: You know, I'm more like hot Cheetos and you're more like ...

Somebody he didn't want to be with anymore. YOU get the point. He is used to dating white girls. This scene never ends.

SCENE 4

THE SCENE in the New England bar resumes. Although MISSISSIPPI concentrates his monologue on YOU, maintaining constant eye contact, he constantly touches TURKEY, rubbing her hand and stroking her back.

MISSISSIPPI: You should meet my brother.
TURKEY: He'd like you. *(Bubbly nod of approval.)* We could all be family!

    MISSISSIPPI goes into his pocket to retrieve his phone and produces a picture of his brother.
MISSISSIPPI: He would like you. You sing?

    What exactly should YOU sing to? A new Civil Rights? Your inner voice becomes political: for males, the goal of social advancement is to supersede the privileges achieved by their parents' generation, making it a task that is, for many black men, associated with proximity to white romantic partners. For females, the goal is the bloodline, maintaining the continuation of an interrace. Our colonization encourages us to simultaneously run toward and away from each other in opposition, a bureaucracy of broken history.

ACT II

Then Jay-Z says, "You know, in the neighborhoods we're in (*"neighborhood" is a reference to any space in which black people develop a sense of blackness*), you know, we have low self-esteem. And then the women and—(*Jay-Z pauses over his Freudian slip, the hypersexualization of children as "women"*) well, the girls—they have low self-esteem as well. So, these are all dysfunctional relationships at a very young age."

The entertainer's faulty logic intrigues you.

SCENE 1

A Thursday night and YOU are standing guard outside the SETTING of a Lower East Side basement bar while your friend pisses in chair pose in the alley. Her parents are from Mumbai but she grew up in TEXAS. She has a friend visiting her from VIRGINIA, also Indian. TEXAS finishes peeing. As they prepare to reenter the bar, TEXAS and VIRGINIA start cracking jokes about their aunties' attempts to arrange marriages between their law student nieces and any eligible Indian bachelors.

TEXAS: I just want to introduce you to some *nice boys*.

She says this with slow, affected sarcasm. Her aunties are worried about the "not-quite-right" ethnics she likes to invite for dinner on her Thanksgiving trips home.

TEXAS AND VIRGINIA spy two young Indian gentle-
men, investment banker types, who have slipped out of the bar
next door for a cigarette.

VIRGINIA: 'Ey husband! 'Usband!

In a grating "auntie" imitation.
TEXAS chimes in. The two girls henpeck, debating which
of them makes the best curries and reminding the cigarette-
smoking boys that they need to get home at six, straight after
work.

It's not that YOU don't date intraracially. It is just that
YOU have felt the pressure from such a young age to be an ideal
partner to someone of your race. As if to be this partner is to be
a good wife to all of your generations of ancestors. You crack
under the expectation, consumed with how much easier it looks
on white television. Everything goes wrong but they still match
perfectly.

YOU do not have a set of aunties but you do have your
interracially coupled friends. These sets of partners seem more
devoted to seeing YOU date inside your race than anyone
else.

SCENE 2
You're having brunch in the actual Financial District in Manhattan. The cast: your half-Peruvian college buddy and his Bul-
garian fiancée.

The house lights lift on a busboy refilling a water glass for YOU.

BULGARIA: *(Enthusiastically trying to set you up with their other one black friend.)* He knows you're a writer. He used to write poetry in high school—he <u>loves</u> open mic nights. *(Beat.)* He's such a great guy. He's so funny!
PERU: We think you two will totally hit it off. You have so much ... *(Beat.)* in common.

Beat.

YOU continue to mull over your croissant until it dissolves on your tongue, bitterly. YOU lick your lips and reach for a napkin. PERU and BULGARIA nod their heads in doe-eyed cross-cultural cuteness, anxiously anticipating what YOU will say in response.

YOU: *(Still wiping your hands with a bunched-up napkin.)* Of course I'll meet him.

PERU and BULGARIA sigh in palpable relief.

White folks always think black people don't date each other, YOU think to yourself as you smile through the last of your brunch eggs. Is this what it takes for YOU to date—intraracially—international emissaries? But, YOU go ahead and meet their pleasant, well-parted gentleman.

SCENE 3

It's the Kentucky Derby. You meet up with HIM, PERU, and BULGARIA at a day-party in Brooklyn. You are braless in a bright blue maxi dress and platforms. He wears Oxfords and glasses, a starched button-down. You have invited your baddest girlfriend to join—her current look is early-eighties dark-chocolate DIANA ROSS with tits. Before DIANA ROSS arrives, YOU try to talk to HIM. YOU watch HIM stuff his hands in the pockets of his staunchly ironed slacks and think he too feels the pressure, the insurmountable burden that this moment, this conversation, even the condensation forming on his cup are the beginnings of some intraracial future.

And this will happen, for HIM, with someone. You have just decided that someone is not YOU. In truth, part of this is because YOU are insecure and convinced he will probably end up with a white girl (at the very least, some interracial fairy tale). Even if YOU like HIM, you want to avoid the inevitable letdown of not being what he's looking for. As his eyes dilate as DIANA ROSS makes her entrance, YOU know this will not be your beginning but it will be fun.

And it is. And two weeks go by and you can't even remember if YOU and HIM ever exchanged phone numbers. PERU does the obligatory check-in when you run into him on the bus home from work:

PERU: *(Nudging YOU playfully as if talking about a Yankees game.)* Hey, how did it go with HIM? He's great, huh?

YOU: *(Knowing nothing about baseball.)* It was good.

Beat, then dryly:

YOU: Did he say anything about me?

PERU: Well . . . he said he met two lovely ladies that night.

Perhaps a preference for DIANA, YOU read between the lines.

PERU: But he liked you both equally.

PERU hopes.

Maybe this is cruel. Perhaps bringing along your hot friend on a blind date is good-natured self-sabotage. Perhaps YOU would rather lose him to her tits—which YOU too could get lost in—than to some childish white girl. This has happened to YOU too.

SCENE 4

YOU go on a lukewarm blind date with a Senegalese guy. YOU and SENEGAL sit down in an Irish pub over a salad and mozzarella sticks and struggle for dialogue. You are surprised when he texts you four days later:

SENEGAL: Would you like to go to an Afrobeats party with me on Saturday?

YOU agree, overlooking the fact he ends his text with the emoji of the monkey with its hands over its eyes—your least favorite—followed by a Donald Duck gif.

YOU: Yes. I love dancing. Let's do it.

SENEGAL responds with a second Donald Duck gif.

YOU and SENEGAL continue to text in the days leading up to the weekend. YOU assume this is a second date. YOU get to the Afrobeats party. SENEGAL and his friend are standing by the bar, flanked by a local girl and her cousin from Montana dressed like The Cheetah Girls.

YOU: *(to SENEGAL)* Well, it looks like I'm intruding.

YOU watch MONTANA, in her tween clothes, getting white girl wasted. YOU think of how completely the phrase describes something YOU can never be. YOU are sober and serious. YOU are not allowed to keep living out your teen fantasies this far into your adulthood. YOU consider this is the "something special" that draws the black man to the white woman, as you have been told by men. Stereotypically, the two share a common social function in each of their communities—they are its most protected people. YOU think of how MONTANA has probably never had to mature into a person who represents her whole race. Given the Donald Duck gifs, neither has SENEGAL. YOU wish someone would be more lenient with YOU. You wish you were not groomed to be this independent.

But then MONTANA starts grinding her way between YOU and SENEGAL. She turns her ass toward his crotch. She jiggles her breasts in front of you, securing them back into her leopard-print tube top. SENEGAL smiles. MONTANA doesn't apologize as she jostles Hennessy all over YOU. YOU finish your drink and leave them to their Disney antics. YOU walk out the club. SENEGAL follows.

SENEGAL: Hey, what's wrong? Is there a problem?
   YOU can't. You can never get caught like this again.

ACT III

Or as Malcolm X puts it, "the most neglected person in all of America is the black woman."

You question the binary in the quote's moral imperative.

SCENE 1

YOU consider the blackness beyond two genders; YOU think how disproportionately HIV affects people of color. YOU consider what it means for black people to live in a time when they are more likely to survive the disease than its stigma. YOU think about how its presence in our intimate intraracial encounters means more black people cannot enter one another without the assistance of a pill or prophylactic. So that we won't kill us.

This feels targeted. As if it is not enough to have the social and the beauty expectations between us. HIV is dividing us, distancing us, digging another chasm to keep us apart. This is our romance. Intraracial dating has always been a complicated type of love. And as YOU try to repair for yourself the intimacy broken by the ownership of blackness, YOU remember it is not just YOU who has been neglected. It is not just YOU who's been rendered unworthy of love.

YOU and your close friend are having cocktails in a bar with beige wallpaper. THEY are nonbinary, and HIV-positive. The bar, dimly lit, feels like Paris.

THEM: I haven't been touched in eight months.

THEY have listened to you lament what has been, thus far, a long experiment in intraracial heartbreak.

THEM: Whatever you do not have, you at least have options in the men that break your heart. Even if I dream a world where I can curl up in a black man's arms, the world still expects me to *be* the black man—
YOU:—to always be that black man.
THEM: The Strong Mandingo!

THEY exaggerate the bass in their voice and pose as if holding the world on their shoulders.

THEM: And the black woman in me is just trying to hold the world together.

YOU rub your hands on their shoulders and hold their hands.

THEM: But I just want to be somebody's baby doll.

THEY chuckle, but the laugh doesn't last past their next sip of their cocktail.

THEM: Is that silly?

Beat.

Black "men" and black "women" still play the lead roles in this love story, an intraracial love story of dysfunction. The truly unrequited exist only in backdrop. The most neglected person in America, you imagine, is the ballroom queen in a book you remember. In her last stages of AIDS, she would dress up in her Chanel suit and take the 4 train during rush hour to feel people brush against her. YOU know what it is like to not be touched, but you can almost always find someone to hold you. THEY are on the outside of the embraceable. What then? What's left?

❧

ACT IV

And Roxane Gay says, "Get yourself a girlfriend."

Not bad advice.

SCENE 1
YOU contemplate this approach as one of your teaching colleagues, a mathematician from TOGO, describes to another colleague, a young woman from UKRAINE, her own expectations of coupling.

TOGO: *(Unbothered, but thoughtfully.)* ... Yes, I imagine I'll get married. Then my husband will cheat and I will have to decide how to take care of our children.
UKRAINE: *(Appalled.)* But that sounds awful!

YOU throw up your hands, agreeing with UKRAINE, your mouth wide in shock. TOGO pauses, stroking her chin with her hand as she contemplates exactly when she, of all black women, became thus indoctrinated. As YOU and UKRAINE exit the scene, TOGO is still thinking...

SCENE 2
YOU want to believe that black men look at you the way you look at women. YOU want to believe you carry in you some

great, longed-for mystery. YOU want to be with a black girl, her impervious beauty wrapped inside your heart in a way so fragile YOU are afraid you will break HER. YOU are afraid of reasserting on women the hurt men have done to YOU.

YOU are walking outside a party holding HER hand. YOU are wearing a shirt that says FRAGILE. HANDLE WITH CARE. (YOU want these things. YOU want inside these things.) Outside the party, a group of men is assembled. A MAN you do not know steps up to you from the group and speaks.

MAN: *(Gesturing toward your crotch.)* How FRAGILE is it, baby?
YOU: Not "it." Me.

YOU let HER hand go to look the MAN in his face.

The MAN stammers as he tries to respond to YOU. The other men laugh at him, and YOU stare at him as you walk away. It never registered for the MAN that the woman beside YOU is your girlfriend. YOU fuck up. YOU are already hurting HER. She knows YOU are not there yet because, even when YOU do not know the MAN, you're still looking for his approval.

ACT V

"You've got to learn to leave the table when love's no longer being served," Nina Simone says.

You try.

But when you have been invited, and nothing has been served, how do you make a graceful exit? You hunger politely. You make pleasant conversation. You pretend you are not waiting. You have always been the most beautiful of houseguests. This is how YOU act.

You do not know how to excuse yourself from the frustrated ambivalence you feel toward love. It is impossible to subside the hunger that builds in YOU.

SCENE

YOU are trying to get dressed to go sit once again at the table but you lie on the floor of your bedroom in complete despair. YOU know the audience is watching. YOU should say something. But YOU don't have the words. Get up! Get up! YOU think to yourself. YOU pick up your jeans, lying in a crumpled heap on the floor, and try to pull them on. YOU stand up and fall back onto the bed. *He doesn't respond—He doesn't respond—He doesn't respond* whispers through your head like a chorus. And the BOYS are all standing there behind YOU: the brother you danced with at the bar, the dancer you DMed after his art show, your occasional hookup, your one-night stand, the BOY who is currently breaking up with you, the BOY who is always breaking up with you, the BOY you have not met yet—the one you have always known. YOU wait for one of them to call. YOU wait for the phone to vibrate. YOU don't want to stand up again until someone is loving you. YOU push. YOU breathe in . . .

YOU stand up.

LOVE SONGS FOR THOTS

A thot is not a slut, Rudo explains. It is three a.m. and you two are sitting in the car with the sunroof open outside her apartment, listening to SZA's song "Love Galore." A streetlamp floods the dashboard and you each have one hand on the armrest. She has recently declared this to be *The Summer of Thots*.

Thot? You've never heard the word and she is trying to break it down for you. "Thot" stands for "that ho over there" or "thirsty hoes over there"—"Thirst" being a particularly important part of the acronym. The Indiana summer is dry. And with the arid freedom of hot days stretching out before you, just for you, to absorb the muddy spring as you start compiling a hot girl summer compendium of new short skirts, midriffs, and pinky-baring shoes.

Yesss, boo! Rudo snaps when you meet her out, applauding your thotty clothes. You both look far too cute and your hair too laid for the dive bars that make up the circuit of go-out

spots in this cornhusker valley town, but you make the best of
it. You carry on romantic entanglements with as many folks
as possible, dancing, drinking, and then debriefing in your car
under the streetlight afterward, the thirst finally quenched.

One of your favorite intrigues happens when one person
you have slept with and another person you made out with enter
the bar at the same time and you have to figure out how to ma-
neuver that moment as you try cozying up to a third. It's a beat
that pretty much everyone else you know did in high school (or
college) while you were the model good kid in glasses and knee-
length skirts. And sometimes you still wear glasses as part of the
seduction. Why not? You are smart and intense, and spent your
early years studying complex themes you rarely expect your love
interests to understand. You pick out a soundtrack: SZA. The
Ctrl album. You turn the music on and talk about how you can
only make love in hyperbole. You replay each intimate scenario.
You analyze every glance and text message, tie your loves to the
bed with nylon hosiery and a heavy theoretical framework. You
look back at the girl you once were and rethink everything she
ever thot.

TRACK ONE

CTRL

Sometimes I wanna break up with a nigga just so I can listen to "Climax" on repeat, says Rudo. It is summer in Johannesburg—Afropunk—but the weather is out of control. You just got caught in a hailstorm, rice-sized nuggets of ice mixed with sleet. You forgo your plan of dancing in the park in thotty outfits and retreat indoors with bad feelings and mucked-up shoes.

It has been two years since *The Summer of Thots.* You shower off the mud. You take out a hair dryer and turn up the music on your laptop. You get into a late-career, early-noughties Usher oeuvre, rapidly cycling through the tracks on *Confessions* to decipher at which point he was definitely sure he had herpes. You dissect "Confessions" and "Confessions II." You and Rudo are both fans of "Confessions," the interlude, a one-minute, nineteen-second melodrama that begins with Usher play-acting a phone call he picks up in the studio in which his friend informs him that his side-chick is pregnant. The interlude ends in a three-part harmony of grieving Ushers deciding that the best way to inform his *good girl* that he's been cheating is to stay in the studio, recording a song about all the mess he's been up to.

The greatest Easter egg of "Confessions II" (or "Confessions Part II," depending on which release of the multiplatinum Usher album you're looking at) is its mention of "Confessions Part I" in its first verse. It's easy to assume, as most people do, that the "Part I" referred to by Usher in "Confessions II" is the interlude called "Confessions" on the American release. But humiliating his beloved through that one-two punch on the second-bestselling album of the aughts wasn't enough for the pop star. Prior to creating "Confessions"—the interlude everyone totally stans for (*Put that on everything.*)—Usher wrote *an actual* song called "Confessions Part I" that ended up as a B-side on the album released in the UK. The four-minute, twenty-second song is complete trash.

You love me? Unconditionally? Usher croons talkily on "Confessions Part I" before he bursts into his fabled falsetto, envisioning how to explain to his real-life girlfriend he's having a baby with another woman through a fake-ass love song. *Confessions* is Usher back in 2004 when he was filling stadiums of screaming teenagers. Back when Usher was basically dimples and five-foot abs. During the *Confessions* tour, he reenacts "Confessions" live, pulling a brick-sized flip phone out the pocket of his low-slung jeans while an industrial fan blows back his orange silk button-down. A half-naked superhero, he stands in the spotlight making hand gestures of anguish and awe.

WE LOVE YOU, USHER!! some lone lady-fan screams in the dramatic pause between Usher's apologetic ab-lib at the end of "Confessions" and the downbeat to "Confessions II," the up-tempo catharsis to Usher's cheating nonsense. He ticks across the stage in the pop-and-lock contortions that made him famous, pauses for a moment, and smiles.

When Usher released *Confessions*, he was dating TLC bandmate Chilli. At the time *Confessions* came out, you were still a closet TLC fan, although the band's legacy had already dissolved into pop passé. TLC was the first female band to make health-conscious sex positivity an integral part of their message. To see Usher date someone who was an artist and not a groupie, someone as successful as he was, felt like filling the lacuna of the black girl achievement gap. Chilli was seven years Usher's senior, and had had a complete career before Usher's *8701* album made him a pop icon—which meant his partner was big in the music industry but not competition. They strode along on red carpets with the easy confidence of a power couple who looked like they could make it, each claiming a comfortable space in the spotlight.

Then, *Confessions*.

It's rumored that Usher decided to wait until it was time to release his seventeen-track list of infidelities before explaining to Chilli what the autobiographical album was about. Instead of coming clean to her while in the throes of his self-flagellating album production, he waited until it was time for him to run through the entertainment newsreels, discussing with the world how the lyrical inspiration for his latest album had been his guilty conscience.

But how could Chilli not know Usher was writing an entire

album about cheating on her? Well, Chilli was busy. She'd essentially stepped out of the music industry by the time Usher got his big break and probably didn't have the energy to get invested in *Confessions* beyond hollering out "Yes, baby, that's my song!" to the opening notes of the album's first single, "U Don't Have to Call." Have you ever dated a dude who sings? Ever dated a dude who wanted you to sit and watch him play PlayStation? Memorized the complete Premier League starting lineup? Blown up your phone data streaming video because your dude plays triangle for the number one band in Eritrea? Whatever sacrifice you have made to keep your love alive is probably pretty much the same thing Chilli did, except instead of getting flowers and a thank-you card, Chilli got a revenge album.

Usher's *Confessions* is a revenge album because Chilli never recovered from the press circus that was its release. Aside from a brief stint on a VH1 reality series, *What Chilli Wants*, Chilli disappeared from the public eye almost entirely. In *What Chilli Wants*, the star of the black girl-band who taped condoms to their baggy clothes and talked openly in their music and interviews about STI education and female gratification is reduced to a rip-off of *The Bachelorette*.

When Usher released *Confessions*, he revealed how little respect he had for his partner's professional background, breaking down the barriers that judge feminine people by their sex lives. His songs on the album separate women into categories— bad and good—the wantonly sexual women he lusts after in the club and the pious, devoted girlfriend (presumably, Chilli) who's sitting at home waiting for him. Thots vs. Wifeys. Both Chilli and Usher wrote panty anthems, but only Chilli's work uplifted people who wore panties. *Confessions* sought to bury TLC's era of nuanced sexual liberation.

If that ain't some mad anti-feminist shade work, what is?

Back in Johannesburg, you switch the music from *Confessions* to "Climax," a song from Usher's deluxe *Looking 4 Myself* album. A song written after Usher's two failed marriages, after his relationship with Chilli, "Climax" sounds tired. You try to imbue a bit of Usher's breathy nineties innuendo into the music and find none. Even if the climax rendered by the song's two characters was intended to be sexual, this song isn't about the end of a romp. It's about the end of a relationship. It's the end of Usher pretending like he has any intention to do anybody right. If "Climax" is about sex, it's about the kind of sex you have when you live with someone, but you love yourself so damn much you don't wanna give you up. You're a bleary-eyed wreck and you're worn out. And you know on the other side of this you're gonna go back out into the thotty uncertainty of your worst-case scenario. But damn it if "Climax" doesn't make you want to be single. "Climax" makes you believe.

You hear "Climax" at a rooftop bar one summer as you are sitting next to a man you desperately want to break up with; the singer covers it as a folk ballad, but its message is the same. You and the man have been dating long-distance for several months before you both decide he should come spend part of the summer in your apartment, a decision that at the time feels very adult. He's supposed to be writing a book, but instead spends most of the summer chain-smoking and fretting—which is basically writing—or getting blazed on legal marijuana and watching *Stranger Things* while you cook and look up art museums to go to, hiking excursions to take.

You were not opposed to this small tryst in monogamy, after the long FaceTime conversations—the weeks you waited to see him, spurning advances from your usual hookups who were not entirely convinced you had an out-of-town boyfriend. For a while, sitting at home alone, and then sitting at home tending to your own personal tortured artist, felt satisfying—very "girlfriend experience"—much like you imagined in your high school sex dreams about Thelonious Monk. You got lost in the romance of it until it occurred to you that you had your own work to get done. And that being the full-time lover of a tortured anything didn't fit your agenda. This is why you are prone to kick men out. But you love him. Instead of writing, you start ordering takeout and spend the rest of the summer beside him, getting blazed on the couch watching *Stranger Things* in thotty protest of your stagnant courtship.

You know you wanna break up with the nigga when you hear yourself on the roof, belting out the climax to "Climax" alongside the folk singer, in full-throated harmony. To belong to nobody. To be unbothered. To mind your own business, like the girl SZA writes about in the chorus of "Go Gina." You got to get him out your house, and bitch, get free. But you wait. You wait until that moment is over. You break up with him months after he moves back to his home city, through a phone call or an email, like a punk.

But really, that was the remix. You didn't just date long-distance. You met at a hotel bar while each of you wrote, both of you on assignment out-of-town. You fell for each other pretty quickly. You made each other laugh until you teared up, and you moved into a bigger hotel room together so you could play house. You were supposed to be a one-night stand. A business-trip fling. But you could barely separate from each other by the time your flights took off in different directions, and you vowed to spend the summer together right there and then.

By the time he landed at the front door of your apartment, his work had taken a momentary downturn. He was chain- and weed-smoking because he was depressed. You both talked about this. You both tried to keep him happy. But the pressure was getting to your sex life. By the time "Climax" hit on top of that rooftop bar, you'd stopped having sex entirely. He couldn't. You had tried a few nights before. He still could not. *Perhaps*, he suggested, *it is because when I met you I assumed you would be a one-off and not my girlfriend. Perhaps I'm not turned on because there isn't any danger left.* You'd turned over on your side and tried not to make noise while you sobbed into your pillow. You woke up with his arms around you long after you'd cried yourself to sleep. You believe that he cares but when he says what you were meant to be—"a one-off"—he shames you. This is something you have no control over. Him saying this is what you always are: fun, quick sex. As if there is nothing to what you feel: like an afterthot.

TRACK TWO

ALT

A thot is not a slut, Rudo explains in your passenger seat under the streetlight. A "thot" offers an alternative to equating
sex with an act that causes one to give up autonomy. A "thot"
does not think of their body as something lessened by sexual
intimacy. Adapting to this new knowledge, you break down the
adage handed down to you by older women since childhood:
nobody wants a "slut." A used woman.

What is "used"? You ask to absolutely no one while naked
in your room alone. You think of the lattice of scars, calluses,
cellulite, and stretch marks that compose your body. Your body
put into practice. Your body put to use. You tried but could not
survive in a glass box. A padded room. You choose to use your
body. You choose.

You and Rudo draw a distinction between "slut" and "thot." You
are a black girl—part of a class of bodies at whom "thot" is hurled
more regularly than "slut," as an insult, and is deployed with a
greater sense of threat. You recognize that the terms were, to the
best of your knowledge, invented by men. The primary purpose
of each word is to destroy you. This language is an alternative to
domination. The words push you into being worthy of a man's

sexual approval. If a slut is a toy, you think, a thot is a trap. "The fantastical nightmare of the thot," Amanda Hess writes in *Slate*, "is a woman who pretends to be the type of valuable female commodity who rightfully earns male commitment—until the man discovers that she's a cheap imitation of a 'good girl' who is good only for mindless sex, not relationships or respect." But you can never think of the concept of sex as mindless. And you have no interest in some dumb man bestowing upon you the honor of his subjugation. If a man can't respect you for this, well, where's the fun in that?

A "thot"? You say to yourself, to no one in particular. You rinse your naked body in your mind. You scoff and wash it off. You lift yourself delicately from the seat of your car, smoothing the wrinkles in your booty shorts and adjusting your sticky thighs. Rudo completes her definition of your Indiana summer. *Well, I'd call that "the girlfriend experience,"* you joke. The two of you just laugh. You are both curious about whether your prudish history makes you immune to a season with "thot" as qualifier. The thot of you, a political act.

TRACK THREE

DEL

So, what is a "good guy"?

After the SZA concert, you get a text from the friend you went with, a man who fits the conventional "good guy" stereotype: clean, good manners, capable of carrying on respectful non-sexual relationships with women. This is why you're surprised when he shoots you an arsenal of text messages after your Venmo request for thirty-five dollars, the cost of his ticket.

Why are you coming at me like this? he asks. I thought the ticket was a gift!

You want to say: Why would I be buying you a SZA ticket as a gift? We ain't fuckin. But, instead, you don't respond.

He follows up with several more text messages:

What is wrong with you?
Are you okay?
Is something wrong?
No, really. You seem to be going through something today.

Yeah, you think to yourself, you owe me thirty-five dollars and want to believe my request for cash is personal. He continues to make it personal, itemizing the things he brought to your house for the SZA concert pregame: a half-drunk bottle of whiskey he finished in your apartment, on his own. A Postmates order he had delivered to your apartment in his name for chicken wings. We're even, he finally texts.

Even. In his words you hear the scene from bell hooks' memoir *Wounds of Passion* where she and her abusive lover are arguing on their way to a Joan Armatrading concert. She tells him he has issues from his childhood that need addressing. He speeds the car up to eighty miles an hour, screaming at her to shut up unless she wants to get punched in the mouth. Then he punches her in the mouth. He drops her off at home and, while she stands in front of the mirror examining her busted lip, her chipped tooth, he goes to the concert alone.

He too was a "good guy"—a patient academic, someone sensitive and political enough to show up alone at the concert of a queer black woman activist folksinger—him, a straight black man. As Joan Armatrading sings "Love and Affection" he seductively smiles at some fresh bohemian girl while bell hooks sits at home searching for a dentist who will fix her broken tooth on a Saturday night. *If I can feel the sun in my eyes . . .* Joan sings, *why can't I feel love?*

What are these men thinking? Your "good guy" friend would never punch you in the mouth, but each text feels like a slap in the face. His comments gaslit, he turns your request for reimbursement into an emotional audit, replacing your need to revisit one receipt (singular) with receipts (plural). Because the two of you used to have sex, and now he renders it impossible for you to request something auxiliary, something that you are owed.

You find the world so quick to categorize men as "good" if they are good at school, and their jobs, and come from "good" families. Because they are good at sports and do everything right for feminism—everything except treat women decently. They buy all the albums. They stand in the front row mouthing all the words.

On a rainy night, a month before the SZA show, the two of you are in your apartment, listening to the whole album. He sits across from you securely singing the highly feminized lyrics of "Doves in the Wind" while you clip open two beers. *Real niggas do not deserve pussy*, SZA sings. Your friend breaks it down for you: *SZA is looking for a good man, not a "good guy."* You don't understand.

You assume you two are bonding as he tells you about his most-recent app dates, which include an entanglement with a leftist vegan who gets mad when he takes her to a pizza shop (*I can't believe you eat animals!*), bursts into tears while they were taking off their clothes, and pauses midstride to pop a Xanax in the bathroom while they have sex. After he climaxes, he calls her a cab. You are worried about him.

The two of you hooked up twice, more than three years ago. After the first time, he texts you: You took me on a journey last night, the message reads. No emojis—straight pleasure. You feel good. Being a good lover is the kind of thing you still feel, or want to feel, good about. When he texts you again, two years later, asking if you'll be his platonic date to a dinner party with his coupled colleagues, you laugh, but say yes. You understand he needs you in this moment; even though you were his hookup, he knows you do a keen imitation of an exceptional girlfriend.

That's one fine woman you have there, his boss says. Your good guy does not correct him. Neither do you; you see little difference between being a fantastic lover and being filled with loyalty.

You wanna smash? you say on that rainy night as SZA closes out "Doves in the Wind," your apartment speakers jostling the sweat off your half-finished beers. You want to delete his strange hookup story from that evening's memory, creating a more loving, intimate narrative. Your friend doesn't *feel like it* but your gesture was more benevolence than seduction. You tell him earnestly this kind of stuff scares you. *That girl sounded like she was going through something*, you say. And so is he, you think, and that sounds like a fast way for sex to get him arrested.

I know, he admits at the time, but you feel certain he takes the question of her consent as a sign that you feel rejected. You feel certain this is the moment he remembers when he asks, *What is wrong with you?*

I know, he says that night as he hurries out of your apartment in still-wet sneakers. He sighs, *thanks for the thot*.

TRACK FOUR

SHIFT

In an interview about the song "Drew Barrymore," SZA discusses the kinship she felt to the medley of sexy siren or stumbling underdog characters that characterized Barrymore's life and career—a catalog of cautionary tales from a girl who in real life developed too publicly and too quickly, but later rescued herself from the realm of the troubled sexpot, the girl-gone-wrong.

Barrymore's characters are often women who may have been loose—or undesirable—but make the shift toward better womanhood, girls whose good hearts and healthy hips might someday be redeemed. They are "slutty" because they don't know they can do better, but they are not thots. This conversation is rooted in whether or not we consider certain women virtuous enough for motherhood. This is the "virgin/whore dialectic" Zadie Smith describes in her *Harper's* essay on Ursula K. Le Guin's *The Wild Girls*, a book Smith heralds for LeGuin's critique of a world "in which women are simultaneously venerated as mothers and debased as sexual property." Whether or not a woman is a "thot" rests mainly upon whether or not she can be relied on to produce healthy children. For a long time, that culture has questioned if black women are healthy enough to be mothers at all.

Case in point: a BBC broadcast from *The Inquiry* podcast titled, "What's Killing Black American Babies?" *The Inquiry* reports that the U.S. is the only industrialized nation where the number of infant deaths is on the rise, and black infants are twice as likely to die as white infants.

In the report, three experts who have been tracking black infant mortality rates for decades weighed in with some background. Back in the eighties, the assumption was that black mothers must be doing something wrong. Then, researchers started tracking black mothers' diets and prenatal care. The babies still died. In the nineties, researchers focused on education, comparing the infant mortality rates of college-educated mothers, both black and white. Black babies still died twice as often as white ones. Neither education nor economics was a significant factor. After nearly two decades, studies had come no closer to explaining the massive mortality gap.

Is it in the genes? the BBC report asked next. The next doctor interviewed had carried out a study comparing the babies of black women born in America to black West African or Caribbean women who delivered their babies in the U.S., and the babies of black women born outside the U.S. were as healthy as the babies of white American women. The same doctor next looked at the birth weights of the grandchildren of black women from West Africa and the Caribbean—the babies of first-generation daughters. Typically, the birth weight of babies increases from one generation to the next. But with the daughters of immigrants, the opposite was happening; second-generation black babies averaged two ounces less than their parents had at birth. "There is something about being of minority status in the United States that is bad for health," the doctors on the broadcast concluded. The stress a black woman experiences in America—as an infant, child, and adult—has a great impact on her reproductive health.

According to philosopher John Rawls' *A Theory of Justice*, "even the willingness to make an effort to try, and so to be deserving in the ordinary sense, is itself dependent on happy family, and social circumstances." Scientists have long held that the stress of injustice often weighs on the body, disrupting the vascular and immune systems; a person's family and social circumstances can directly factor into the rate at which cells age. Based on this evidence of repeated stress's wear and tear on the body, Dr. Arline Geronimus developed what she called the "weathering" hypothesis. She posited that the "double jeopardy" of injustice leveled upon black women through both gender and racial discrimination causes their health to deteriorate more rapidly than other groups. Their bodies shut down any function that is not required for survival, infant mortality being one of the many forms of disease that disproportionately affect black Americans (along with "cervical cancer, asthma, diabetes, and cardiovascular disease," a follow-up article in *The Nation* reports).

⮌

On September 2, 2017, the day after her daughter Olympia's birth, Serena Williams suffered a pulmonary embolism. She knew the signs; a predisposition for blood clots had nearly killed her in 2011, and she took a daily anticoagulant medication to ward them off, but stopped in preparation for a C-section. When Williams noticed her body shutting down after the surgery, she informed the nurses that she needed further treatment immediately.

"I was like . . . I need a CT scan and a heparin drip, Listen to Dr. Williams!" Williams later said of that day in a *Vogue* magazine interview. The nurses told Williams the pain medication was making her confused, but she insisted on follow-up treatment. In the six days following the birth, Williams experienced blood clots, hemorrhaging, a burst C-section wound, and a large hematoma that flooded her abdomen. Had she relied on the nurses' assessment, she would likely be dead.

In thinking about Williams' story, consider what black women go through to get medical treatment, to go to the doctor, and to give birth. You could enter a hospital to deliver your baby—one of the richest, most powerful women in the world—and still suffer as Williams did. It doesn't matter who you are. Your black girl body enters into this country at a state of disadvantage.

You recall a line from the *Slate* article: A thot "is a woman who pretends to be the type of valuable female commodity who rightfully earns male commitment." If the most "valuable female commodity" is birthing healthy babies, can a black girl ever be valuable? Is that thot even possible?

TRACK FIVE

CAPS LOCK

Black Twitter wasn't a fan of the Solange-produced music video for SZA's song "The Weekend." I DON'T GET IT!!! says one tweet about the video, all in uppercase. Since the song's lyrics were dedicated to the perils of being a side-chick, lovers of its synth-laced melodrama expected the video to feature a nineties-style R&B narrative—like Brandy & Monica's "The Boy Is Mine"—a triangle featuring some notable matinee idol balancing his time between the two lavish apartments of his romantic interests, culminating in a scene where thotty, man-stealing SZA gets her ponytail grabbed by the girlfriend and a hand thrown in her face; everyone's wearing a halter top.

What they got instead was a video with no plot. Solange directs wide shots of SZA—her gymnast's legs and effervescent curls—draping her unaffected girlishness across pieces of Modernist architecture.

Think I got it covered, sings SZA.

WTF? said fans.

What's beautiful about "The Weekend" video is the way it bucks against the expectation of how a thot is meant to feel. From Millie Jackson to Nicki Minaj, black girl recording artists have offered a catalog of complicated love—the recorded history of jump-offs. But the obligatory soliloquy in these songs has always erred on the side of asking our forgiveness: I'm sorry I'm doing this, I shouldn't admit this to you, but I love them. The singers use the song to sway you with compassion for their plight—caught between a rock and a record deal—their group lament on the other side of a wife.

In their book *Sex at Dawn*, Christopher Ryan and Cacilda Jethá explore a wide range of sexual mores across the globe, including in the matrilineal Mosuo people of China, a culture in which women brag about having hundreds of sexual relationships. Once a Mosuo girl has reached a state of sexual maturity, she receives a house. At the back of each house is a private entrance that leads into the girl's "babahuago," or "flower room," a space in which she can entertain her many sexual partners. There are no rules regarding who a Mosuo can and cannot sleep with; children born into Mosuo society are viewed as the sons and daughters of everyone who has participated in their love-making, and requesting a vow of fidelity from a romantic partner is viewed as shameful.

The video for "The Weekend" shows SZA romping through her very own "flower room." She tries on cute outfits and primps her hair. She doesn't give two shakes about how you feel about a side-chick. She sings about the possibility of more days with a man she desires, a man she is willing to share. She admits to being motivated by self-interested desire and does not apologize for it. She struts around in broad daylight, her love interest absent, like he's following the Mosuo's one rule for guests, to be gone by daylight.

It would be easy to assume that the thot SZA heralds on her *Ctrl* album is an unmoored woman, someone who grew up without an acute moral compass, but SZA speaks openly about being raised in a devout Muslim household—and spending her younger years oscillating between the decision to wear or leave behind her hijab. "I used to wear overalls and baggy clothes because modesty is a big thing [in Islam]," she said in an interview with *Complex* in 2013. ". . . [Islam is] very rigid, but it's safe because you can trust it . . . I like the clarity." It isn't that modesty does not appeal to SZA, or the character she plays in the video. It is that, when it comes to the reality of her romantic choices, this kind of groundedness does not exist.

The ability to be both unapologetic and earnest remains one of the greatest unsung attributes of "The Weekend." The belief that, through love and fidelity, one can maintain ownership of another person can sound like the cure to a deeply alienating loneliness. But recognizing the frailty of these expectations, relying on oneself as the benchmark for worth or pleasure, is a much heavier reckoning to carry. The goal of "The Weekend" is not to live without feeling but to live alone in feeling. To be thotful.

TRACK SIX

TAB

Y'all wanna holler bout how we had *a black president* and *a black Disney princess* but why nobody talking about how she the only princess who ended up with a light-skinned nigga with no job?

This. Is. Facts.

In fact, the original story was called *The Frog Prince*. In the fairy tale, the *frog* is a *prince*. Story's whole lily pad sits on the idea you can't judge a book by its cover. In the black girl Disney version, it's *The Princess and the Frog*. Nigga, "PRINCE" ain't even in the title. The prince ain't even a prince—he cut off.

First: he a broke nigga who sings.

Then: he a frog.

Then: he's just a light-skin nigga who sings. A broke-ass light skin running around with a mandolin while his girl out working three jobs and kissing amphibians and still being both THE PRINCESS *and* THE FROG WHISPERER.

In the movie, the frog meets the "princess" at a party where she's dressed fresh to def, networking with rich people to get start-up funds for her bakery. Ole Light Eyes makes her out to be the palace princess. He's wrong, there's a blond chick he misses in the room. But the frog gets the black girl to kiss him anyway—working his magic, ruining her life—so he can go back to writing songs in his Creole-family castle basement. She agrees (? Disney never bothered to explain what she got out of the bargain) but since the white chick is the actual princess, they end up both just frogs. They both frogs, so they decide it's time to hightail it to the bayou and live their lives as a broke-ass, quasi-happy swamp couple—which, if you've ever tried dating a nigga who carries a mandolin, there it is.

Mad that he can't push that mixtape in the bayou, in the delta, in a condo his girl's paying for with her rainy-day savings fund and delayed dream, neighbor to a washed-up trumpet-playing alligator named Louis (whose minstrel presence is never fully explained, but best guess is he too had a sugar mama he has long since eaten), the light-skinned mandolin frog-rapper decides to get back to the city, find himself that white chick he missed at the party, and finally get himself out of his own fool-ishness.

He seduces the white girl with whatever opening line mandolin-playing light-eyed rapping frogs have been using since their invention. But, just as he thinks he set to upgrade, ready to ruin one princess-frog's life after another, he kisses her. *He stays a frog.* He stays his broke-ass rapping frog-self and goes crawling back to his frog "princess" by the stroke of midnight.

The frog "princess" takes him back on the condition he locks this shit down for real this time—like—a wedding. He does and they do. So now she's legally obligated to be financially responsible for a nigga with a mandolin. *ONLY THEN* does a black girl's version of a fairy godmother—Jenifer Lewis (*praise hands*) wearing a boa as a boa—show up to tell her:

Surprise, bitch, you a princess now! by decree of some nepo-
tistic contractual loophole written in the Constitution of Putting Up with Broke-Ass Rapping Mandolin Light-Skins. At the
end of a regular Disney fairy tale, the prince and the princess
kiss and ride off in a converted Cadillac pumpkin. At the end of
the black Disney princess fairy tale, they open a restaurant.

Poof! Issa black girl fantasy.

(Now that's food for thot.)

TRACK SEVEN

ESC

And you were too hard on Brandy. You rewatch the 2002 episode of *Oprah* where a twenty-three-year-old Brandy seizes her pregnant belly, the girl-next-door dimples unimpeachable but her eyes wincing in tragic horror. In the interview, Brandy announces to the world her joyful good news—her secret marriage and her new day job as an expectant mother.

You remember this moment as you are riding from L.A. to Santa Monica with some friends in a Lyft manned by a young-blood driver who doesn't mind dispensing all his worldly wisdom to you in under forty-five minutes, including business lessons from his other side-hustle running a drug delivery service (which incidentally is probably the best advice you've ever gotten: *You get your three thousand dollars and you get out of the game*).

He tells you his real goal is to become a songwriter. *My dream is to work with Brandy*, he says, *more than any other singer on the market right now.* You think he's being ironic, chauffeuring a carful of Brandy-aged black girls. The mean girl in you snorts.

What are you on? he asks. *Brandy's hands-down the best vocalist of our time. You ever listened to the vocal playback to "Angel in Disguise"? Heard her hit those rungs?* He flips on the track and you realize that you never really had.

You hated Brandy. In the middle school locker room, as you and your classmates attempted to shield every mole, zit, and un-shaved surface from the exacting eyes of bullies, the one thing you all could do to distract from the disgust you felt for your own bodies was to hate on how cute Brandy thought she was. You hated the way she held her neck in her braids—knowing full well the heaviness Kanekalon brought to the crown and nape of your own head—her beanpole body, her ethereal brown skin.

How can you say that girl is ugly? your mom would ask as you frowned through episodes of *Moesha*, sitting on the living room carpet with a hot comb and a plastic basket of sponge rollers—a phase you were going through—doing hair and watching televi-sion, disapprovingly shaking your head.

You couldn't love her. You couldn't love a girl who looked like you—a "good girl," like you, from a "good," hardworking family like yours. You couldn't love her because she reflected what *you* looked like—not the sassy comeback-ready queens or the half-black, good-haired ingenues that populated most music videos and television shows—an honest-to-goodness awkward, skinny black girl emerging right in front of your eyes: her crackly alto, her hopes for prom.

Everything up until Brandy had told you that you needed to be someone different to be good with yourself. You took cop-ies of *Black Hair* magazine to salons, pointing out impossible styles worn by grown women with nearly silky hair textures, straw-straight relaxers, or waist-length weaves—believing that with the right amount of spray and grease, you might achieve the unattainable: to be lovable to boys, to not be teased, to go through a day without confronting your own savage beauty.

In truth, not even Brandy was allowed to be good with Brandy. In those first few moments on *Oprah*, as Brandy pretends not to be an unwed mother, you can almost feel her pulse quicken as her own mother is brought to the stage to corroborate her fake fairy tale with a quaint family anecdote. In the audience, Brandy's fans bring their cupped hands to their faces, elated to be some of the first in the world to learn their crown princess, the black Disney *Cinderella* of their childhoods, has finally claimed her throne.

"So, you finally found somebody who treats you the way God loves you?" Oprah asks the singer.

"Yes," she answers emphatically, staring at her sham-prince, who's seated in the first row of the audience. The adoring smiles the counterfeit newlyweds exchange during the interview is the only thing in the broadcast that still feels real. Two years after the announcement of the wedding that never happened, Brandy and her partner end their coupled bliss. Brandy's prince, the one who "treats you the way God loves you," goes to the press. He announces to the world he and the singer were never married, that the marriage was fabricated in order to maintain Brandy's "good girl" appeal.

A decade after the fake wedding announcement, Brandy and Oprah reunite.

"It was a sin," Brandy says of having her baby out of wedlock. "It was not something [back then] that people praised." Brandy's celebrity engine wanted to keep her dedicated fan base from knowing what she had become—a thot, a fraud, everything a "good girl" was never supposed to be—the stigma of which she feared she'd never escape.

"I was afraid I would lose my career," she tells Oprah, admitting the pressure she felt to maintain her impeccable image. Brandy's ex announced the marriage fraud one month before the release of her fourth studio album. It sold less than half as many as her third had.

Was she right?

I was afraid to lose my career, Brandy said. Her career, she said. This echoes in your mind, the thought almost breaking you. All those years you spent listening to Brandy and watching her on TV, pretending you were too cool for her music and too hardened for her goody-two-shoes appeal, you had ignored her deep professionalism. Brandy had talent and access, yes, but, manager-parents aside, Brandy made an empire happen through goals and grit. It couldn't have been easy to sell *Moesha*, a show headlined by a dark-skinned teenage girl in a middle-class family, to network television. Up until Brandy, nobody in the nineties could have told you your adolescence would include Brandy as *Cinderella*, tiara done up in a crown of box braids. Impossible. The fact you never noticed was another part of her acumen. You should have seen how hard she fought. You should have looked up to her and seen grace. Why didn't you?

I dare you to find another singer her age who's got that kind of sound, the youngblood says as he pulls up to the Santa Monica Pier playing "Angel in Disguise" one more time. He is right.

They are keeping her down, yo, the labels. Brandy's been in the studio for years making all kinds of hit records. But they keep them in a vault—keep putting out more trash one hits from new stars they want to promote. He insinuates that he has inside knowledge of the industry, hinting that he's the son of some producer whose name you would know. *They know if they let Brandy release her music, this other shit won't sell. She got too far for them. Got too good. That's why she's been trying to get back on that reality TV shit.* Dancing with the Stars? *She's trying to make enough money to buy back her masters.*

You give the Lyft driver five stars on the app, thinking about Brandy, all caught up in your own stuff. All that time you had spent distancing yourself from Brandy, believing it was a radical sign of independence, you had been distancing yourself from yourself—so as not to be thot less.

TRACK EIGHT

COMMAND

A heavy portion of SZA's *Ctrl* album is devoted to accepting love with the clear understanding this love is handed down at a depreciated value. The songs are love songs but the love songs are sad. Her protagonists strut by in high heels with proud hair flips but they are never the princesses, never the main love interest, never the center of the narrative. It is hard to tell if the girls SZA writes about are happy but it is easy to say they are not alone.

It is hard to tell if you are happy, but it is easy to say you are never alone. You're surrounded by a crowd at the penthouse apartment of the man you are currently fucking, swaying to "Prom" while wine spills out your stemless glass. It's the kind of party this person is known for throwing, like a manic-depressive black Jay Gatsby quietly observing the bacchanal fray. The fact you've been fucking your host you tell no one, save the person you drove there, your only friend in attendance.

The friend doesn't believe you. He looks around at the setting—the lavish fireplace and furniture, the wall of windows overlooking the river—and can't imagine you in it. Why not? you think, ambivalently. He was there when you picked up Gatsby at a charity gala, while wearing a red backless evening gown at least two people you saw that night are still asking you about.

You flirt with Gatsby from his kitchen island—twisting your hips or hair like you don't notice him, occasionally making eye contact. You flirt with him in the way you must touch anyone who is prone to keep you at a distance—private and cool—in a way that prevents you from being someone for whom anyone else is responsible. Your friend notices your aloof host smiling hazily in your direction, and decides to test you, to mar this small mark of approval.

Sid thinks we're fucking, your friend says loudly, referring to a girl-crush of yours in your social circle, imposing his body in the space between yourself and your quiet flirtation. *Sid thinks we're fucking and, if so, she wants in*. You are neither shy about, nor easily shamed by, your interest in a wide range of love arrangements. Despite the prudishness of your past, you have never been shy in admitting you could see yourself with multiple people as easily as one. And your friend has no real interest in this kind of loving you. You know that he's not proposing that he fuck you inasmuch as fuck you over, inasmuch guarantee it is clear to this penthouse, to this new suitor, to this apparent luxe upswing in your situation, that you will never be a hoe turned into a housewife.

This confuses you. You are part of a generation whose members seem so open about multiple sexual partners, often referring to themselves as "polyamorous." But this is a misnomer. You find what people more often mean when they refer to themselves as capable of polyamory—or loving many—is that they want to distance themselves from promiscuity—sexual transience—a term that more aptly describes them. You do not have to be promiscuous to be polyamorous and yet, the possibility of love stretched out across multiple genders, across multiple people, across multiple warmths at the same time, can still be leveled at you like a threat. A good girl would never desire more than one sexual partner, in one room, at one time. Your friend knows this and propositions you the way, if you were good, no one would.

You don't know why people feel the need to take things from you. Your friend isn't the first "friend" who has decided, upon learning that you are loved, to put a wedge between you and that feeling's possibility. The new tableau destroys their image of you. In all their talk of sexual liberation, it is impossible for them to believe that the thot you are might actually seduce someone they consider respectable. You get propositioned all the time now. Mainly by people who know your aloof love interest, mainly by people convinced you're deceiving him.

It is impossible for you to understand why so many people feel comfortable weighing in on the sex lives of women. You spend far too much time thinking about the moment when former *Fresh Prince of Bel-Air* actor Tatyana Ali came on *The Wendy Williams Show* to explain a *Huffington Post* interview in which she'd offhandedly mentioned her "guiltiest pleasure" to be "one-night stands." Wendy drums up the audience like they're at a feminist rally, asserting if a woman has "her own keys" and "her own place" she should be able to invite over

whomever she wants. She also reminds the crowd that Ali graduated from Harvard—as if this news should have some bearing
on the value of her vagina—but barely lets the Harvard graduate speak for herself. When Tatyana does talk, Wendy's voice
drowns out that of the entrepreneur, one-time pop star, and current early-education advocate, as if Wendy is afraid "Thotyana"
will come out and give Wendy's good girl resuscitation a throat
punch. Wendy takes it personally, Ali undoing the rich girl-
next-door, the dark-skinned American sweetheart she spent
eight years portraying on television, as if Ali's promiscuity is a
reckless character assassination of the fictional sweetheart she
played on TV.

In truth, Tatyana Ali's admission, giving equal weight to
"one-night stands" and "bread pudding with chocolate" on her
list of guilty pleasures, seems pretty on-brand for a grown-up
Ashley Banks. There is a running joke in the show's later years
in which Fresh Prince Will chases after teenage cousin Ashley
in multiple episodes, covering her thot-fits with his signature
denim bomber jacket. The punchline always implies that Ashley's sexual awakening is the penitence required of the Prince
for the way he thinks of women, since she's usually going off to
flirt with boys who act like Will, wearing outfits that replicate
the costumes of actors who played characters he dated on the
show: Nia Long, Tyra Banks, Jada Pinkett (whom casting directors labeled "too short" to be Will's girl on-air but whom Smith
met on set and later married in real life).

On Jada Pinkett's show, *Red Table Talk*, three generations of
black women (Pinkett; her daughter, Willow; and her mother)

talk openly about sex. There's an entire episode dedicated to Willow's interest in polyamory, one that Willow opens with a PowerPoint slideshow on the benefits of a "polyfidelitous" relationship in a world where monogamous unions are falling apart. When Jada candidly answers an audience question about whether or not she's ever participated in a threesome, Willow playfully shields her eyes as the two laugh heartily, taking in this confession from her mama as information that's possibly "too much." You laugh too; you black women envision yourselves so vastly.

And you make no apologies for who has entered you nor what is you inside.

Years after black Gatsby has given up his penthouse parties, he calls to ask if you'll take a trip with him to an expensive tropical retreat. You are intrigued by the thought of spending time with him on the beach and by how well his lavish proposition fits your climaxing thot archetype. You pack to leave but tell almost no one of your plans, though the friends you do tell voice concerns that accepting his proposal crosses some moral threshold. You do not try to talk-show spin or straighten this up for them. You delight in their complicated apprehension. They have no idea what he thinks of you. They do not need to. They do not know that he called you a month before and told you he loved you, that he wanted to marry you, while you sat on the curb outside a bar where you'd been scheming on someone else. They do not know that he has little interest in sex with you. That he keeps you around, mostly, like he'd keep a pretty pet.

You take the trip, having considered all factors, feeling like this is a situation you have command of. Command, a false sense of control. You spend five days ordering room service to his elaborate suite overlooking the ocean and swimming naked in the private pool just outside it. You wake him up to watch a rainstorm take over the rainforest in the valley below. You dress well for dinner. You kiss him and wrap your limbs around him and fire back at all his jokes. People mistake you for his girlfriend. His partner. The hotel staff refer to you as Mrs. _____. All of a sudden, you are his wife. But you're no fool. Each time he recounts the story of how you met, at a gala, he describes you as drunk and gorgeous. The party girl next door. You acquiesce. You know he wasn't lying when he told you that he loved you. But, Love, you are much easier to keep as an amusement. At the end of another night of dinner and cocktails with the happily coupled resort guests he parades you around in front of, you go back to the room alone and strip out of your party clothes. You dip naked into the dark of the private pool. You float on your back and look at the stars, whispering the words to SZA's "Anything." *Do you even know I'm alive?* you wonder. You sink. As your bright breath skims the vibrant waters, you are your only thot.

THE TOP 10 SADDEST APHORISMS ON SZA'S *CTRL* ALBUM:

. . .

1. You love me.

TRACK NINE

RETURN (ENTER)

You never entered into the world an unmarked girl. As early as you can remember, your sex was a pervasive thing that required discretion. You wore princess costumes, but understood them even then as costume—a thing that existed only in the realm of make-believe. By the age of five, you already understood the fairy tale as a world that held no place for you. When your mom asked you, *What do you want to be when you grow up?* and you said a princess who got rescued by a knight on a white horse, she did not encourage the fantasy; she looked back at you with dark sad eyes. Much of your parents' sadness you internalized as a measure of your value. It was not. They brought you into a world that was already hostile to them. They didn't know how to protect you from this hostility through anything other than the truth.

"Do you know where your children are?" a television commercial would ask every Friday night during your freshman year of high school. *She is right here*, your mother would answer, beaming proudly. You felt ashamed. You felt like your parents locked you in the house like a creature in a fairy tale, but you didn't feel much like a princess. You wanted to be outside like the girls you knew who were not black or brown girls—not dark girls in any fashion—girls with their own pocket money, and their own plans for their free time, making their own decisions.

You would see those girls at the bakery, in soccer socks and 5K-run T-shirts and sweaty ponytails, while you stood in line flanked by your parents in your Sunday morning regalia: your father's suit and lemon starch, your mother's floral hat and your childish dress that matched it. The other version of girlhood served no realistic purpose for you. You barely carried a purse before you started college, so rarely were you not in the company of an adult and in need of something that was personally yours—a pen or ChapStick. Being a "Normal Girl," as SZA pleads to be in her song, felt as distant to you as being dry does to water.

It was not that you resented your parents' desire to keep you sheltered from the outside world; it was that you hated their inability to see that their attempts did not protect you. Being sheltered did not keep you from being hurt, it did not keep you from being abused, it would not protect you from sexual assault. You were never an unmarked girl. That was not how the world imagined you.

You realized that, just as many white children are raised with the notion that they are good and the world is safe, black children are raised to understand the opposite. To succeed at being a "good" black girl would mean appearing as if the world never got to you. You gave up the fantasy of being rescued; you role-played your independence. You stopped trying to be normal. You apportioned a large part of your fantasy world to being a woman unbound. You would smear makeup on your eyelids and lips, swinging to Tina Turner's "Private Dancer," your hips still unformed. Or you would bump along the furniture with the strap of one of your mother's old lace slips falling off your shoulder, warbling like Miss Hannigan—the orphanage head-mistress played by Carol Burnett in *Annie*. "We love you, Miss Hannigan," you imagined your stuffed toys saying in refrain as you barked at them, taking fake swigs from a closed thin-necked bottle of Mr. Bubble and miming a provocative strut. This may have been fun but it was also grooming—as child's play often is. You were training yourself to live in a world that would take everything from you. That would not protect you. The dress-up was you girding yourself.

❧

You are at the beach. Your little black dog is running vast am-bitious circles into the surf when he finds a half-exposed seagull carcass sticking out of the sand, and begins pressing it against his cheeks and ears, then onto his back so the deep musk scent of the acrid bird can engulf him completely.

Isn't that just like slutting? says your friend Annie, watching the way the dog revels in the carcass of the bird, lustfully rub-bing his body into it without regard, metaphorically reclaiming a slut's agency. You take two steps in to try and detach the dog's wet body from the dead bird. The dog pauses momentarily be-fore diving back in, smiling at your disgust.

Like a dog to a dead bird, a slut's interest in sex is recreational. It is not survival; it is not work. A "slut" desires sex but won't need anything beyond that. By comparison, the fact that "thot" is an acronym of "that hoe over there" or "thirsty hoes over there" associates her with being needy and ravenous. Which would be more "like slutting" if a thot's insatiable desire was a need for sex and not a need for things. "Thots are criticized based on sexual behavior," explains Amanda Hess in *Slate*, "but they're more broadly identified via their consumption habits; this makes it possible to denounce them on sight even when their sexual histories remain private."

Here Hess hearkens back to the difference in cultural assumptions made by white culture about black children. In the same way black boys are disproportionately labeled rebellious as soon as they enter preschool, black girls, from the time they are very young, are disproportionately labeled thots. Young girls of all races are forced to manage sexual expectations at ages in which these adult concerns should be no child's prerogative. Regardless of whether a young girl is labeled a "slut" or a "thot," any slur leveled upon our young has severe consequences for their reputation and developmental health. But the crucial difference between a thot and a slut remains that a thot can be *born* and a slut is made. A slut's accuser uses the word to claim they have proof of the person's sexual activity. This is why the word "slut" can be redeemed as a badge of honor for those who choose—as part of adult agency—to have casual sex. The word "thot" does not carry that dignity. It is attached to a chasm of want and lacking the thot-bearer cannot distance themselves from. Even when reclaimed, the word "thot" carries a color, an undeniable stigma: a thot needs things, because without them, a thot can't prove she is valuable.

The fact that thot entrapment can include (according to

social media and rap music) believing a person is "high class" or providing them with "emotional support" suggests the real downfall of the thot is *not* that she will do whatever she needs to convince someone to love her. Her real downfall is that she is someone who is born undeserving of love, of "happy family and social circumstances." In this, the terms "thot" and "black girl" are basically the same. What makes a "slut" dangerous is when she doesn't need someone in order to be valuable. What makes a thot dangerous is that she does.

TRACK TEN

FN

When SZA sings "Supermodel" at the close of the concert you attend, the audience sways back and forth, linking shoulders and arms. She fills the theater with a chorus of self-doubt, the audience awash in the stage's pink reflection. Her face lights up as she turns the mic to the audience—her freckles and crooked teeth.

But SZA didn't really end the show that night with "Supermodel." Instead, she ended her concert the way she ended her album, with "20 Something," a song wishing you good luck as you go about this world, in all the ways you will survive.

You turn the thot around in your mind. It is a word that inks, as much as it doesn't suit, you. You try to wipe it off but the mark lingers and smears. You recognize the stain is permanent, and do the best you can to tighten its edges, to clean it up. You think of it as lipstick. You take a hard look at yourself while you reapply. You try to fit a thot's description. But how can it be that the "thot" you are looking at so closely resembles a girl, just a girl, coming into her own, growing up?

You know why you are driven to remember the end of the SZA show differently. You want to believe the SZA concert is your life in metaphor, that you close out the show telling your lovers to believe in you and to see you. That you stand out, like one bombastic track. But that isn't the truth. You didn't end where they began, at the place where you were trying to find yourself, turning yourself into a powerful glitter, an unapologetic pop star. You end in you. You end in self-doubt and indecision. Or perhaps you don't, praying your punch-drunk self won't kill you. Either way, you love.

You are surprised how much you need this love.

You are surprised how much love motivates you.

You are surprised by the things you do to function. You lift your hands in the air and ride the wave of SZA's voice, closing your eyes. You are surprised you still function. You are surprised. You still function. That is what you always thot you were—a surprise.

CAKE IS CANCELED

You put on a pretty dress and do your hair like you did pre-marriage but now you're post-divorce. You're getting ready to go out with the Colombian man you met while trying to cross "make out with a guy at a party" off your Newly Single Bucket List.

Don't worry, he says halfway through a date, when you've progressed from dinner to drinks, *you'll be on Tinder soon.* He's a few years further into his own uncoupling than you are.

The fuck you mean? you say to yourself, thinking about the hour and a half it took you to flat-iron and exfoliate. You aren't trying to get married again (oh God, no!) but you were at least planning to get through another date. Maybe two or three. Maybe hang out for a while in that zone of enjoying and being enjoyed without having to worry about dating. But Tinder? Tinder . . . and soon?

What is Tinder? you ask the Colombian. You have a vague

idea but you are trying to keep this one date going and pretend the answer will be the least bit interesting to you.

It's this app where you get to meet people in the area—you know, "swipe left, swipe right?" he explains, animated by the possibility of being your envoy to this new dating world. But you're thinking he could be a much more useful envoy by fucking you, which doesn't happen because, he's got a girlfriend, he explains, or rather *I'm kind of in a relationship*, which you would have known had he bothered to update his status to "It's Complicated" on the Facebook profile you hunted down in your obligatory pre-date internet stalking. But *the notion of updating your Facebook relationship status is a bit outdated, isn't it?*

So, you decide to try Tinder, or better yet, Tinder decides to try you. It's about six months and as many dating attempts later. They've all had code names: The Colombian, The Unicorn, The President. Little Finger—the date after which you decided maybe you'd give up altogether and start binge-watching *Game of Thrones*. But then you tell yourself it's probably psychologically important that you stop masturbating to episodes of *The Wonder Years* with an ice pack and a half-bottle of cheap wine. It isn't the sex that bothers you. Or the lack of sex. Or the intermittent, or the impotent sex. It's the fact that when you're coupled, you're inundated with propaganda that describes the single world as an openhearted nation of freewheeling promiscuity where people are adults, and people are responsible, and even when it doesn't work out no one gets hurt very badly. You think it can be. But you're scared. You've been told by single people it's time you got back on the horse (the horse?), or the wagon (the wagon??), but it's a scary-ass world out there and you're not sure you're comfortable with a situation involving your genitals that uses agriculture as a metaphor.

You'd spent most of your married life in the Netherlands near a sheep farm and a farmer's market—a housewife, learning how to make soufflés. The two of you move back to America so you can go to graduate school, and you spend the first year there wearing an apron—still a housewife, canning tomatoes from your neighbor's backyard garden.

It is in year two in America that you need to get an STD test. You're still married, but your husband's fidelity has become . . . complicated. You fill out the form:

1. How many sexual partners have you had over the course of your life? <u>One</u>
2. With how many sexual partners are you currently engaged? <u>One</u>
3. Are you currently sexually active?   _____

It's a drop-in health clinic. You've come under the pretext of a cold you don't have, because you were too ashamed to write down the reason for your visit on the patient intake form.

And by the way, I'd like to take an STD test, you tell the doctor as the visit is wrapping up and he writes you a prescription for drugs you probably have at home for symptoms you don't. He looks at your sexual history. He says, *you don't need an STD test. Give me the goddamned STD screening*, your face

says. *Full-panel spectrum.* The nurse gets the needles. He prepares the gloves and clamps. Now that you're alone, you want
to know your body is okay. Okay in a way a hospital test can't
tell you.

  How are you going to go back into the world? your soon-to-
be-ex-husband asks you one afternoon, after the STD screening, after you've separated but have ended up back in what is
now only your bedroom when he comes over to do his laundry.
How are you going to go back into this world, he says, *as much as
you like sex?* You were a good girl. You turned into a, regretta-
bly, better wife. Conversely, the critique women like you get
is that they haven't invested enough time in being virtuous. By
women like you, you mean black. For every one of you, there
are at least a dozen men telling you the reason you're not married yet is because you haven't learned how to "act like a wife."
About a half-dozen of these men are famous, and making hundreds of thousands of dollars capitalizing off the concept of the
"undateable" black woman: Pastor Gray, D. L. Hughley, Ralph
Richard Banks—and there was a time you couldn't walk down
125th Street in Harlem without seeing a black woman carrying
a copy of Steve Harvey's bestselling *Act Like a Lady, Think Like
a Man.* (Steve Harvey. The man with three marriages and two
restraining orders. The man enmeshed in a $60 million lawsuit
for beating and cheating on his first wife.) But you didn't need
slut-shaming from a waiting room full of megachurch comedi-
ans to keep you good and decent. You had an overtly suburban
conservative Christian family in your background. You prayed.
You sang the hymns. You cooked all the meals. You kept your

legs closed all the way up until your white-veil wedding night in your late twenties. You still ended up here.

I'd always been taught that life was a beautiful five-course banquet I was meant to partake of carefully, methodically, savoring each hors d'oeuvre and entree with immense tactile pleasure, you tell Rudo when she asks you about your decision to remain a virgin until you married. *So, that's what I did. I staved off my craving for sweets with a fruit course—maybe a little pasta—but stayed dedicated to the idea that at the end of this meal* THERE WOULD BE CAKE. *So, I got married. I had a wedding . . . and there was cake. Three fucking tiers of cake. Cake for an eternity. Everyone was anxious to watch me eat it. I cut myself a dainty sliver and ate politely, chuckling with the wedding guests and covering my mouth. I spent the next few years turning that cake into the best possible version of itself it can be before thirty. The wedding's long over but cake's supposed to stick around forever. I rose from the table to cut myself another slice. But cake has vanished. Cake is gone. "Cake is canceled," cake has written down on a sticky note.*

So, you decide to try Tinder because you've decided you want to try to have a one-night stand; you've heard of these encounters, mostly conducted by spies in movies in which two people come together in the Biblical sense, preferably at a hotel where they can still make a joke about the dresser drawer containing a Gideon Bible. They wear all black and ravage each other and one walks out of the room the next morning while the other one is sleeping or shoots their lover in the head like a Black Widow/

Rihanna/ex-wife. You download the Tinder app and stop re-
lentlessly referring to yourself in the second person.

～

I decide to organize my first one-night stand while I'm out of
town at a conference, a writers' conference in Minneapolis.

 *He's a picture of Saturn, Peter! He's replaced his face with
a picture of Saturn!* I say to my fellow writer and close friend.
We're in a dimly lit dive bar rapidly swiping left through a series
of unacceptable men's photos on my phone. After carefully cu-
rating a collection of my cutest photos (some shots with friends,
some close-ups, that photo of me in Venice where my abs are the
MVP, no selfies) and one Outkast quote (*Real guys go for real
down to Mars girls*—major, right?!), I did something good girls
are never supposed to do—I'd made my dating {profile} public.

 Eventually, you're going to have to pick one, Pete says, not quite
in the tone he might use to encourage me to buy a pair of pony-
hair stiletto boots bound to put me into overdraft, but more in
the one he used a few months ago as he inspected a clogged drain
in my upstairs bathtub. Each day, I'd been showering quickly
and crossing my fingers that the gray sludge wouldn't creep in
between my toes. The pipes grumbled like they were getting a
divorce. *Eventually, you're gonna have to get someone in here to fix
this*, he'd said with a bit of exasperation, pulling back the shower
curtain then clapping his clean hands together, a job well done.

 We continue to scroll through the dating offerings of
greater Minneapolis. This city feels like a solid place for me to

try out my first Tinder profile. I figure the odds are slim I'll run into anyone who knows me. Minneapolis is the ancestral home of Prince—whose music was the soundtrack to which I was conceived—plus, Minnesota is my birth state. This return brings a delightful circularity to my sexual cotillion, my coming forth, my birthing a new identity. I find a photograph of a guy named Ricky. His smile looks cheerful but mischievous and his eyes seem to dance a little in the light of the photograph.

I finally swipe right.

The next evening, Ricky and I meet at the same dive bar where I'd sat with Peter and swiped on his profile. There are only a handful of places I know how to get to in Minneapolis, and I've established a pattern of visibility in this bar. Plus, in case Ricky decides to murder me on the spot and a group of my writer friends have to be called in by the police to identify my body, at least I'll be in a location they can easily get to.

As for the spy-level seduction, the only black outfit I packed was a miniskirt that has the Wu-Tang Clan logo printed all over it. Too obvious. I pick a slim-fitting, backless, navy blue dress, and arrive early to look calculatedly cool while sipping a sweaty Manhattan in a well-worn leather club chair. Ricky enters the bar on time.

According to—well—everyone, the two most "undateable" demographics on social dating apps are black women and Asian men. I could back this up with stats—I'm a Virgo, a spreadsheet is basically my love language—but any internet search on dating app discrimination immediately reveals articles with titles like:

RACIAL BIAS AGAINST DATING BLACK WOMEN AND ASIAN MEN IS VERY REAL (*BUZZFEED*)

"SEXUAL RACISM" AND LIFE ON TINDER AS AN ASIAN MAN (*MEL MAGAZINE*)

WHY BLACK WOMEN AND ASIAN MEN ARE AT A DISADVANTAGE WHEN IT COMES TO ONLINE DATING (*TORONTO STAR*)

AND:

ARE TINDER LIKES RACIALLY PREJUDICED? YES, OBVIOUSLY (*METRO* UK)

OkCupid's report "Race and Attraction, 2009–2014" shows black women and Asian men on the lowest-ranking scale for QuickMatch scores. The diagrams use colors to signify how a person's racial designation stacks up against their perceived attractiveness based on the racial preferences specified by members of the opposite sex. In a series of charts in which "average attractiveness" is defined by the number of times members swipe right and is represented by boxes in verdant green, the "attractiveness" level of Black women and Asian men is marked in stoplight red representing ratings in the negative—less than 0 percent—failing test scores that the stereotypes of neither Asian men nor black women would find acceptable. In this abysmal landscape, OkCupid's report concludes with this advice to undateables:

One interesting thing about OkCupid's interface is that we allow people to select more than one race, so you can actually look at people who've combined "white" with another racial description. Adding "whiteness" always helps your rating! In fact, it goes a long way towards undoing any bias against you.

Ricky is Vietnamese. About twenty minutes into our date he tells me he and his sister were adopted by a British couple as babies and imported to America, where their parents taught at Midwestern colleges.

So, you're basically living someone else's American dream, I joke. He laughs and looks down at his Coke. He doesn't drink. I catch him giving a side-glance through the bar window to a pair of big-haired, big-booty girls passing by. I'm not mad. We like what we like. It seems obvious this isn't his first time at the Donna Summer disco. I ease into the idea that I am not an anomaly for him, that I may even be one of his racial preferences on this dating app.

So, you like black girls, I say, and he gives his body a quick shake, a little embarrassed I caught his glance. It isn't something I'd ever normally say—so uncouth. But I'm out of town, starring in my own spy movie, and so I'm testing out the dialogue.

It's not that. (It was that.) *It's just one—one of the girls reminded me of my ex. She had big hair. I do love big hair.* He settles into his chair with a flirtatious smile, looking unbothered and confident. Though we don't speak of it, I can tell he's latched on quickly to the idea that the two of us are starring in our own movie, one Hollywood should really cast us in. *Have you ever had an Afro?* he asks.

I find his question arousing. I smile at the possibility of my slicked-back sisterlocks disappointing him as he returned in his mind to my Tinder profile. They could have been braids. They could have been housing some immaculate forest of peonies and coconut oil he could lose his face in, had he caught me on a day in which I had chosen to unleash my hair.

We talk and walk between a couple of bars before we land outside in the Minnesota spring chill while he smokes a cigarette. He doesn't drink. He smokes. I don't smoke. I drink. We are obviously not getting married. I've asked him about what he likes to do to keep himself occupied in town.

I keep a bunch of paints at my house, he says, *a leftover habit from childhood. I think my parents thought I'd become a famous artist, but I'm not any good. I like putting stuff down on canvas.* We'd skirted around it long enough. It's the moment in the script where one spy has to decide if they're going to throw the other one up against the wall and kiss them or slink off into the night to resume the fight against bioterrorism.

What would you like to do with the rest of your Friday night in Minneapolis? Ricky asks.

I think I'd like to paint.

❧

Ricky takes me back to his place in an Uber, to a sleepy neighborhood of brick houses interrupted by two-story apartment complexes. His apartment is warm and trimmed in old-school hardwood wainscoting. The front door opens into the living room, where I see a large glass-topped coffee table and an over-sized black leatherette sofa, the kind single guys are so often fond of. I sit on it, resting my bare feet and legs under my hip, shuffling my short dress a little up my thighs to assume a sexy, yet comfortable position. I quickly glance at the open bedroom; he fixes me a drink.

What do you like in your tea? he asks. You, I think.

Nothing, I say. *This is great, thanks.*

Ricky goes into the bedroom and brings out a blank canvas and then heads to the hall closet, where he pulls down a box filled with tubes of acrylic paint. The box is clean. Tender. I'm touched by his neat arrangement of the beloved acrylics he's turned over and over in his hands, their immaculate expectation of possibility. I act indifferent and raise my eyebrow, balancing my head casually in one palm while lifting my teacup in the other, a bold move for someone who, since ten, has spilled a glass of water across nearly every dinner table I've encountered. I sip my tea and attempt to look seductive.

Ricky begins to paint. We are *actually* painting. I pull a brush from the spotless Mason jar and join him. I try to think of it as foreplay. I think about brushing the top of his hand with a swipe of blue, the two of us ending up in a sex-paint-filled tussle, but I don't know how to do this. I am shy and a little nervous and this is the first time I've ever been in the apartment of a man I just met. I could be killed, I think, remembering the safeguards I'd placed around the beginning of the evening,

realizing that none of them actually included a one-night-stand
escape hatch. I think about texting Peter, but don't want Ricky
to think I'm distracted. I decide that if Ricky is in fact a serial
killer the best way not to end up in his next bloody Rothko is to
keep him talking.

   Do you have a favorite paintbrush? (Yes, that's good.)

   Probably the one you've got in your hand, he says, using his
brush to dot the top of my hand with an eyelash of black paint.
It was a gift from my ex . . . you know, the one with the hair. He
smiles. I ask him about her. She was a singer and a single mother.
She had full hips and full breasts and I see half-moon visions
of her dancing in his eyes when he tells me about her. The two
of them pulling all the covers out of the bedroom and onto the
living room floor when the heater in the bedroom broke one
Minneapolis winter. They'd stroke each other and laugh and
talk while they listened to En Vogue. But that was some years
ago. (He loves her, you think, the thought of them lying down
and listening to R&B tinder to the spark of his memory, a vivid
paint.)

   In some strange way, hearing him talk about loving her, I
feel loved in a way I haven't felt in years. We are flirting and
laughing and the Spotify playlist switches to En Vogue. We
are carefully leaving flecks of paint on each other's hands and
cheeks and the tops of our bare feet. We move our faces in to
kiss and the doorbell rings.

   Let me get that, he says, trying not to look nervous, but it's
late—almost one a.m.—so anyone ringing the doorbell at this
hour either has not made a mistake, or hopes to. He tries to talk

through the intercom but the speaker is spotty. He heads downstairs. I wait.

Ten minutes. I wait.

He bursts back through the apartment door, no longer trying to hide his concern.

Have you seen my phone? he asks. Confused, I stammer as I uselessly search for it. He finds it anyway; he doesn't hear me.

He bolts out of the apartment again.

By this time, I figure it's a good idea to start mapping out my date night contingency plan. I pull my phone from my clutch, and call my best friend, Dan, my conference roommate, whom I'd left in the hotel room earlier saying "Don't wait up," with an exaggerated wink. He doesn't answer. I text Peter. I update my phone settings, giving both of them permission to track my location for the night.

If anything goes wrong, Peter texts back, our safe word is "Oyster."

Thanks, I write, reassured but curious about the kind of situation in which texting *Oyster* would be the mother-fucking protocol.

Ricky returns, holding a purse. *It's my ex*, he says, placing a sable Coach bag with white trim and a pink keychain on the dining table.

Lana? I say, instead of *the black one.*

No, Lilly.

The number of times in our five-plus-hour conversation the name "Lilly" has appeared is exactly . . . zero.

It's—Lilly and I started dating over the summer, but we broke up a couple months ago. *She'd gone on a date tonight,* he continues. *It hadn't gone so well.* She was drunk. She walked to his house. She rang the bell. *When she realized I had somebody here, she got really upset. I came up to get my phone to try to call her a cab, but by the time I got back downstairs, she'd disappeared. All I found was her purse.* As he speaks, he's frantically punching letters into his phone.

This is no longer my spy movie. I sketch out a new script. Despite having no real reason, I feel ashamed of myself. I'd been sitting in a strange city with paint on my face, about to have sex with someone I didn't know. Someone I don't know who turns out to have a girlfriend he didn't mention, with whom he's desperately trying to make things right. I start feeling all the same things I've been taught to feel about myself, about "women like us." I start to think of his tenderness as a ruse, a trick, some sympathetic put-on he's constructed to sleep with black girls. The easy demographic. The angry demographic. The ugly, "undateable" demographic. Preying on the women for whom no one else will swipe right.

I swipe that thought right out of my mind. Nearly every black woman I know is goddamned fantastic. If anything, lucky Ricky has managed to unlock the Rosetta Stone of dating happiness—he's nestling comfortably on a settee in the kingdom of peonies and coconut oil and good. Like, real good. Like shea butter, curvaceous hips, and big hair good. Like apple-slick lips, and smart looks, and smoky-voiced good. And if there's one good thing all those years of good black girl wifedom have taught me, it's how to be a hostess.

I shake the bad-girl-spy game off my navy blue minidress, girding myself for the Hollywood role black women are most apt to play, The Fixer. *Well, she couldn't have gotten far*, I say. *Do you have a car? We should go look for her.* His expression eases from one of anguish to one of relief.

You wouldn't mind that? Okay. Let's go. He's a bit brusquer and more distracted than I would like, given the coy dedication I'd given him all evening. But I've already resigned to the fact that sex is not happening. Sex has been hijacked. Sex has turned out to be someone else's date.

Ricky slides into the driver's seat of his white nineties-era Mazda and turns over the ignition. His paint set is pristine but his car is filthy. We are not getting married. He rounds out the driveway. We cruise down his block at fifteen miles per hour, and spot a woman who I assume has to be Lilly. She's tastefully club-dressed in a cropped cream moto jacket and a floaty, flowery, thigh-high skirt with chunky heels, her barrel-curled hair winking from under the streetlight. I size her up, combing through the dating app bias data in my mind: she's in the highest-rated app dating demographic of all, Asian women aged 20–25. We see that Lilly is trying to explain how she got here to a white hipster couple who seem to have landed a two-for-one deal on tan Patagonia fleece. Ricky parks the car and starts rolling down the window. I place my hand on his on the gearshift.

Maybe you should get out of the car . . . I say softly.

He sighs in agreement, and I watch his forearm flex in his white T-shirt as he puts on his coat. Damn, he's cute.

Lilly! What are you doing?! Ricky screams as he gets out.

He looks both angry and terrified, the way Tim Riggins gets on *Friday Night Lights* when he knows Julie Taylor shouldn't be outside the Pizza Hut drunk in a miniskirt after the big game. If "Ricky" (Riggins) does nothing, "Lilly" (Julie) might end up in the back of the white van these fleece-wearing white people have parked around the corner, but as he comes barreling toward her, nostrils flaring like it is kickoff on game day . . .

No! Don't TOUCH ME! DON'T! TOUCH! ME! Lilly yells, swatting her hands in the air to keep Ricky away. I watch from the passenger seat as the Patagonia couple prepares to protect her with a *Wait just a minute, there* and a *Hold on there, buddy* that escalates to a full Police Academy Women's Defense Class blockade. I look at Lilly. Her beautifully stiff curling-iron waves. Her matte MAC Honeylove. I can almost smell her Prada Candy perfume sliding its tongue through the crack in the slightly opened passenger side window. *Hell, I'd sleep with her,* I say out loud to myself, with a sigh. Outside, Ricky tries to pull Lilly toward the car by the arm and Patagonia Jane gets all Her-Body-Her-Choice, and Patagonia John looks like he's about to pull a rape whistle out his pocket but instead reaches for his phone—which is worse because nobody goes home happy tonight if this ends in a person of color being carried off by the boys in blue. I sigh and start to open the passenger's side door to get out of the car.

Hello everyone, I say, putting my hands in the air, the universal gesture of Victoria's Secret fashion show models, talk show hosts, and "I come in peace." Hello, nice hipster people! Hello, former Tinder date! Hello, hot, drunk, inexplicable appearance of an ex-girlfriend! I give the trash fire of bad news forming in front of me my best Tyra Banks.

Hello—hi! How is everyone's evening going? Yes—I was just in the car . . . so, I noticed we've all gotten ourselves into a bit of a kerfuffle. [Nice white people], I'm sure this must look pretty terrible on your end and I understand completely, [Jane], why you wouldn't want to leave Lilly alone in this situation—believe me, sister, I get it—but I do want to let you know I was on a Tinder date with this nice young man right here and Lilly stopped by briefly and . . . you know what—she happened to leave her purse. Which we now have, in his car . . . I open the back door on the passenger side, where Lilly's Coach bag rests innocently. Lilly whimpers a little, sobered slightly by the sight of her purse. *Now I know you [nice white people] probably don't feel comfortable with Lilly getting into this car, given the circumstances, but you also have to imagine how he feels watching his girl . . . friend meeting a couple of people on the street that they don't know.* It's the first time the fleece couple has considered that approaching this situation with do-gooder enthusiasm may have done some harm. They blink at me as if awaiting instruction. I beam a little on the inside. As much as people don't listen to black women telling them what to do, most times the only thing they want is to have a black woman tell them *exactly* what to do.

I go on. *Ricky, what do you think would be the best way to solve this?*

Ricky reaches in his pocket and starts to free a couple of keys from a key ring. *Lilly, here are the keys to my place. Walk back and wait for me right there. I will be right back.* Lilly takes the keys and collects her purse. *Right back*, I think.

Oh, says some dumb pit inside me. *It's settled, then.*

∾

I got married in Brooklyn. I boarded a plane the morning after, the morning after the night I lost my virginity, and moved to the Netherlands. Before we took a taxi to the airport, I bought a cupcake, buttercream frosting with a hint of lemon, and ate it, the sugar dissolving in my mouth. The day before, in the hours while he was still my fiancé, I'd texted my husband a note, while the women in our families helped me get into my wedding clothes and my college best friend, Vidyuta, took photographs. I love you so stinking much that if you ever try to leave me I'm going with you, it said, and I did. I followed him around the world until he decided to go crazy, the one place I could not.

My date with Ricky was ending. Since that night, I've been on dating apps every once in a while. Sitting across from each new stranger, I cannot escape the feeling there is somewhere or someone else that we each love but can't get to. We set up a profile. We make an avatar of ourselves. We play the game, but this isn't us. I know people, black girls in particular, who have managed to cut through the bullshit and used Tinder to meet their husbands and partners. But this isn't that story. This is the moment where I feel like no one is waiting for me, that no one will ever be "right there" for me ever again.

But Ricky does not know this. Right now, the two of us

are riding in his car, in the blue-breaking first minutes after
three a.m., in complete silence. He does not know how much it
hurts me, the quick, translucent way in which so many people
abandon me, my attempts to circumvent the inevitable by being
perfect, perfect for someone, tender, if only for one night. But—

—*Wait. There's Lilly*, I say, pointing to his ex. We have just
passed Ricky's apartment in the car and Lilly had walked
straight past it, blocks away, shivering as she tries to hold her
thin moto jacket closed. *At this point, maybe it's going to be better if you put her in the car.* Ricky pulls over, unfastens his seat-
belt, and strides into the street. He scoops up Lilly in one deft
move—purse, keys, flash of thigh, the skirt watermarked with
vodka tonics. He opens the door with one hand and slides her
in the back seat like the disgruntled dad, the gesture strong and
tender. *Damn*, I think to myself. But not for long. Lilly places
her hand on my shoulder from the back seat, and I turn around.

    I'm sorry, she says, tenderly. *I'm so sorry*. And it is—sorry—it
feels sorry for all of us. There's something about her that I find
precious. I am as unseductive as possible when I address her,
overcompensating, *Hey Lilly, it's okay. I didn't know Ricky was
with anyone. If it makes you feel any better, we didn't even have
sex!* Lilly lets out a sound halfway between a cry and a swan call,
one that's everything I feel like inside, then passes out in the
back seat.

    *Lilly? Can you hear me, Lilly? I'm taking you to your par-
ents' house. I'm going to call your parents*, Ricky prattles on from
the driver's seat while she sleeps, but his dialogue is mostly for

show—mostly a flirtatious finger that pokes at my rib, and asks me to remember the finer points of the evening. Perhaps even Ricky's realizing the error in his instinct to abandon his hot painting session black girl date for a sad drunk damsel-in-distress. While we idle at a stoplight, I get a direct message to my Tinder profile.

I told you this would be a night you'd never forget, says Ricky's Tinder photo. I smile at him, beside me in the driver's seat. I touch his real face.

The next afternoon, when I'm back in conference sessions, Ricky will send me a photo of the abstract painting the two of us made: tan with cream and purple spatters, a streak of midnight blue.

Beautiful, I'll write. We make beautiful music together [Edvard Munch emoji face]. He'll apologize and ask if he can take me out that night to make it up to me.

I'll reply a few minutes later: Yeah . . . Nah. As much as I love a good story y'all were a little too much of a scripted melodrama for me—and I'm at a writing conference.

He'll respond with an emoji wink and an LOL; I'll probably never see him again.

But it's still early morning and the two of us aren't there yet. Right now, dawn is trying to crack open on the Tinder one-night stand that never was. With Lilly curled up in the bucket seat behind me, her legs tucked under her, she looks like she could be our kid, the three of us one big happy family on a daybreak-tinted road trip. As Ricky drives toward Lilly's parents' house, I spot the glint of my hotel's skyline. I see my face refracted on its surface through the smudged window—all slick and gleaming against a starless sky. I know where I am now. I point one elegant Dorothy Dandridge finger toward the all-glass high-rise, and speak up politely.

Would you mind dropping me off where I'm staying? I ask him as he starts to turn. *I'm pretty sure that's me right there. I'm pretty sure it's me just up there on the right.*

LET HER BE LAUGHTER

*I love myself when I am laughing . . . and then again
when I am looking mean and impressive.*
—ZORA NEALE HURSTON

As a child, I loved *Song of the South*, a 1946 Disney adaptation
of the Uncle Remus folktales featuring Br'er Rabbit, Br'er Fox,
and the Tar Baby. The film combines animation with live-action
footage, a feat that used to look like magic to me. In the film,
Hattie McDaniel smiles broadly while she bakes pie in the
kitchen, essentially reprising her Oscar-winning role as Mammy
from *Gone with the Wind*, replacing the acerbic wit of that character with placid singing. Eventually, in the late 1980s, *Song of
the South* was banned from distribution because of its racist de-
pictions of a happy plantation where infantilized slaves lived in
peaceful harmony with their white masters. I must have seen the
film right before it was vaulted, on VHS or the Disney Channel,
during the film's fortieth anniversary in 1986.

One of the most memorable moments in the film was its rendition of the Uncle Remus folktale about the Tar Baby. The Tar Baby was a doll made from pitch and turpentine, whom the villain Br'er Fox creates in order to lure the story's hero, Br'er Rabbit, into a trap. Tar Baby, a black girl, cannot speak. The black girl is a construction. From a young age, I understood this as a presumption made broadly about dark girls, that our greatest value to a story is often how well we fit into the background or the conflict. Yet, I always laughed when Br'er Rabbit passes the Tar Baby on the road and gets stuck. This was my favorite part of the story. There is something subversive about being sticky; this too says something about black girls. Br'er Rabbit says *Good day* to the Tar Baby. Because she does not respond, cannot respond, he punches her in the face. I liked this part of the story. I knew what it was like to stay quiet, because you have to, because you have been told to, and still be punched in the face. I liked to believe the next time this happened to me I would be like the Tar Baby, my stillness incisive. My skin, adhering. In the end, it is me who is safe and them who get stuck.

For most black people, "tar baby" is a racial slur that stems from classic American literature—like "Little Black Sambo" or "Uncle Tom." When I read Toni Morrison's novel *Tar Baby*, I saw where the author might have wrestled with the tar baby's implications as a child, and derived a certain satisfaction from tenacity as a conceit. Morrison once said to an interviewer that she used it as the title of her fourth novel to represent how black women hold things together, her mouth in a wry smile.

In *Tar Baby*, Morrison casts a black girl named Jadine Childs at the center of the novel, not as a plot device. She is the novel's protagonist but is also deeply unlikable. This is what makes me care the most about her. Because, just like Br'er Rabbit, most of the time I just want to punch Jadine in the face. Jadine is self-interested and materialistic. Jadine doesn't believe in the white disenfranchisement of black men. She despises motherhood and eschews any association with it. Jadine evades every opportunity to look after the aunt and uncle who raised her, who are servants in the home of a rich white man. She defends this man, who's paid for her education at the Sorbonne in Paris, and instead of putting her expensive liberal arts degree to use, she works in Europe as a fashion model and appears comfortable with, or at least ambivalent about, the ways she is fetishized. At the end of the novel, Jadine visits the former plantation house in which she was raised—where her adoptive parents still work as veritable slaves—presumably to say goodbye but in all likelihood just to retrieve an expensive sealskin coat before fleeing back to Europe. If Remus' Tar Baby, when gifted with language, turns out like Jadine, it seems little wonder why in the rest of literature she's always remained the personification of a tar-sticky silence. But Morrison gives her a mouth.

Why? I'd argue it's because, although *Tar Baby* was published in 1981, Jadine feels like an emissary from the future. A place and time in which a black girl can be unlikable and still be the center of attention. This is important to me because we are still vying for a world in which even a likable black girl can command any attention at all. Society prefers that we use our tongues to sing rather than deliver sharp observations. That we smile instead of laugh. When I think of Jadine, I think of her audacity in defying expectations, which is for me the very essence of delight. I feel Jadine is rooted in a "delight" that bypasses our everyday use of the word and takes us back to its etymology, stemming from the Latin "delectare," which derives from the same word "charm." What "delight" truly means is the capacity one has to distract, to detract, to pull away. This is Jadine— the difference between a smile meant to appease and a laughter meant to unsettle—a difference in the use of delight.

I often smile to prevent people from being afraid of me. There is, for instance, the grin I painfully affix to a nine to five workday. It began at my first full-time architecture job, a gig I took shortly after my return from Italy. I'd moved back in with my parents in Lexington, Kentucky, and was saving up money to move to New York. I'd stare at a screen drafting bathroom details, repetitively inserting toilet paper fixtures and the design number for certain styles of commodes into CAD drawings. I was in my early twenties, about Jadine's age. There was nothing about working at a desk that pleased me like Venice and the delightful internship I'd held at the Peggy Guggenheim Museum.

What's wrong? my white colleague might say, peeking his head over the top of the desk divider. There was nothing the matter with me. When I concentrate, my face appears stern and focused, but this wasn't what he wanted to see of me. He should have been more worried when I got lost in a delighted face— part chuckle, part daydream. In those moments, I was back in Campo San Barnaba kissing other expats under streetlights, and regularly leading tours through the museum's collection, an expert in modern art. What sounded like a dream was actually a memory, one that made me smile in earnest.

This wasn't the only time I've been reminded in the workplace to smile. I have had white bosses tell me in performance reviews that I am *so much more approachable* (or some other euphemism for "pretty" or "attractive") when I smile. Interacting with colleagues is so much easier when you smile, they might say. You should feel lucky to be here, they say. They need to know I am a grateful servant. A smile would prove this.

In Venice, by contrast, I felt conveyed to myself every time I crossed a canal bridge. Of course, racism was rampant throughout Italy, and I experienced it regularly from my young managers at the museum, but it was the first time in my life that my status as an American—a black American—held any cultural capital. I represented a world that both the Italians and the expatriates I worked with wanted desperately to know intimately. They cared about what I thought, my interpretation of what it meant to be black. Unlike Jadine, I would never be the type of person to say that Europe is a place where my darkness flourished. What I can say is, *I* flourished because the provocation in my darkness set me apart. I was sticky and I liked it. I liked the way, like the Tar Baby, it wasn't quite right.

I loved the Tar Baby because although she was silent, she seemed smarter than the villain who made her. I don't remember any scene in *Tar Baby* in which Jadine smiles, but she inspires in me a deep laughter. Delight played loud. She lounges naked on the bed in that sealskin coat while her aunt and uncle labor downstairs. The image is perverse. There were many times in the novel where I cringed at Jadine's behavior, but she possesses both a patience and petulance I admire. She hears the other characters calling to her but answers to no one. At the end of the book, she leaves the handsome prince to find her own destiny. (I have done this myself a few times.)

As the Tar Baby, though, Jadine is also the glue that holds the characters in the novel together. The adoptive parents who adore her, the white sponsor who desires her, his white wife who aspires to be her, the lover who gets lost in her grasp. When Morrison says that black girls hold "the world in place," I don't believe she is saying we are meant to hold the world together like tape—to uphold, to stitch the existing structures back in place. I believe she is saying that we are adhesive in ways that are self-sacrificing and supportive but also provocative and threatening. We absorb. We arrest. We suffocate. We attract and defy. We disrupt. We delight.

⬎

It is January 15, 2018, and in an upstate New York middle school, four black and Latina girls were heading to their school cafeteria for lunch, laughing. Unnerved by their excitement, the school's assistant principal demanded the girls remove their clothes so they could be probed for drugs. They were strip-searched. The girls were twelve years old.

This news story didn't surprise me. When I was in elementary school, the only thing I wanted to be was quiet. In

Kentucky's tightly wound Bible Belt, I associated silence with piety. I was a bright child, an enthusiastic student. I desperately wanted the people who taught children things to like me, but I knew I was not terribly likable. Sometimes I still feel like this. I often associate this dislike with my insatiable desire to know, reminded of how the serpent tempted Eve with fruit by saying to her if she only ate from it she would become wise. She did, and learned she was naked. I see this too as a kind of laughter; the pleasure of knowing brings me delight.

Laughter is a form of embodiment. It requires the power of one's ribs and diaphragm, the respiratory and circulatory systems. When you're unhealthy, you might be able to smile, but it can be very difficult to be in physical pain and laugh. This is what was wrong with our four dark girls that day. They were healthy. They felt safe among each other, and unafraid. Their laughter, its open and remarkable power, posed a threat to their white superiors. It was dangerous for the world to know they were happy when a little smile would suffice.

NBC News reported that the white assistant principal who ordered the strip search claimed she was "afraid" to be alone with the twelve-year-olds, and so enlisted a school nurse. During the ensuing police investigation, it came out that the assistant principal and school nurse humiliated and shamed the girls by making derisive comments about their developing bodies as they disrobed—comments described by Governor Andrew Cuomo as "traumatic sexual harassment" in his official public statement. Moreover, the nurse described the four girls as "loud" and "disrespectful," as "having attitudes," language that, according to NBC News, "evokes all too common stereotypes."

During the 1990s, films about white children who "had attitudes" were very popular. The movies featured either fictional or real-life child prodigies, children who knew things: *Searching for Bobby Fischer*, *North*, and *Matilda*. I was obsessed with Jodie Foster's film *Little Man Tate* from the moment my parents took me to see it. There's a scene in which child genius Fred Tate constructs a collapsible dodecahedron out of pencils and rubber bands. A few weeks later, I built the exact same structure from communal supplies in school. I proudly displayed it on my desk for at least two weeks. My teacher should have marveled at my construction, and perhaps briefly did. But a day came when the whole class got lost in a rowdy, raucous wave of laughter, and our teacher lost her temper and shouted at me, sitting in the front row. She demanded I destroy the dodecahedron. To put all the pencils back. I did it. I wanted so badly for her to like me. Everyone had laughed, but I was the one who was punished.

The student my teacher adored was Bethany. Bethany was the amiable daughter of a Baptist preacher from Georgia who joined us a few months into fifth grade. Bethany was plump, a half-foot taller than all the other fifth graders, and an out-of-towner. I'm sure the transition was hard on her, but Bethany was white. I was not a quiet child; Bethany showed me all the ways I was not as beloved. Our teacher would praise the way Bethany spoke, barely above a whisper. During free time, for absolutely no reason I could see, Bethany would break into soft hymns. Instead of scolding her, our teacher—who was Catholic and had mentioned to us offhandedly that she was in the midst of a messy divorce—would praise Bethany's singing and clutch her heart. When it came time to answer questions in class, I would shoot up my hand while Bethany held her palms together like a prayer book. The teacher would call on her anyway.

Well—Bethany would begin in her southern lilt, *I believe . . . when I'm in church . . . with all my church friends . . . sangin' . . .* I was confused by the pride our teacher radiated whenever Bethany rambled on because it seemed clear to me that she didn't know much.

Can you believe it . . . ? Bethany said one day, coming up to me, overjoyed. Our teacher had selected Bethany as Citizen of the Month, for the second month in a row. I kept my lips shut. My silence disappointed her, but it was my inability to stay quiet that always got me into trouble. I was not a preacher's daughter, but I was the child of a devout household, as exemplary as any preacher's daughter, as any white student. I knew my blackness marked how far my young body had already fallen from Biblical perfection. They couldn't see me as an eleven-year-old, especially through my audacity. When I spoke, they saw Jadine—outspoken and decorous, knowingly rubbing her naked body into the ink of a black sealskin coat.

By that winter, I'd started to develop tension headaches. I was convinced it was due to the visible mold in my classroom, and convinced my mother of it, too. She fought for weeks to have me transferred to another classroom, and during that time,

I stayed at home frequently, worried and anxious under the covers of my bed. Looking back now I see I was sick because I was trying to explain to myself the pain I felt trying to fit my tar into a box. I did not have the language to explain how my stickiness felt to me. That I felt like I was no good. That I was traumatized.

It was the strangeness of watching her once-joyful twelve-year-old stop playing music, stop playing with makeup, start staying in bed all day, and start trying to hurt herself that alerted Chanderlia Silva, the mother of one of the four strip-searched middle school girls, that her daughter had experienced trauma. According to an interview *Essence* magazine conducted with Silva, no one at her daughter's middle school informed her or the other parents about the strip search. The parents were *never* asked permission for their daughters to be undressed by school officials, nor were they informed afterward that it had taken place. It was only after Silva and the other parents had witnessed the physical, emotional, and psychological toll that day had taken that they finally extracted the story from their daughters.

According to Silva, after her daughter returned to school, she could not focus. No longer safe at school, she and the other girls missed several days' worth of classes. Silva's daughter was afraid she was being followed; the girls were afraid they were under surveillance. After several weeks, all four dark girls were transferred to an alternative school, a school whose primary function is the discipline of unruly students—one in which those bright, cheerful twelve-year-olds, whose only crime was laughter, would wait out their middle school years receiving instruction only in math and language arts—the only subjects the school offers. This is not a solution. It is imprisonment. This is not an answer. It is a trap.

This is the story of Tar Baby. This is what happens to our girls, to the things they take delight in. To the ways we charm and distract. Like Br'er Rabbit, the world punches us, rips through us, tries its best to pull us apart.

In my recollection of *Tar Baby*, Jadine never smiles, but I believe she possesses a deep laughter. Whether Jadine is struggling or strutting through the story, I hear her laughing, even if it is not written in the text. She does not labor over the task of a suffocating existence. She opens herself to her vastness. She knows.

I know I've finally mastered the task of becoming a quiet person in my mid-thirties, the day an advertising agency I'm working at brings in a photographer to take staff headshots. I apply my plastered smile and face the camera. [Click.] I strike another pose, trying to glare into the camera, look cold and imposing, but this too is nothing like me.

Can you do anything else? the photographer asks.

Like what? I say.

I don't know, laugh! he says. He says, *laugh.* And I do. I laugh, hesitantly at first and then sincerely. My laugh is not a smile, it is an intractable happiness. It is like something to which God has adhered delight to, as the scriptures say, "Make a joyful noise." There is a time for quietness, yes, but we have been brought forth through song and the explosion of stars. Us beautiful-throated beings. Who dares to steal that bright bird from inside us?

I can still hear it when I see that photograph, the sound of my own laughter. My deep and pleasurable delight. The sound is a heavenly one. My laugh a broad inheritance. Within it, you'll hear Zora and Hattie and Jadine. And my mother. It digs its fingers into the tar-dark earth we are rooted to. It knows things. It decides to be pious or not. It says: Let there be an end to silence as goodness. Let there be loud dark girls. Let those girls hold giddiness in their bellies until it becomes a thunder roar. Let their sound be our holy book. Let there be no end to their stickiness. Let us cling to them. May they disrupt and destroy us. (And God said, "Let there be light.") Let our dark girls be delight.

DIANA ROSS IS MAJOR

It is 1997 in Bessemer, Alabama, and Diana Ross is enjoying a rib. It is a cliché to say she looks iconic in Ruven Afanador's black-and-white photograph capturing the moment, but I don't have another word. She wears a slip dress; a stole slides down her shoulders. Her wide eyes look forward, deep-set, into the future. She holds the rib in her right hand at a distance, discarding it as if its taste in the ridges of her own flesh proves more filling than the meat itself. She wears her hair styled in a "Love Child"–era Afro; she looks far too young to be the woman who played Dorothy in *The Wiz* in her thirties, twenty years earlier. She looks past the camera with a level of seduction that makes the backdrop dramatic and high-fashion—a difficult thing to do when the staging is a deserted street, a couple of cars, an overturned La-Z-Boy, and half-eaten barbecue, but you can make all of this work if you're Diana Ross.

When Ms. Ross posed for the iconic photograph in Bessemer, Alabama, I was a fifteen-year-old high school kid in Lexington, Kentucky. I would not see the photograph for at least another ten years, but in 1997, I was trying to turn myself into a Diana Ross of my own making. I was sitting in the first drama club meeting of my sophomore year, petitioning for *The Wiz* to be our spring semester musical.

What's The Wiz? asked the drama club, composed mostly of white kids who tap-danced or dabbled in a cappella barbershop quartets. I was stunned. The 1970s musical reboot of the 1939 movie was the bedrock of my childhood memories—the black *Wizard of Oz.* I stumbled to find the words to answer but I was losing my audience. I panicked. I blurted out:

It's the only movie where we get to see Diana Ross' real hair! My classmates chuckled. It was the nineties; the "real" or "fake"-ness of black women's hair was a popular, ongoing, derogatory conversation topic. I didn't realize it then but my comment was basically reinstating the criticisms surrounding fakeness that had plagued Diana Ross' whole career—an attempt to make her more common, less mythic, less graceful in order to put her back in her place.

By the time I was trying to become my high school's Diana/Dorothy, I had stayed in my place for about a decade. I knew I shouldn't dare to be a diva, a woman who stands out and sticks up for herself. But I wanted to be. And my sole petition for my high school to put on a musical in which I could play the lead was my first step to becoming major, just like Diana Ross. By the time I was a sophomore in high school, Ms. Ross had been a multimillionaire for twenty-five years, declared by the *Guinness Book of World Records* as the most successful female music artist in history. By 1997, I was a small southern girl finally coming into my own and Ms. Ross was in Bessemer, devouring a rib like the bones of someone who had crossed her—an enemy, not a victim. She strutted through a deserted Alabama downtown, taking its ribs hostage, thoroughly enjoying it.

Diana Ross is major. Diana Ross is the black girl glorified. Both shimmering and imperfect. These qualities attracted her to the role of Dorothy back in 1977. "I started doing a lot of reading," she said in a *Rolling Stone* interview. "[I] found out that [the author of *The Wonderful Wizard of Oz*] never ever described who Dorothy should be . . . because everybody, all women, all men, have a Dorothy, a youthful something inside them that's searching for who they are." I know I certainly did. I also feel certain Diana Ross knew how well that statement described her. She is a person whose youthful energy and quest to define herself had already, by 1977, influenced a generation. But casting a thirty-three-year-old in the role of Dorothy was not a foregone conclusion. At fifteen, Stephanie Mills was receiving stellar reviews in the Broadway musical and a lot of people couldn't see how a thirty-something Ms. Ross could compete with the young ingenue for the role. One of those skeptics was Berry Gordy Jr., the head of Motown, whom Diana Ross had worked with ever since she was a teenager, the man who had helped make her a star.

Up until then, Gordy had been one of Ms. Ross' biggest advocates; Diana Ross, Gordy's muse. A few years before *The Wiz*, the two had had huge success on the big screen with her Oscar-nominated film debut as Billie Holiday in the 1972 biopic *Lady Sings the Blues*. But Gordy did not see Diana Ross as Dorothy, he thought she was too old.

What Gordy didn't understand is that Diana Ross is from the future. Diana Ross couldn't have predicted this, but her portrayal of Dorothy as a single adult who can't seem to move out of her family's house is a pretty accurate forecast of black girl millennials. We've grown up in an era where the space between 18–35 has looked less like adulthood and much more like an extended adolescence. Many of us, like Diana/Dorothy, have had to move back home into our childhood bedrooms, as we take inventory of our college degrees, career goals, and the constantly rising cost of living, while we try to figure stuff out. When I watch *The Wiz* now, I see a twenty-something school teacher living with her aunt and uncle and understand this Dorothy so much better. She is much more relevant to us than any other Dorothy could be.

When I finished college in my early twenties, I was living with my parents. I thought I'd be out in the world the minute I got my degree, but I was wrong. I spent a year on my parents' couch, taking odd jobs when I could but mostly debilitated by illness. This wasn't what I expected my life to look like. I think of Diana Ross as a post-collegiate Dorothy, lying back on her middle school comforter engulfed in a flower pattern she considered fashionable as a preteen, staring at putty marks where posters used to hang from her ceiling, attempting to convince herself her life is in the midst of some bohemian interlude. And her family has people over. And Dorothy hears her extended friends and family downstairs gathering for dinner. And somebody in the family has probably invited some nice-enough young man they know to be the only other single twenty- or thirty-something in the area. I just don't know what's wrong with her, but I believe she will get past it, they say as they gather around the table to say grace.

Even back in the 1970s, when *The Wiz* was just a screenplay, the motion picture was setting itself up to be a film of its time—funky, edgy, and Afrofuturistic—something as mature and forward-thinking as Diana Ross. The 1974 Broadway musical version of *The Wiz* was set in Kansas, like the book. It depicts a blackness that has just emerged from the Civil Rights era. Its themes were rural and hopeful, imagining a Black American experience that brought us back "home" to our agrarian roots. But the 1978 film was set in Harlem and Brooklyn, culturally black epicenters that sandwiched a metropolis. The Emerald City was an opulent place filled with Afropolitans, an upwardly mobile black social class. When Ms. Ross' Dorothy sings "A Brand-New Day" during the film's climax, she liberates throngs of black people from the tyranny of the Wicked Witch's sweatshop. They disrobe from their weighty, minstrel-inspired costumes and strip down to gold underwear, their dark, slick bodies androgynous and beckoning. I remember the sexual stir the scene used to build in my preteen body; I wanted to put my lips on all of them. Sorry, teenage Dorothy, a fifteen-year-old could not have played the lead to all that eroticism and joyousness. But Diana Ross brings the black and free into salvation. They lift her high in the air, their savior, the only black girl of the time who truly could.

Securing the lead role in *The Wiz* isn't easy. I couldn't make it happen for myself in high school and it almost didn't happen for Diana Ross. Ms. Ross made the role happen, though, in what film critic Pauline Kael called "perhaps the strongest example of sheer will in film history." Gordy's Motown production studio was just getting off the ground and *The Wiz* was meant to be its inaugural production, which meant the film needed support from a bigger studio. Diana Ross bypassed Gordy and brokered a deal for that backing. She got Universal Studios to guarantee they would fund the film if she played Dorothy. What industry savvy. What determination. What moxie. But power plays like this garnered Diana Ross heavy disapproval, her reputation constantly under siege, the battle between public admiration and ridicule she fought for years.

"Why do they call you a bitch?" Barbara Walters asks Diana Ross in a 1989 interview.

"Because I'm just like you!" Diana Ross responds. Walters interviews Ms. Ross in the singer's gorgeous Connecticut mansion, and during the anchor's introductory voice-over, the broadcast plays footage of the mansion's tastefully decorated rooms and of Ross' recent wedding to shipping magnate Arne Naess Jr. When the camera cuts to Ross on the interview couch, she looks poised but tense. Ross' daughters are not in the frame, but Walters mentions that they are standing guard. Interviewers have been notoriously unkind to Diana Ross. The three teenage girls have given Walters a polite but firm schooling on giving their mother a chance to defend herself.

Diana Ross telling Barbara Walters they are the same is a bold move, but the evidence is unassailable. They are both powerful women who know what they want—visionaries with high standards. If they were men, they'd be called geniuses or moguls, not dogs. The Diana Ross who calls this out is the Diana Ross I love. Her takedown of the word "bitch" is poignant and calm, the ease with which she explains herself akin to the way she performs her music. Ross came of age during an era in which the only kind of black woman vocalist Americans listened to was the big-voiced, full-bodied chanteuse. Although their music is indispensable in the canon, she offered something these women did not. Softness. A slowness. A self-preservation. There is a quiver in her voice that suggests it's okay to hold some notes back, to hold something back. Despite Ross' strong soprano belting range, her voice is best known for its breathy swoon, a sound that pulls me close; I want to put my ear to the speaker or the television set, feeling like I'm listening to her fall back upon a Victorian-era fainting couch, draped in silk chiffon.

This isn't the music assigned to black girls. Up until Ms. Ross, our sound was gospel and blues—sex and penitence. We were the music of heavy labor and hard living followed— hopefully—by a righteous retribution. As much as we were encouraged to emulate her style and confidence, our parents and the media raised us to think that becoming this kind of gentle, easygoing, yet unapologetic woman was unrealistic. We could never be the girl in the pretty clothes lying back on the fainting couch. A fainting couch, nonetheless, that we paid for and selected. Aspiring to that image was treacherous because it removed us from the slave narrative we were meant to buy into—the rewards of hard work and piety—the version of *The Wiz* that takes us back to our sharecropping beginnings without taking for ourselves any of the advantages of Emerald City. But who in the music industry has proved more hardworking than Diana Ross, the Detroit-bred black girl who started singing as a teenager and by forty had bought herself a mansion in Connecticut? Yet, black women like me were raised to sort out real black girls from fake ones based on the color of our skin and how closely we stuck to where we came from.

"I was never on the cover of *Ebony* or *Jet*," said Nina Simone during an interview. "They wanted white-looking women like Diana Ross—light and bright." Simone wasn't the only one to notice Ross' mass-market appeal. A 1982 article in *Marxism Today* referred to Diana Ross as "one of the most spectacular examples of someone who has been allowed to be a success [in the ways of] white male Americans." With the qualifier of "allowed to be" economic philosophy cosigns Nina Simone's observation, exposing a difficult truth. Dark-skinned women have fought a long and vicious battle to be seen in media, even black-owned. Black culture's relationship to colorism runs deep. "Prettiness" in our community is often defined by how closely our physical features reflect an idealized whiteness, from the shape of our bodies to the size of our noses. Culturally, we are not alone in this, but the competitive edge this prejudice gives "lighter," or less dark-skinned black people has been a problem. And is still a problem. But when we're talking about Diana Ross, we're talking about a woman who is successful beyond the spaces that have been kept open for a marginalized people. We are talking about a black woman who is successful in ways that, according to white people, give her more capitalist power than white men. Nina Simone isn't wrong. As dark girls, we still fight against the stigma that makes the Afrocentricity of our hair, our curves, and our complexions second-rate; we fight that battle outside of and among our own people. But Diana Ross' hair, complexion, and features have always definitively represented the black woman. When Simone refers to Ross as "light and bright," she brings awareness to the color bias against women with darker skin but ignores the fact Diana Ross made black women visible in a time when we weren't seen at all, and definitely not in our entirety. Without photographs of both Nina Simone *and* Diana Ross we would not have a complete vision of a black girl: political, charismatic, passionate, and indisputably powerful. Nina Simone chronicled our civil rights as a woman whose Pan-African style highlighted our pride and intelligence; Diana Ross created the black woman whose nation-building was so ubiquitous, white people had to acknowledge it as equivalent to theirs. Of course, we weren't supposed to like her. We weren't supposed to like either of these women. And yet, they took on a world rife with prejudice as infidels, girded with a deep personal, and cultural, black girl love.

Diana Ross is at her black girl best on stage at her 1983 concert in Central Park. When it starts to rain, she powers through her indelible hit "Reach Out and Touch (Somebody's Hand)" in a form-fitting orange jumpsuit. The winds are torrential as the song begins and a stagehand drapes her in an orange chiffon cape. Although Ross powers through the change in weather, the audience gets anxious. Umbrellas go up; people begin to shove their way out of the park. Ms. Ross must have noticed that the exodus alarms the park police, and encourages the audience to join her in singing. She tells them to put their hands in the air and feel the music. When this does not quell the tension, she yells at them with gruff playfulness, *Don't push!* When I look at Diana Ross' face as she tries to calm the crowd, it is clear to me how much she genuinely loves them, her racially diverse but noticeably dark—noticeably black—Central Park audience. Diana Ross is no stranger to the danger a nervous police force poses to her fans. Her girl group, The Supremes, integrated television, looking lush and desirable on *The Ed Sullivan Show* during the 1960s (*the 1960s!*), a time when it was still illegal for white Americans to acknowledge the esteem they felt for black people by marrying them. America had no public models of legal, respectful human relationships between black and white love interests before the *Loving v. Virginia* Supreme Court ruling in 1967. The Supremes helped pave the way for the white acceptance of black people who would enter their homes as family members, through the adoration they built as mainstream integrators of popular white television broadcasts. Two decades later, Diana Ross was still lovingly integrating America in a televised Central Park concert, performing through torrential rain. She kept orderly an event that could have easily melted into mob violence, a race riot: the Wicked Witch of the West.

We might treat these markers of black pride in Ms. Ross' multigenerational pop presence as accidental or inadvertent, but I don't think they are. Diana Ross has been miscast as a "light and bright" music diva whose affinity for white capitalist America made her a celebrity. This is not true. Diana Ross loves herself. This is a good thing. For a black woman to love herself despite the world's insistence she shouldn't is both a generous ambition and a revolutionary act. Her love has prevented her from letting herself be typecast as someone smaller, someone less influential, someone black women are more used to seeing ourselves as.

Even her hair reflects this: we've seen plenty of stars, black and otherwise, completely undone by overly fussy hairdos that are unprepared for the perils of performance. But Diana Ross lets the rain pour down on her. A stunt that is, especially for women of her era, a black girl no-no. Diana Ross was not wearing a wig. She was not hiding the texture of her coiled hair to prevent the possibility of her audience catching her in an unkempt natural state. This *was* Diana Ross' real hair augmented by glamorous extensions that highlighted the airy volume of her black girl hair texture. If I had a time machine, I'd pick up my high school self from 1997 and take her back to 1983 when Diana Ross sang to us, completely exposed in a rainstorm; I'd school my teenage self in some black girl history. In 1983, as scholar Daphne A. Brooks points out in her essay "Let's Talk About Diana Ross," NO ONE WAS WEAVING BLACK WOMEN'S HAIR.

The 1997 me, who made that hideous joke about Diana Ross in drama class, was still trying to disguise the fact my coarse natural hair had been braided through with tightly curled synthetic extensions. My braids only mimicked an Afro because I was too scared to see how the world would treat me if I wore my real texture. If I had worn my real hair to school on a rainy day, braiding it up the night before and letting it out in the morning to achieve its greatest volume, I would have run from the rain. I would not have been okay with exposing my hair, in its wet, shrunken state, to an audience of my harshest critics. Few people are, regardless of race.

But Diana Ross let it all come loose, she let herself be real in front of thousands of people. And she looks beautiful. Her hair and makeup applied, not as an artifice, but as skilled armor. Who do we have to thank for the way Diana Ross held up in the rainstorm of glam squad Judgment Day? According to her actor daughter Tracee Ellis Ross, her mother styles herself. Diana Ross studied cosmetology as a teenager and has used those skills ever since as a performer to produce the look she has become iconic for on stage. Gotdammit, Diana Ross.

When I look back on my life, it has been hard for me to love Diana Ross because it has been hard for me to see myself as someone that radiant, that stunning, that deeply free. When Diana Ross spins around in rainbow-colored chiffon in the film *Mahogany*, her joy is upending, bursting from the dress at every ruffled end. Are we allowed to be that happy in our own skin? I let myself feel that way once. I was living in Venice, Italy. I was getting ready to move out of my basement apartment and had invited over my lecherous old neighbor and all my bon vivant friends. My neighbor was a very famous artist, according to him. He burst through the door of my basement party carrying precarious amounts of red wine, each bottle labeled with illustrations of the large thighs of thoroughbred horses—a tribute to my Kentucky return.

I survived three American wives! he boasted, his voice taking up as much space in the room as Ms. Ross spinning in a dress. Venice is the only place in the world where I have been called by someone, by many someones, a Great American Beauty. The multicultural expatriates who made up the cast list of my Venice life regularly complimented my complexion, my gracefulness, my trips down the canal in brightly colored sundresses. My sketchbooks filled with watercolors, dreams, poetry. I told them this was who I was and they believed me. I was *Mahogany*, a beautiful commodity. In Venice, I was an American export. It was 2007 and I was playing the role, in real life, that Diana Ross epitomized, right before she played Dorothy in *The Wiz*.

If you haven't seen *Mahogany* yet, that's okay. In 2007, I hadn't either. As a child, I remember my mom fretting about whether or not I was old enough to watch the cult classic with her. She wasn't ready to introduce me to the movie's glamorous life of sex and drugs but she was dying to show me the clothes—if you want to know what pretty much every black woman wants her closet to look like, look at Diana Ross' garment rack in *Mahogany*. Diana Ross' character, Tracy Chambers, starts out as a Chicago shop girl who dreams of being a designer. She is scouted by an influential fashion photographer who convinces her to move to Rome and become his muse. As a model she's a hit, but she never loses sight of her ambition to take on the world with her talent and not white people's approval of her "prettiness."

Mahogany begins with Tracy Chambers achieving her goal, with a runway show that's the talk of Rome. Pretty much everything else that happens in the movie's next two hours is a flashback. Tracy Chambers/Diana leads us through a two-hour journey of women who are underestimated, exoticized, and meant to stay in their place. Even in today's world, the movie crosses controversial territories: she defends herself from the white men who are convinced they own her body and the black men who ridicule her for stepping outside her black neighborhood to achieve her goals.

I'm reminded of Diana Ross as I'm sitting down to brunch with my friend Shannon at a restaurant in Portland. I don't live there anymore, but I am visiting her and my other friends on a work trip. I picked out a new restaurant with a "$$$" price tag on the internet whose flavorless dishes I continue to send back to the kitchen. Our conversation is peppered with the phrases *I don't want to sound elitist, but . . .* , *I don't want to be difficult, but . . .* , *I don't want to be a "bitch . . ."* but, why is that? We have things black girls shouldn't have. We're talking about things black girls shouldn't talk about. Like not caring for a man just to have one. Just because it benefits our people. We're thinking about a Facebook screenshot that's gone viral; it tells black women we are single because we don't know how to be the type of girlfriend who gets a guy on his feet, helps him open up a checking account and fill out job applications. We've both taken that advice before . . . and since dropped it.

If they give you five years, I say to Shannon, *you'll be the type of CEO who opens up a whole foundation to help men open up checking accounts.* We laugh. Because it's true. Shannon is already a director at Nike, on the fast track to becoming a VP, and I'm a professor at one of the most prestigious liberal arts colleges in the country, the director of Creative Writing. It's not bragging. We're literally bosses. Shannon is from the Bronx and I'm from the south. We came from places where nobody ever expected black girls to amount to anything. Yet, here we are. (*We've finally made it*, as the Lyft driver told me years ago, looking at the aspirational apartment in Portland I have since left behind for the Northeast.) We've finally made it, and we're not done. And we're not new to being called bitches, or privileged, or difficult, in a world that does not want to see black women have beautiful things and feel confident about themselves. We demand excellence from ourselves in the way we run our business and from others in the way that we're treated.

Shannon talks about being called "light skinned" by another black woman as an insult. A woman whose complexion is as brown as hers. The woman uses the term as a commentary on how she perceives Shannon's "prettiness," the only thing that makes Shannon's career possible, a space within the mainstream the woman feels isn't hers. As if Shannon doesn't fight to take up space in every boardroom. As if Shannon didn't earn everything she has gotten. I know dozens of successful black women who feel guilty about what they have earned because they have gotten things we are told black women should not have. Self-confidence. Great jobs. Healthy bodies. Nice homes. Happy families. Respectful partners, lovers, and friends. Instead of feeling as if we deserve these things because we have worked hard and earned them, black girls are supposed to feel lucky. Grateful. Humbled. We are not supposed to shine when we are successful. We are told to attribute our gifts to something outside of us. We are not supposed to feel we've earned anything we have.

I say "earn" so much because, as a black girl, I often think that we can only take ownership of what we've done if the ownership looks objective. We are not allowed to say (as Diana Ross once did in a 1980s *Rolling Stone* interview) that we are "satisfied" with ourselves. It feels treacherous. The biggest stereotype I carry about black women, as a black woman, is our patient, unsung toil. I grew up surrounded by women who would deprecate themselves after bringing the baddest macaroni and cheese to the cookout: *Oh, I just threw this together* or *You know, sometimes it turns out a little good.* Although I still find beauty in being this type of woman, that kind of effacement rarely gets us past the cookout, the dinner table, past our first jobs, past "125th Street," as Aunt Mae tells a timid Dorothy at the beginning of *The Wiz.* Some of those women I knew growing up, and the girls I grew up with, did alright. But many of those women ended up in isolating marriages, abusive relationships, continuing to work jobs in which they are neither appreciated nor recognized, and perpetuating a system that tries to destroy them. We stay in our boxes because we are told to stay in our boxes, because we are told we are not enough outside them.

Sometimes I can look at myself and see I am exceptional. I wasn't supposed to be here but here I am. I used to believe I could never be as perfect, or special, or (as Nina Simone put it) "bright" as Diana Ross. Black women have always had limits set upon what they should be—how big, how sexy, how successful, how accommodating, how black. And in the case of Diana Ross, her bigger critics have been black girls themselves—people like me, in fact. Some of my ability to say this about myself comes from Diana Ross, from the version of the black girl she gave us that wasn't owned by anyone. This is her gift. She is a woman who kept loving us even when we let the world deride her.

As a black woman, I think it is overwhelmingly important that we talk about what Diana Ross has offered us, a mainstream image of an us who is powerful but with whom the world does not feel too afraid to get intimate. Diana Ross' intimacy is an icon all its own. I can't tell you how many times I've been told I am difficult, intimidating, impossible to get close to, even as I do my best to let people in. I love a *Real Housewives of Atlanta* champagne fight or a *Love & Hip Hop* rant on pussy maintenance, but mainstream culture has trained us to accept black women who are explicit instead of intimate. We mistake candor for vulnerability. When we see a girl on television take off her wig to "beat down a ho," I associate this behavior with being "real" because I have been trained to accept that these are the things real black girls do. And sometimes we do. And sometimes we all need to. But sometimes we extend our beautifully manicured fingertips to a crowd of adoring fans like Diana Ross did that day in Central Park. "Reach Out and Touch" starts. She calls the song her favorite. She walks up to a stage platform that overlooks the whole audience and leans against a podium.

The rain is just beginning and the winds blow back her hair and costume with the strength of an industrial fan. She can barely stand, but she stretches her elegant fingers out to the audience. She embraces us.

Sometimes I catch myself being critical of Diana Ross because the laid-back composure she exhibits on and off stage seems impossible to uphold. She can't be real, I think to myself, when I read her *Interview* magazine conversation with Andy Warhol in which she says the secret to her film figure is that she doesn't eat very much. She and Warhol are at lunch, she orders a burger with fries and a chocolate mousse for dessert. *She has got to be kidding me*, I think when, in a 1977 *Rolling Stone* piece, she glides into the backstage after-party of a Los Angeles lounge performance so aglow with the energy of the audience she announces she's going to do a second show every night. Where's the sweat and exhaustion I feel in my daily performance? Where is Ms. Ross' tired, grumpy indifference? How does she keep it together? Most days my biggest achievement is that I haven't menstrual-cried over climate change or destroyed something breakable (and let's be honest, you can't expect that I won't do both). But then, this is all just perspective. I have to accept there are ways in which other people feel they will never measure up to me. Little me, with my slight lisp, and all my clumsiness, and my stupidly abundant love.

I have realized the biggest difference between Diana Ross and me is that she accepts herself. She is patient with herself. She is patient with her talent and her image. I believe this is what has kept her going all these years. Critics have always said Diana Ross' singing wasn't strong enough for her to compete with the big R&B voices of her generation—but she has out-performed all of them. Critics said her face and body were too gangly and strange to make her a sex symbol—at seventy-five, she still is. Diana Ross has survived because she has taken care of herself first. Instead of trying to prove us wrong by pushing her voice and body past its limits, she has let her longevity speak for itself.

These days, when I listen to Diana Ross sing "Home" on *The Wiz* motion picture soundtrack, I hear all the confusion and longing that has been my adulthood. Her performance on that track is so intimate it scares me. She breathes each word in the first two verses as if she is on the verge of tears that may be of hope or fear or both. By the time she belts the word "home" in the song's final line, I feel like I'm running into the infinite blackness of a final curtain call, a tear in space that will take me back to wherever I belong.

In my own bit of *Wiz* moxie, I reached out to Diana Ross' representatives for permission to use her photograph in this essay, the "rib" one. For someone as big as Ms. Ross, I assumed I would never hear back from her people, let alone that the person who responded would email me back saying Ms. Ross is out of town but will respond to your request as soon as she returns. Ms. Ross? Responding to me? I assumed these kinds of decisions in the life of one of the most influential people of our time would be taken care of by a team of handlers, never the artist herself. I've encountered a fair number of "divas" as a person who writes about music and interviews people. Diana Ross isn't one of them.

In the end, we did not use the photograph. To get you to understand what Ms. Ross means to me, you don't need it. I took a look at the essay I had sent to her and it looked less like the woman who moved me in her iconic image and more like a picture of her I'd drawn in crayon with my fist. I took a hard look at what I was saying about Ross, about black women. I didn't love it. I threw it out and started again. I have to do this a lot with the ways I look at myself. I am not immune to the stigma of what black women are supposed to be. I was not immune to the skeptical claims I've heard leveled against Diana Ross all my life. But here, as much as I could, I wrote about all that I see in Ross that makes black women amazing—intimate and invincible— drawing my image of her, and all of us.

Diana Ross is major. She changes both what we have done and what we will do. As she eats a rib in Bessemer, Alabama, in 1997, she returns to her origin story, her grandparents' farm town, the place where she learned to sing. Like Dorothy, she reclaims the land where she found her voice. In the photograph, she holds the gaze of someone coming down the street that we can't see, but whatever her fate, we know she will be in control. She sets aim on a target—not a victim. She looks to kill what the mainstream might deem seduction, sophistication, or better logic. She upends all expectation, thoroughly enjoying it.

～

Diana Ross is you. Diana Ross thereof. Diana Ross potential. Diana Ross as love. Diana Ross as icon. Diana Ross as whole. Diana Ross as fashion. Diana Ross as goal. Diana Ross as model. Diana Ross as truth. Diana Ross as color. Diana Ross as youth. Diana Ross as primer. Diana Ross as role. Diana Ross as world. Diana Ross as more. Diana Ross as owed. Diana Ross as thief. Diana Ross as legend, Diana Ross motif. Diana Ross as Dorothy—Diana Ross pastiche. Diana Ross is real, Diana Ross is us. Diana Ross is major: Diana Ross as fuck.

YOUNG, DRIFTED & BLACK

First time I heard Nina Simone, I was young, gifted, and black. I'm in the driver's seat of my first car, playing "To Be Young, Gifted & Black" on CD the summer after I graduated from college. Windows open. Nina plays emphatic chords while a fast wind in the speakers batters the belted notes into vibrato. Nina Simone records and releases the song after Lorraine Hansberry loses her battle with cancer in 1965 at the age of thirty-four, in honor of Hansberry's posthumously published memoir and theatrical work by the same name. I carried a well-loved edition of *To Be Young, Gifted & Black* inside me as a teen, long after I'd returned it back to the public library. As an adult, I'd comb through Lorraine's collected papers at the Schomburg Center in Harlem, looking for anything I could that told me what these women talked about together.

During Lorraine's last days in the hospital, Nina sent her a greeting card with the printed message:

WHY WOULDN'T YOU BE SICK

MIDDLE CLASS MEDIOCRITY EVERYWHERE…

SONGS CRYING OUT UNSUNG

YOUR UNTIMELY GENIUS LOCKED IN

CHOKED BY THE FACELESS CITY…

BLANKETED IN QUIET FURY.

Leave it to Nina, I said to myself, pulling Nina's greeting card from the library's collection of Lorraine's personal letters. Leave it to Nina to be the friend who sends the card that cries out, *This silence cannot appreciate you.* The character on the front has tears in her eyes, she holds a coffee mug and a cigarette. I can see how Nina saw this card and thought of Lorraine. Nina must have thought of Lorraine all the time.

Sitting amidst cozy hardwood bookshelves and in front of a stack of archival papers, I read a Nina Simone interview by a *Seventeen* journalist. Nina's first question: "Are you going to write something about me in *Seventeen* magazine?" A reasonable question. But the interviewer says, "She comes on strong and direct." The interviewer goes on to describe Nina as "intense," and "alternately attractive and homely depending on what the angle is." Unlike the other interviews I studied in the *Seventeen* archives—Sade, Diana Ross—Nina Simone appears to be the only singer for whom the interviewer seems at a loss. Compelled by this silence that does not appreciate her, Nina asks her own follow-up question: "Why does it take so long for someone with a little talent to gain some success?" The question is never answered. Aside from a few notes, the rest of the page is blank. I try and figure out why Nina's interview is never finished. A librarian and I search through the archive folders, checking to see if a second page was misplaced. We never find it. It is weeks later when I am going through my notes, alone, on New Year's Eve, finding the dark and its advent a perfectly good time to write a riff on my favorite misconstrued singer, that I realize the *Seventeen* magazine interview of Nina Simone was conducted on the day Lorraine Hansberry died. I sat in front of my laptop and coffee mug and cried.

All Nina wanted to be when she was young was the world's greatest black concert pianist. To be surrounded, I believe, by black genius. To shake the bedrock of who was major. A major key. I think about the "alternately attractive and homely angles" the interviewer commented upon in Nina's face, "blanketed in quiet fury"—how unconcerned Nina was about being formidable. Both Nina and Lorraine had more than "a little talent." This is what made them intimidating, especially to the white establishment. Much of Lorraine's redacted FBI case file details the transition of *To Be Young, Gifted and Black* from Broadway play to TV movie. Because Nina wrote Lorraine an anthem, Nina was in the case file. Yes, the FBI has monitored and critiqued the work of talented black writers for generations. (As you read this, consider yourself party to a grand conspiracy.)

Hearing Nina sing "To Be Young, Gifted and Black" for the first time, I wrestled with the words; I didn't believe it was alright for a black girl to love herself enough to say so out loud. It is a gift to be inimitable. I am eighteen when I listen to the song in my car and I turn it off, still not ready to love me yet. When I slow beside another vehicle at a stoplight, I hear Nina saying that I am brilliant and better and I turn the volume way down, roll the windows up to half-mast. I grip both hands on the steering wheel as if cosigning a pact of war—against my hometown, against my country, against my own survival. It is dangerous to be young, black, and gifted. It is dangerous to be an instrument of light.

❧

First time I heard Nina Simone, I was sinnerman. I was the staccato of the piano, Nina on keys, I was the breakdown in the lyrics where you can't hear the difference between *O, Lord* and *I run.* My voice was something I didn't know could be taken away from me. But my sound was being replaced by static and discord. I was in my early twenties and finishing up architecture school. If this had happened ten years later, I would have known that I had SIBO. I would have known that years of lingering infections in my small intestine had caused a spasm in my diaphragm, which meant each time I breathed I was swallowing extra air. But I was fifteen years from a diagnosis or a treatment plan.

All we noticed—my doctors, my parents, the people who had been my friends, and me—was the loudest symptom, my voice replaced. You could call it a burp, the sound that took over, but I would call it a note. The tinny repetition of Nina in "Sinnerman"'s piano solo as she stumbles through a series of single keystrokes, the whole song urgent as sin. I was like that. I would belch and swallow. The orchestration rushed and limited. I was *Oh, oh, oh* and *Lord, Lord* and occasionally *rock*. I would echo low, *pray, pray, pray*.

Just like "Sinnerman," my life at the time was Southern and rooted in prayer. We Southern prayers are not a gentle people. Our love is a grooming by a rough, hard tongue. But the doctors weren't any different. Specialist after specialist informed me that there was no cure for my delusions, the burping presumed to be psychosomatic—a learned behavior, a tick. As I made my music through an upper endoscopy, the technician laughed. The doctors all ran from my disruption; the specialists recommended I see a psychiatrist. I gave him my sins, I told him everything I knew about who I was then. I took his Lexapro like a sacrament on my tongue, penitence paid. But the medicine swelled my tongue. I can't tell you if it is more painful to lose the voice inside you or have a tongue enlarge until it covers your gums. If I had only known that the swelling was a side effect of the antidepressant, coupled with dehydration, partnered with the dilation pills the gastroenterologist thought would soothe my esophagus—instead I was told it was a delusion. I watched everything Nina said *the Lord said* betray me.

When it came to our Lord, I relegated myself to the back room on Sunday services to run from my deep guilt: over being wounded, over being sick, over carrying the sign of the sinner in me. I believed that in the presence of God, my own sound should be something silent. I never overcame this. Not my disease and never my belief, even after I got back my voice. If I learned anything from the time in which I was silenced, it was that I was *powerful*, like Nina said. Beyond comprehension. I listened to her sing. I locked in my delicate throat a storehouse of things I would say if I ever could.

After a year and a half without a diagnosis, another set of specialists recommended speech therapy so that I could mask the sound that bled from my insides, if not control it. I continued to mask that noise for over a decade. I would have small flare-ups, and would occasionally visit an acupuncturist. On one such trip, in my first months in Oregon, I told my new acupuncturist about my symptoms and she gave me the phone number of a naturopath who was among the first in America to diagnose SIBO as a disease. He was working out of a local teaching hospital. When I went there, I put on a gown and he stuck his hand under my rib cage while a half-dozen new lab coats watched and scribbled notes on clipboards. He pulled the muscles on my diaphragm. The spasm released and I felt as if the bubble that locked my voice would never overtake me again. "Can you feel that?" he asked. *Oh . . . Oh, yes.*

First time I heard Nina Simone, I was feeling good. Like after the rain, when the sky comes in two colors. Yellow chartreuse. Cornflower blue. I bought one J. Crew V-neck sweater in each hue, at full price, with my own green bills. From selling felted handbags I made while I was feeling down, I'd stashed away enough money to purchase small luxuries, like sweaters and lavender syrup to pour into sparkling wine. Ushering in a new year, I got drunk off the heavy, gold-labeled, emerald bottles. I bought a cast-iron teapot that I kept on my bookshelf, telling myself I'd carry it to my first apartment whenever I got well enough.

In the year I couldn't speak, I could still sing. Although this did little for my speaking voice, it did everything for my confidence. It allowed me to keep performing poetry. I figured out I could still do open mic nights if I sampled songs. Something about holding a low G in my belly felt calmer than a sentence. The silences in "Feeling Good"—where Nina breathes before she speaks to us, allowing each line to live, not as a verse but as a sentence—I was like that, *birds flying high*. I mean, I understood her.

I took to the stage at the open mic night my close friend from architecture school, Jared, was running out of our college's Martin Luther King Jr. Cultural Center. We had both graduated college but were still circling the grounds. He'd taken on the job of directing the center; I was still searching for treatment for my illness, and as a part of my self-prescribed recovery plan, I audited one poetry class. Since I could only speak a couple of words at a time without burping, it took me a long time to read my poems. But I had to. I wasn't who I used to be, someone who wrote to be seen by other people; the words had become the only place I could recognize myself. I hadn't done an open mic since I was probably fourteen and all the slams were in pubs and I couldn't drive so my mother would take me to every single one and stay to watch. That night, I had driven my mom. She sat in the shadows with her purse in her lap, like she'd done when I was a kid.

The title of my poem was the same as the song. I wrote its sentences in short measures so I didn't have to read more than five words at a time (*You know how I feel*). I'd recite the poem and sing Nina's lyrics in between. I'd sing about the breeze and blossom. I had become much more accustomed to seeing things slowly now that I couldn't run. I would sit under the shade of my parents' deck and watch the way wasps hovered. I knew I wanted to do that with words, become something beautiful I could barely see. I was a strange song. (You know how that feels.) I was clunky and nervous, but ambitious enough to believe I could belt a high, flat B.

Because the audience was good and dear, and my mother was there and the host was Jared, I'm sure they clapped and shouted but I was too flushed in my face to hear it. I sat down by my mom. Afterward, at the reception, we all ate cookies, and an older woman from the audience tugged at my cornflower sweater. *I know what that poem was about*, she said. *It was about being happy.*

❧

First time I heard Nina Simone, I was here comes the sun. It is night and I'm standing outside my car and my Discman is dying because we were all transitioning to iPods and I barely took care of it, only kept it around for mix CDs. How do you tell someone you love them, now that all the music is digital? We're standing four feet apart from each other, in the dark, under the night-blooming jasmine, the tension so intricate I watch the soft dew heavy the spiderweb woven on the branch behind his ear. Although it'd been years since we were together, my very first boyfriend has written IT RAINS . . . IT POURS . . . DEPENDING ON THE WEATHER on the top of a CD he ripped for me. Perhaps we'd grown nostalgic. I set the disc upon the spindle and slip on the spongy headphones. Nina tells me it's alright to come outside, when I'm already outside. Little. Darling. An eleven-track EP of contiguous love. This is how I learn that the life of my Discman is ending: unless I press the forward button, it only plays one song. Somewhere in the bright, brief months that follow, the hand who scrawled IT RAINS across the top of the mixtape will ask me to marry him, but I have come through the clouds. And the sun keeps blinding the horizon, and I haven't found my horizon yet.

I transferred the mixtape to my iPod and played it in my gummy earbuds in waiting rooms before doctor's appointments. "Here Comes the Sun" played as I completed speech therapy. I was getting healthy enough to make a trip; since I had no horizon, I could pick one. It was late, the night I stumble across the overwrought romance of the mediocre mainstream movie *Under the Tuscan Sun* on television while I'm recuperating. I watched the movie's last scene knowing the era since I had seen the sun was finished.

My travels had always been the most romantic part of me. From my family's car trips to coasts and mountains and national monuments, to the still-undented passports Jared and I used in college on an architecture trip to Barcelona. While I watched *Under the Tuscan Sun*, I cried. Not because I was moved by the image of a woman finding herself abroad, but from the complete absence of any black women in it. There were never any black girls going abroad and finding themselves in books made into Hollywood movies. But I had already read our autobiography. I was Zora and Nina and Josephine; I was Jadine from *Tar Baby* and Diana Ross in *Mahogany*, a black woman protagonist, a black girl adrift. I was going to move to Italy. As the credits rolled on the film, I skipped to the next track on the disc.

꠸

The first time I heard Nina Simone, I was misunderstood. Nina wrote a very impassioned letter to James Baldwin in 1977 from Grens, Switzerland, most of it an extended postscript. She is headed to Paris in a week to perform and hopes to see him. "I need to hear from you, man," she writes, "I'm very homesick—."

Love.

Nina.

I find the letter in the archives of the New York Public Library. I had spent the last twenty-four hours with a tall skinny man; he thought himself very pretty. We had met dancing—we had cuddled then napped, then told each other every funny story we could think about ourselves in the morning over yogurt and honey. I give him my well-loved copy of a favorite book, *James Baldwin: The Last Interview*, with all my love notes and annotations. I don't know why. He felt like I was traveling. We took the train up to Harlem. My stop was before his so we kissed as I stepped out of the train, onto the platform. I never do this in New York. So rare are these moments when I am home and still visiting another country.

I have never been homesick while abroad; I have cultivated a little talent for striking up small, short intimacies. Seven years after my first move to Italy, I return over the winter holidays to write a new poetry collection. I live in an exquisite dormitory attached to the library of the Cini Foundation in Venice, on an island whose only inhabitants were monks.

There are times where the monks and I both take the last ferry of the night back to our respective sleeping quarters. On one such night, I've been partying at a speakeasy at the bottom of a bell tower so filled with smoke and candlelight and ambiance that I could never find it again if I tried, as if it dissipated in the fog. I smile across the ferry at the Father in his habit and rosary beads, wondering where the long night that found him had led.

I don't get homesick abroad, but I do get lonely. When that happens, I do what I am too timid to do in my own country. I put on some lipstick, as my mother taught me, and wander the streets as if I have plans for the night, as she didn't. I stop at the first place that calls to me—tonight, the restaurant Amarone. I'm wearing a yellow chartreuse jersey dress and a black leather jacket and I hover at its doors like a speckled bumblebee. The window is misty. It takes me a moment to focus my eyes on a table of about a dozen people. One of them quickly recognizes me:

Johann. He is a close friend of the boyfriend I had adopted, like
a sly stray cat, during my last Venice stay. It is Johann's father's
restaurant, and he and his wife are hosting a birthday party for
an Irish painter, Claire, who recently moved to the city. They
make room for me. For the next two years, I'm in and out of
Italy, in and out of Amarone, working on that manuscript.
During one visit, they have me write a poem in their guest book,
certain that one day I will be famous; no one in my life has been
more convinced I was meant to be someone. My Italians held on
to the way I put words down on paper or in my mouth as if my
song housed something meaningful, something understood. It
is a shame, when I come home, that I feel so much less a part of
the world. It is so painful to be so misunderstood in it.

In Nina's letter, she tells James she wears his scarf all the time.
She encloses an article torn out of *Variety*, an unflattering story
about a Cannes performance at which she'd accused the industry of exploiting her. "Since then, [I] have stacks of encouraging
mails [*sic*] from home urging me to come back," she tells him.
But can I ever go home? I imagine she asks as I hold the letter in
my hands. *Don't let me be like this*, I hear her plead. "How can
you leave me so all alone without even a phone call?" she writes.
"I feel so fucking lost."
      When I moved back to America eight years ago, it didn't
have room for me anymore. It was a spotty coalition of mis-
shapen ideologies residing under one, coagulate flag. Blue
bruise. Red war. White blood cells. America the beautiful rent
through, an unfree and huddled mass irreparably torn by the

less-than-quiet fury that accompanied Obama's second term. Somehow, white America hadn't understood that a dark-skinned president is exactly what our centuries would eventually yield, a more perfect union. But what do I know? I'm just human, I move houses every three years, mostly out of circumstance. Wherever I am now is not the last place in which I'll end up. I don't regret this; I feel a homesickness.

First time I heard Nina Simone, I was four women. I was in the hallways of my high school spitting a Lauryn Hill verse. A metaphor: defecation, the vehicle; Nina Simone its tenor. But I didn't know who Nina was. I'd gloss over her name every time The Fugees' "Ready or Not" track played, making up the words, determining my own meaning. Then one day Kadijah stopped me.

What did you say?

I mumble something indecipherable.

"Nina Simone," that's what she says, she tells me, sweetly condescending. I put a Nina Simone disc in my monthly order of BMG Club CDs. When it arrives, "Four Women" is the first song I listen to.

In 1963, when Nina Simone first heard that four little girls had died in the bombing of a Birmingham church, instead of taking to the streets, she took to her garage to build a zip gun. I am not unfamiliar with the spirit that brings a woman to a gun. One of the stories I always return to about the women in my family is that my great-grandmother shot her husband in the foot and ran off, leaving behind him and their seven or eight children. She sounds like a verse in a Nina Simone song.

"I had it in my mind to go out and kill someone," recalls Simone, referring to the murders in her autobiography, *I Put a Spell on You*. It was only when Nina's then-husband and manager convinced Nina to come out from the garage, reminding her that her best means of intervention had always been her music, that she went to her piano and composed "Mississippi Goddam," her first protest song.

What I take from both of these black women is that our collective survival depends on self-preservation. Although my great-grandmother was inspired to use a gun because of domestic violence and not domestic terrorism, the instinct feels the same. Black women have battled against backbreaking labor and brute force, against bombs and abuse, subjugation and silence, to ensure the next of us women survive. It is not a pleasant narrative. My family rarely talks about the event that led to my great-grandmother abandoning all her offspring, including my grandmother. She returned years later to retrieve her children but by that time many of the boys had grown into men and my grandmother, the only girl, was a mother with kids of her own. I have one other story of my great-grandmother. My grandmother is in her early twenties and the man she is dating threatens to beat her in front of my young mother, aunt, and uncle. The children run across the street to get their grandma, in the house she now lives. She follows them back to the house brandishing a heavy cast-iron skillet. The man's back is turned to her as he lifts his fist to hit my grandmother. *If you hit her*, my great-grandmother says, *imagine what I will do to you with this.*

The violence that erupted from these women is provocation and necessity. Had Nina Simone taken to the streets with a gun that day, we would have lost her voice. Goddamn. To think of my life without Nina singing in it, singing into it. I cannot imagine the kind of woman I would have become without either Nina or my great-grandmother. I have always been a woman on the verge of a gun. My anger is quiet. Reserved. But I feel so close to the edge of a trigger I can feel the metal cool and codify in my hand. I grip a pen instead of a song, or a skillet, or a trigger; I do not consider this strategy for assassination a passive action.

It is hard to tell the story of who black girls are without a hidden massacre. The dark is our beauty but it is also the lot to which we have been cast: to the shadows, to the margins, to the places most people shield their eyes because they do not want to see. In "Four Women," we are a field worker, a sex worker, the child of rape, and we are also murderously angry. It is to the shame of humanity, not our bodies, that we have been these things.

I have seen "Four Women" examined as a reclamation of the lives of the little girls killed in Alabama that day, but it's not an interpretation I agree with. Nor do I see Nina displaying the opposing tragedies of African Americans based on their hair textures and complexions, the song ending in the voice of the *bitter* and *brown* Nina herself. For me, the "Four Women" are all Nina Simone—the conjoined creation of one Eunice Kathleen Waymon—the woman who became the singer, the activist, and the pseudonym, the young black girl from North Carolina who dreamed of becoming a concert pianist. Instead, she surrounded us in genius. She made us a history. She wrote herself into who we are.

In the second-to-last set of verses of "Four Women," the song points a gun at the past, the song's final narrator telling us her bitterness stems from being the descendant of slaves. *What do they call me?* Nina asks as her piano playing makes the ground tremble with dramatic tension. She answers, gathering her girls together in the plurality of one name: *Peaches.* A metaphor: the fruit, the vehicle; us, the tenor. The foliage wide, the blossoms fragrant. We, the tart, taut, and petulant. We, the sweetly gnarled fruit fallen to the bed grass, nestling in the ground to begin anew. We have survived the hostile soil. Our hard pit. Our ripe flesh. Our tree feeds the world. Some of us given. Some of us ripped from us. Some of us still unfurling. But we keep the orchard alive. We keep us alive. I write to you, nestled under our dark canopy. I hear you, pressing my cheek to the stiff dark bark. I hear you: *My skin is.*

& JUST IN CASE YOU FORGET WHO I AM, I AM

The Madam C. J. Walker of millionaires,
The Carol's Daughter of good-smelling drug stores,
The Queen of Sheba of self-care,
The June Jordan of soldiers,
The Queen Dido of elephant marches,
The Mae Carol Jemison of motherships,
The Dr. Rebecca Lee Crumpler of whatever kills you.
The

          Carrie Mae Weems of spotlights, dinner
          tables
                    & cigarettes,
The Rebecca M. Johnson of high school principals,
The Dominique Dawes of backflips.
&   The Gabrielle Union of honesty.
I am the Susan L. Taylor of executive-level cornrows.

The
                Mary Fields of backwoods gunslingers.
    The Lena Horne of bayou high notes
&   The Kathleen Battle of making a hell of an entrance.
I am the Debbie Allen of dance sticks.
    The Natasha Rothwell of laughter.
I am the Dr. Marijuana Pepsi Vandyck of PhDs
    The Queen Latifah of U-N-I-T-Y.
I am the Keke Palmer of spelling bees
&   The Amandla Stenberg of first kisses.
I am *the* Sonia Sanchez.
I am the Nikki Giovanni of love poems; love poem tattoos.
I am the Skin of British punk rock
&   The Dorothy Dandridge of the ruched red dress.
I am
    The Bessie Smith of queer.
    The Ma Rainey of queer.
I am the Roxane Gay of *GAY*
&   The Audre Lorde of proud black lesbian woman
                          warriors.
I am the Billie Holiday of holding back in my throat
    nothing—then mink, puppies—then nooses.
I am the Zora Neale Hurston of loving myself when I'm laugh-
    ing (& when I am not, looking mean & impressive).
I am
    The Ms. Immortal, Henrietta Lacks of cancers.
I am the Lieutenant Uhura/ Nichelle Nichols of answering
    the galaxy.

I am the Whoopi Goldberg of starships, enterprise,
    the Zoë Kravitz coming back down-to-earth.
I am the India.Arie of free birds.
I am 2 Dope Queens
I am
       The Arielle (my sister) of Little Mermaids
&   the sisters—Chloe x Halle—locked & chorusing.
I am the Donna Summer of flipping my hair back.
I am the Mary J. Blige of dance moves.
I am the Aaliyah of dance moves.
       The Martha and the Vandellas of street-dancing
&   The Lizzo of posing my sweet ass in photographs.
I am the Pointer Sisters
I am the Chaka Khan of sex.
I am the Thandie Newton of sex.
I am the Tyra Banks of rooting for you
&   The Omarosa, of apologies.
I am the Janet Mock of realness,
       the Condoleezza Rice of violin concertos,
       the Issa Rae of Stanford graduates with good teeth.
I am the Yvonne Orji of fur coats,
       The Lisa Leslie of dunks
       The Normani of the basketball booty pop.
       The Missy Elliott of back-break bass beats.
       The MC Lyte of microphones,
&   The Lady of Rage of Afro puffs.
I am the Leslie Jones of Saturday night.
I am the Kelis of colors

I am
     The Lauryn Hill of acoustic, wearing my scarf & my
     guitar & making my broke-open look badass.
&   the Da Brat of big-lipped sneers & out-sized jeans.
I am
     The Eve—of Ruff Ryders,
&
     The Leikeli47 of wearing the mask.
I am
     The Wakanda Warrior Women of If-your-bitch-ass-ever-
     tries-to-come-for-me-again . . .
     The Big Freedia of "You better slay, bitch!"
     The Tina Turner of "The Bitch Is Back,"
&   The Danai Gurira of & a bitch better be dead.
I am
     The Kerry Washington of taking shit on,
     The Wanda Sykes of standing up.
     The Viola Davis of struts,
     The Gina Torres of swank,
     The Lena Waithe of goddamn swag,
&   The Angela Bassett of the gotdamn side-glance.
I am the Terry McMillan of strutting from burning cars.
I am the Left Eye of setting fire to burned men.
I am the Angela Davis of black leather
&   The Elaine Brown of power fists.
     The Shirley Chisholm of power legislation.
     The Fannie Lou Hamer of sick & tired;
I am *the* Sweet Honey in the Rock.

I am *the* Anita Hill of advocacy (Thank you.).

I am the Tarana Burke of me (Thank you.).

I am

      The Diana Ross of whomever the fuck I want

&   The Solange in the elevator of whatever the fuck I please.

I am

      The Beyoncé of homecomings;

I am the Nefertiti of homecomings.

I am the Jamaica Kincaid of papaya-thirst sentences,

      The J. California Cooper of straw hats,

      The Joan Armatrading of love songs.

I am the Phylicia Rashad of high-waisted hip grips.

I am the Tressie McMillan Cottom of thick.

I am

      The Mariah Carey of being carried

&   The Marsai Martin of boss little girls.

I am The Keshia Knight Pulliam mouthing blues on the stairs

      on *The Cosby Show* of little girl duende.

I am the Sarah Vaughan, of the earth, of paradise—

                                      singing.

I am

      The Gloria (my mother) of black catsuits, short Afros &

      serving Bambi eyes in black & white photographs.

I am the Ruby Dee of brownstone windows.

I am the Voletta Wallace of mothers

      The Donda West of mothers.

&   The Afeni Shakur of raising our sons.

I am the Assata Shakur of exits.

I am the Leontyne Price of divas, feathers—storytellers

&   The *Aïda*, of bedtime stories.

&   The Glory Edim of open books as open invitations.

I am the Ruby Bridges of grammar school as first steps.

I am

       The Gloria Naylor of opening front doors.

I am the Alice Walker of what we love can be saved.

       The bell hooks of passion.

I am the Grace Jones of knowing when a fierce note is

                                                    grace.

I am the Sade of "King of Sorrow"

I am the Four Little Girls of sorrows

I am

       The Eunice Waymon of sorrows breaking white piano key
       silences

&   The Nina Simone of, come pack your gun.

They call me

       The Rihanna of poetry   but really,

I am

       the Rihanna of $600-million heirs—an empire of beauty
       & lavish charity.

I am the Minnie Riperton of loving you.

I am the Zora Neale Hurston of walking on red lights

       because the green ones were never for me.

I am

       the Toni Morrison of noble.   Peace.

Didn't I tell you, I was grand?

                    & it wasn't just some dumb dream
I had; some perfunctory way of telling myself I was
special? I had
a vision. I don't remember even
      the half of it but, you were   *glorious.*
You shimmered & basked.
& when I hold my eyes open . . .

                          There you are.

ACKNOWLEDGMENTS

Honey, listen, I couldn't have written this book without the support I received first from Vidyuta Rangnekar, Dan Bernitt & Brian McQueen, who have told me, longer than anyone, *you can do this* and *this is the only thing you was put here to do.* Thank you to Chet'la Sebree (no relation) & Bükem Reitmeyer (some relation), who are the readers I could not live without: would not have made it to the end of this book without; if there is anything in here that speaks to you it is because of them. Thank you to my agent, Kerry Sparks, who very matter-of-factly told me—a poet—that I should consider writing an essay collection & then stuck by me when I spent nearly a year chickening out and then turned me into an author, my dream. Thank you to my editors, Emily Griffin and Amber Oliver, who told me on our first meeting at HarperCollins that *you have a voice* and did everything they could to make sure I cultivated that voice on the page. Thank you, HarperPerennial. Thank you to Phillip B. Williams for vegan chocolate donuts and sitting with me talking about our books on my couch. Thank you to francine j. harris for the raucous laughter that always accompanies all of your best advice. Thank you to my mother, Gloria Butler-Lawson, who taught me how to dress and taught me how to love sitting at home watching movies on rainy days and who took me to my library. Thank you to my sister, Arielle Lawson, who taught me how to dress and teaches me every day . . . strength. Thank you to my father, Dr. Willie Travis Lawson Jr., for telling me after college that I shouldn't get a job in architecture because my passion was writing—I still did, but here you are: you were right. Thank you to the Essandoh family: Nana, Justin, Nina, and Louis, without whom I would not know all the stories that I do about growing up in Minnesota—all our love and home videos, and family photos. Thank you to Linda and Zacc Day for always being my family. Thank you to Lorene Higgins and Shelly Johnson and Renee McGee and Rene Barnes and their families—you, all of the family who made me. Thank you, Jaeden and Jalea—I learned to love me because of how much you loved me—it has been an honor watching you grow up. Thank you, Santi Elijah Holley, for your home. Thank you, Nicholas Nichols for Twitter. Thank you, Annie Russell, for writing across from me. Thank you to the women I interviewed or referenced in this book, among them: Ava McCoy, Lisa Jarrett, Aaliyah Bilal, Marisa Parham, Rudo Mudiwa, Shannon Slocum, and others— our stories made this possible. Thank you to the cast of my high school rendition of *For Colored Girls*, I am thanking them collectively here to preserve their privacy, but I want each of you to know I wouldn't have made it this far without your beauty and resilience; I am so very proud we were girls together. Thank you to Rosa Bounds for loving to gossip about book characters the way I do—this one is for you. Thank you, Maud Newton, for being the kind of reader and advocate the world needs, bless you. Thank you to Judith Frank for your text message "can I help yous" and thumbs-ups throughout the year I wrote this book, my first year as an Amherst professor. Thank you, Amherst College, the MacDowell Colony, Yaddo Artist Colony, the Kentucky Foundation for Women, the Carnegie Center for Literacy & Learning, and Kentucky Governor's School for the Arts for your support. Thank you, Crystal Wilkinson and Kelly Norman Ellis, my first black-woman writing teachers. I know I'm missing some people; y'all know I'm thankful. But most of all: thank all of you girls for being black.

APPENDIX

The essays in this book are indebted to the following resources:

American Girl Dolls Wiki, https://americangirl.fandom.com
/wiki/American_Girl_Wiki (December 3, 2018)

An Indigenous People's History of the United States by Roxanne
Dunbar-Ortiz (2014)

*For Colored Girls Who Have Considered Suicide/When the
Rainbow Is Enuf* by Ntozake Shange (1976)

"Researchers unclear why suicide is rising among black children" by Justin Wm. Moyer, *Chicago Tribune* (March 8,
2018)

"Carefree Black Girl: The Life and Death of Karen Washington" by Anita Badejo, *BuzzFeed* (March 24, 2014)

"Karyn Washington, Founder of *For Brown Girls* Honored,"
MadameNoire on YouTube (October 21, 2014)

"How I'm fighting bias in algorithms" by Joy Buolamwini,
TEDxBeaconStreet (November 2016)

THICK by Tressie McMillan Cottom (2019)

A Burst of Light and Other Essays by Audre Lorde (1988)

Gender Shades by Joy Buolamwini, http://gendershades.org/ (March 25, 2018)

"Plantation sharecropper Lonnie Fair's daughter dressing for Sunday church services in sparsely furnished room" by Alfred Eisenstaedt, https://www.gettyimages.com/photos /50526364?family=editorial&phrase=50526364&sort=best #license (1936)

Dreams Are Colder Than Death by Arthur Jafa (2013)

"Saartje Baartman: Her life, her remains and the negotiations for their repatriation from France to South Africa" by P. V. Tobias, *South African Journal of Science* (March/April 2002)

"Tituba: The Slave of Salem" by Rebecca Beatrice Brooks, *History of Massachusetts Blog*, https://historyofmassachusetts .org/tituba-the-slave-of-salem/ (January 2, 2013)

"The Real Story of Marie Laveau" by Gina Dimuro, *All That's Interesting* (blog), https://allthatsinteresting.com/marie-laveau (October 5, 2019)

Homecoming: A Film by Beyoncé by Beyoncé (2019)

"The Racism Discussion with Oprah and Jane Elliot, Part 1," *The Oprah Winfrey Show* (1992)

"Diversity Day," *The Office* (2005)

"Freaky Friday" by Lil Dicky, featuring Chris Brown (2018)

"Kendrick Lamar halts performance mid-song after white fan he invited onstage says N-word" by Ilana Kaplan, *The Independent* (May 21, 2018)

"The White Negro: Superficial Reflections on the Hipster" by
  Norman Mailer, *Dissent* (1957)

Sister Outsider: Essays and Speeches by Audre Lorde (1984)

Bulletproof Diva: Tales of Race, Sex, and Hair by Lisa Jones
  (1994)

What Was the Hipster?: A Sociological Investigation edited by
  Mark Greif, Kathleen Ross, and Dayna Tortorici, tran-
  scribed by Avner Davis (2010)

"What Will Replace the Hipster" by Joe Bish, *VICE* (December 17, 2015)

White Trash: The 400-Year Untold History of Class in America
  by Nancy Isenberg (2016)

"Oregon Was Once Ku-Ku for the Klan" by Dana Alston, *Willamette Week* (August 17, 2017)

"The Vanport Flood" by Michael N. McGregor, *The Oregon
  History Project* (2003)

"How Oregon's Largest City Vanished in a Day" by Natasha
  Geiling, Smithsonian.com, https://www.smithsonianmag
  .com/history/vanport-oregon-how-countrys-largest-housing
  -project-vanished-day-180954040/ (February 18, 2015)

"There's Another Vanport" by Mona Albertson, *Oregon Journal*
  (August 3, 1947)

"Why Aren't There More Black People in Oregon" by Walidah
  Imarisha, Diverse and Empowered Employees of Portland
  (DEEP) lecture available on YouTube: https://www.youtube
  .com/watch?v=7Lcm1LDZZXg (November 9, 2017)

Vanport Mosaic, https://www.vanportmosaic.org/ (November 27, 2019)

"Fifty years later, Legacy Emanuel Medical Center attempts to make amends for razing neighborhood" by Casey Parks, *The Oregonian/OregonLive*, https://www.oregonlive.com/port land/2012/09/post_273.html (September 22, 2019)

"A *Thot* Is Not a *Slut*: The Popular Insult Is More About Race and Class Than Sex" by Amanda Hess, *Slate* (October 16, 2014)

"The *Harper's* Columns: *On Wild Girls, Cruel Birds—and Rimbaud!*" by Zadie Smith, *Feel Free* (2018)

"What's Killing Black American Babies?" *The Inquiry*, https://www.bbc.co.uk/programmes/w3cswqt4 (April 30, 2018)

"What's Killing America's Black Infants: Racism is fueling a national health crisis" by Zöe Carpenter, *The Nation* (February 15, 2017)

Sex at Dawn: *How We Mate, How We Stray, What It Means for Modern Relationships* by Christopher Ryan and Cacilda Jethá (2010)

"Who Is Sza?" by Insanul Ahmed, *Complex* (September 8, 2013)

"Tatyana Ali Reveals Her Odd Workout Routine, Penchant for One-Night Stands for HuffPost's #nofilter" by Kiki Von Glinow, *Huffpost* (October 21, 2013)

"Tatyana Ali on One Night Stands and Drake" *The Wendy Williams Show*, https://www.youtube.com/watch?v=Q0E2Xx N0iCA (March 19, 2013)

"Unconventional Relationships: Can Multiple Partners Work?" *Red Table Talk*, https://www.facebook.com/watch /?v=419568041972431 (June 20, 2019)

"Race and Attraction, 2009–2014: What's changed in five

years?" *OKCupid* (blog), https://theblog.okcupid.com/race -and-attraction-2009–2014–107dcbb4f060 (September 10, 2014)

Tar Baby by Toni Morrison (1981)

"Four girls at N.Y. middle school subjected to 'dehumanizing' strip search, lawsuit says" by Erik Ortiz, NBC News (April 30, 2019)

"4 Black Middle School Girls Allegedly Strip-Searched at New York State School" by Breanna Edwards, *Essence* (January 24, 2019)

"Diana Ross: An Encounter in Three Scenes" by O'Connell Driscoll, *Rolling Stone* (August 11, 1977)

"Giving Face: Diana Ross and the Black Celebrity as Icon" by Nicole R. Fleetwood, *On Racial Icons: Blackness and the Public Imagination* (2015)

"'Love Child': Diana Ross and the 'Small' Black Female Voice" by Emily Lordi, MoPop Conference (April 2017)

"Diana Ross Goes from Rags to Riches" by Michael Thomas, *Rolling Stone* (February 1, 1973)

"A Singer, a Throng in Central Park, a Deluge" by Leslie Bennetts, *New York Times* (July 22, 1983)

"Let's Talk About Diana Ross" by Daphne A. Brooks, *Let's Talk About Love: Why Other People Have Such Bad Taste* edited by Carl Wilson (2014)

"Q&A: Diana Ross" by Jill Hamilton, *Rolling Stone* (November 13, 1997)

"The Summer and Fall of Diana Ross" by Ben Fong-Torres, *Rolling Stone* (August 11, 1977)

"Diana Ross" by Richard Dyer, *Marxism Today* (June 1982)

"Interview with Nina Simone" by Anne Fulchino, *Seventeen* Magazine archives (New York Public Library) (January 12, 1965)

Nina Simone and James Baldwin correspondence, letter, March 3, 1977, Schomburg Center for Research in Black Culture (James Baldwin personal papers)

I Put a Spell on You: The Autobiography of Nina Simone by Nina Simone (1991)

ABOUT THE AUTHOR

Shayla Lawson is the author of the poetry collections *I Think I'm Ready to See Frank Ocean*, *A Speed Education in Human Being*, and *PANTONE*. She grew up in Lexington, Kentucky. She is a professor at Amherst College and lives in Brooklyn, New York.